ISRAEL AND AFRICA:
Forty Years, 1956-1996

ISRAEL AND AFRICA:
Forty Years, 1956-1996

SAMUEL DECALO

Middle East Studies, No 1

FAP Books
Florida Academic Press
Gainesville and London

Designed by Rob Evans
and set in Calligraph and FrizQuadrata
Printed in the United States of America

Publisher's Cataloging in Publication Data
Decalo, Samuel, 1938-
    Israel and Africa: 1956-1996
    1. Israel—Foreign Relations
    2. Africa—Foreign Relations
ISBN 1-890357-01-4
LCCN 97-75052

    10 9 8 7 6 5 4 3 2 1

For Henry Wells

CONTENTS

FOREWORD

When I was first invited to assemble for re-publication some of my writings on Israel's four decades of interaction with Africa, I was somewhat hesitant. The articles, written over a considerable span of time and for different audiences, at times mesh together nicely, but elsewhere to some extent duplicate each other. As I had never favored "retrospective" editing, or for that matter artificial cut-and-paste jobs, that seemed called for in this case, I was not sure if the book could hang together without altering some of the original articles.

I was nevertheless persuaded to proceed with the project by the argument that otherwise the record of the first decade and a half of Afro-Israeli relations—on which I had written so much—was likely to be forgotten. The "era of tachlis" (acute pragmatism) in Afro-Israeli relations, as Frank puts it, is upon us, and the early years of wine and roses have largely receded into distant memory. It is in this spirit that this collection of articles is offered. An epilogue and an additional selected bibliography, specially written for this volume, are intended to bring the book completely up to date.

ACKNOWLEDGEMENTS

The author gratefully wishes to acknowledge prior publication of ten of the thirteen articles in this book, that appeared previously as follows:

"Messianic Influences in Israeli Foreign Policy," originally published as *Occasional Papers in Political Science No. 2*, University of Rhode Island, Kingston, 1967.

"Messianic Influences and Pragmatic Limitations in Israeli Foreign Policy," originally published in Marion Mushkat (ed.), *World Society*, The Hague: Mouton, 1974, pp. 373-382.

"Israeli Foreign Policy and the Third World," originally published in *Orbis*, vol. 11 no. 3, fall 1967, pp. 724-745.

"Africa and the Mid-Eastern war," originally published in *Africa Report*, October 1967, pp. 57-61.

"Africa and the Middle East," originally published in the *Middle East Information Series*, no. 22, February 1973, pp. 2-7.

"Afro-Israeli Technical Cooperation: Patterns of Setbacks and Successes," originally published in Michael Curtis and Susan Aurelia Gitelson (eds.), *Israel and the Third World*, New Brunswick: Transaction Press, 1974, pp. 81-99.

"Libya's Qaddafi: Bedouin Product of the Space Age," originally published in *Present Tense*, vol. 1 no. 2, winter 1974, pp. 50-54.

"Africa and the U.N. anti-Zionism Resolution: Roots and Causes," originally published in *Cultures et Developpement*, vol. 8 no. 1, 1976, pp. 89-117.

"The Rise, Decline and Rebirth of the Afro-Israeli Entente," originally published in the *Journal of Contemporary African Studies*, vol. 8/9, no. 1/2, 1989/1990, pp. 3-25.

"Israel and Africa: A Selected Bibliography," originally published in the *Journal of Modern African Studies*, vol. 5 no. 3, 1967, pp. 385-399

1 | MESSIANIC INFLUENCES IN ISRAELI FOREIGN POLICY *

Foreign policy is necessarily a function of the political and socio-economic order of a nation as well as of its sustaining store-house of myths, and mystiques. The "national interest" of a state, as determined by the policy-making strata, is a product of concrete existential factors such as security considerations, economic and geopolitical realities, the International power-hierarchy, etc.; it is, however, also influenced to a greater or lesser extent by the plethora of cultural and ideological outcroppings prevalent in the nation at any particular moment in the time-continuum. Foreign policy as an extension of a nation's internal hierarchy of values, may thus be equated—if the analogy is not pressed to the extreme—to the behavior patterns of an individual's specific personality make-up.

The foreign policy of Israel is the end-product of a variety of intermeshing factors and influences. Some of these are constant and their effect upon policy-formulation may be decisive; others linger in the background coloring policy-formulation and enunciation and only occasionally assume paramount importance. Of the latter kind are what may be called the messianic features of the Israeli polity.[1]

The messianic features of Israel have their philo-theological origins in the biblical designation of the Jews as the Chosen people. Theirs was the mission, thereafter, of bringing all the pagan nations to the bosom of the Lord. By setting an example to humanity they were to attract admiration and emulation until an era of True Faith, peace and social justice dawned across the world.

Imbedded in the Jewish collective consciousness the biblical concept survived throughout the ages. Kept alive by the prophetically-foreseen destiny of Israel as future spiritual leader of the world, it was embroidered by lore and legend, elevated to the status of an all-encompassing national mystique differentiating Israel-in-exile from other peoples, it became the major source of psychological comfort in times of persecution. And the entire heritage was transferred to modern Israel

---

* Originally published in University of Rhode Island, Occasional Papers in Political Science No. 2, October, 1967

to perplex the country's leadership once Independence was achieved. For inevitably the question arose, unremittingly demanding an answer: what is Israel's "role," "mission," in the twentieth century?

The re-emergence of a sovereign Israel after an eclipse of two thousand years was viewed by many religious people in the world as a fulfilment of an ancient prophecy. The non-religious viewed the event as a grave and momentous historical milestone. To Israelis, independence was both a modern-day miracle and the logical culmination—indeed, vindication—of their bitter struggle for a National Home. And the long dammed-up emotions set loose by the declaration of Independence could hardly have not left their mark upon early formulation of Israeli foreign policy. The new state was regarded as endowed with certain unique characteristics and a world historical role recognized implicitly by the Great Powers by virtue of their immediate recognition and support of Israel. Even the no more than slightly bizarre outcome of the unavailability of suitable accommodations for diplomatic missions, in the Tel Aviv of 1948, leading to the housing of both the United States' and the Soviet Union's delegations in the same hotel (with their flags flying side by side over the same roof) was taken by Israelis as "proof" of Israel's "uniqueness." As the Director General of the Israeli Foreign Ministry, Walter Eytan, wrote In 1958:

> Israel beset by Arab armies, could lean on the support of the two mightiest nations on earth. More than this—there was a feeling that Israel had somehow brought East and West together. If they could act in concert, or at least in step, on Israel, why should they not come to agree on other things? The messianism latent in the Jewish soul, stimulated by the miracle of Israel's rebirth was ready to embrace the whole world. With the fulfilment of the Biblical prophecy, a new era of peace and goodwill could be dawning for all men.[2]

Acting on the above presumptions (retrospectively highly utopian) Israel's first steps in the international arena were characterized by a strong desire to steer a strictly neutral course between the two world blocks. It was felt that such a policy was only befitting a young state neither interested in getting involved in what appeared to her to be remote issues of conflict, nor willing to alienate either of the two major Powers towards which she felt gratitude for diplomatic and military support rendered during her struggle for national self-determination. Such a neutralist policy also seemed expedient—and extremely congenial if not necessary—from the domestic point of view.

Moreover, non-identification was viewed in those early days of enthusiasm and messianic idealism as "Israel's way of serving world peace, of making specific her contribution towards preventing a widening of the breech and perhaps, within her restricted means, of helping to narrow and heal the breech."[3] Stressing pointedly, therefore, that part of her cultural paternity and current social ethos came as much from the West as from the East, and that her peculiar national interests were such as to preclude alignment with either (more so since her self-conceived international role was to reconcile the two blocs.) Israel attempted to walk the tightrope between the opposing camps.

The degree to which such a policy was based upon idealistic misconceptions of international realities may perhaps be judged by the fact that less than two years after Independence the Israeli government was carefully-weighing the advantages of an outright alliance with the West. The intensification of the Cold War in the world in general and in the Middle East in particular, and the outbreak of the Korean War quickly shattered the early exuberant expectations of Israel playing an immediate role in the promotion of international peace. Indeed, totally immersed in the three-pronged struggle for national survival—namely, resettlement of the massive refugee-immigration, strengthening the country's extremely shaky economy, and warding off the threat of military annihilation by the Arab world—Israel's ventures in the international scene tended to be pragmatically-oriented. The early zeal for an international role flagged, though it did not die.

The re-emergence into the public limelight of Israel's quest for an international mission had to await the normalization of the power-status in the Middle East and the recession of the Arab threat, both apparent in the years following the Sinai campaign. With the alleviation of some of Israelis harshest security problems after 1957 public debate could latch on to the niceties of less palpable issues. Moreover, the incessant foreign praise heaped upon Israel's phalanx of cooperative institutions and practices, coupled with the beginning of a small but highly significant stream of visiting socialist leaders and Afro-Asian cadres, generated amongst Israelis a deeper awareness of their country's growing International importance as a socioeconomic laboratory.

Israel's enhanced international stature was possibly best attested to by the fact that newly-independent Ghana's first Ministerial delegation to travel abroad included Jerusalem as a focal point in its itinerary. Widely respected John Tettegah (Secretary-General of the

Ghana Trades Union Congress) exclaimed at the end of his 1957 visit to Israel: "Israel has given me more in eight days than I could obtain from two years in a British University."[4] Similar sentiments were voiced by numerous other leaders from the Third World. As the stream of visitors assumed the proportions of a minor deluge—and began to include numerous visiting Heads of State—Israeli policy-makers redoubled their efforts to redefine the contemporary meaning of, and mission of Israel.

"We cannot rest content with being an ordinary people of two million, living its life like every other nation," candidly confessed Histadrut Secretary General Pinhas Lavon in 1962.[5] "Hardly a week passes without our being given a lesson concerning our being a chosen people and our obligation to be a light to the world. What does this mean?...in what way can Israel be a light?"[6] "Are we really able—is it really our duty—to solve the problems of the human race, or to make an important contribution to their solution?" queried Ben Gurion rhetorically before giving a resounding affirmation, adding that:

> I have no sympathy with those clever people who regard messianic yearnings and the aims of the Hebrew prophecy as some kind of mysticism unfit for the attention of the modern man. Nor can I share the satisfaction of those sections who have already attained comfort and tranquillity and believe that we are a people like all other peoples, and a State just like the rest.[7]

It is generally conceded in policy-making strata that Israel's role is mostly in the spiritual realm.[8] The most common view is that the Israeli role lies in the conception, formulation and promotion of fundamental social values and mores applicable equally in relations between nation-states as in relations between man and his fellow-beings. According to Lavon, for example: "We can be a light to the nations only to the extent that we know how to create a people which will not be a copy of other nations but one shaping a way of life and a regime morally, socially and humanly expressing some redeeming idea for all mankind."[9] And Israel—according to Ben Gurion—is eminently suited for this, her self-imposed task, because:

> A universal attachment to social and international justice is...engraved deeply upon the nation's soul. The passion of our prophets was launched against all violence, oppression and lawlessness in human and international affairs...The State will not be faithful to its

prophetic testament...if it fails to follow gratefully and with deep respect for truth every venture that has it to advance righteous and merciful relations between men and peoples and to build human society on foundations of equality and mutual help, not of rivalry and exploitation.[10]

Thus envisioned Israel's "role" has two basic components. The first centers around the creation in Israel a model socialist society based upon social justice, cooperation, progressive values and ideals.[11] This is necessary not only for the sake of the modern Israel polity, but also because "...a model kind of civilization can emerge..." as a result of the Israeli effort.[12] By creating a model society Israel can become a "light to the nations" evoking emulation by others. And the fact that so many cadres from the developing countries have been sent to Israel to study communal developmental methods (cooperative farming, youth organization, trade-unionism, promotion of civic consciousness, soil redemption, etc.,) is cited by Israelis as proof of international recognition of the global significance of the Israeli innovations and leadership in these spheres. Indeed, a number of scholars, European as well as Israeli, view Israel as one of the "three or four developmental models relevant to the Third World. (The other most frequently cited are China, the Soviet Union and Yugoslavia.)

The second facet of Israel's "mission" is her obligation to help promote the emancipation and development of the *Tiers Monde*. Though a definitive study of Israel's foreign policy vis-a-vis the developing countries is yet forthcoming, enough has been written on this topic to preclude a lengthy digression at this stage. The friendship and international support of the forty-odd non-Arab states of Afro-Asia is vital to Israel within the framework of her rivalry and dispute with the Arab bloc. There are other pragmatic and tactical aspects to Israel's policy in Afro-Asia. These, however, need not eclipse the purely ideological and messianic influences coloring Israeli policy-formulation. As the *Manchester Guardian* stressed pointedly: "Israel's policy towards Black Africa should perhaps be seen in wider terms and should be recognized to be not just part of its defence line against the Arab world, but also of a genuine desire to be of help. Africans respond because they recognize this."[14]

This "genuine desire to be of help" rests partly upon psychological and partly on ideological grounds. Psychologically, Israel—long a recipient of international aid—derives great satisfaction from participation in programs of technical cooperation with the developing world in which she is the contributor. This satisfaction should not be under-rated and it assumes even greater significance if viewed in conjunction with the fact that until the late fifties Israel was scorned by many of the then existing Afro-Asian nations. In a sense, therefore, Israel's program of technical cooperation is a re-assertion of her sovereignty and a unilateral declaration of the country's coming of age; of its economic maturity and political independence.

Ideologically, aid to Afro-Asia is based upon a moral conception of the universe according to which all nations are interdependent and responsible for the security and well-being of one another. "In the entire cosmos...there is nothing which can live by itself...Everything is interdependent. It is a world cooperative commonwealth which we ought to aim at, built on freedom."[15] "It is now the duty of the rich and the developed—for the sake of their own peace and liberty and fu-ture—to offer their devoted assistance to the backward peoples..."[16] And Israel's role is to spearhead this drive for the final emancipation of the developing world. For, according to Ben Gurion: "Israel has been granted the great historic privilege—which is therefore also a duty [!]—of assisting backward and primitive peoples to improve themselves, develop and advance, thus helping solve the greatest problem of the twentieth century."[17]

This theme, that Israel has a deep moral obligation to assist in the process of development and modernization of the Third World, has been stressed by many Israeli policy-makers. It is not a policy enunciated solely by a few prophetically-minded leaders such as Ben Gurion. (Lavon himself hardly fits into this category.) No less "prag-matic" a figure than Mapai Secretary-General Mrs. Meir (a political power, in her own right who split with Ben Gurion at the dramatic 1965 Mapai schism) has been enunciating much the same views upon which rested, in part at least, the guidelines of Israel's Afro-Asian policy. In her 1963 review before the Knesset, Mrs. Meir (then Foreign Minister) stressed that, "Israel has always assumed, is assuming, and will continue in the future to assume, an active role in every operation and every objective meant to consummate the restoration of human and national dignity to once downtrodden peoples in Africa and in every place on earth."18 This unequivocal Israeli commitment to the emancipation of the Third World is based, according to Mrs. Meir, upon "...a conception of the world which considers it her own moral duty as well as that of the community of nations, towards the developing countries."[19] Further expanding on this theme at a Paris press conference, the then Foreign Minister reiterated that Israel's assistance to Africa "...conforms with our conception of International obligations. We do not believe that the world can or should tolerate much longer the economic and social differences that separate the new nations from the older nations..."[20]

On no other issue coming before the *Knesset* is there such a unanimity as on the issue of international technical cooperation with Afro-Asia. A consensus encompassing both the coalition and the opposition parties exists in connection with Israel's moral obligation to help those states less fortunate than herself. Though party divisions do crop up as to whether a specific country should receive extensive aid (e.g., Ghana, Cuba, Mali, etc.,) the principle of international cooperation has never been the center of controversy as it has been in several other countries with far greater resources than Israel. Indeed, in several instances it has been the opposition parties that have pressed the Government to increase its technical cooperation appropriations. Moreover, the majority of the population and the information media support the policies of the Government in this domain.[21]

Israel's commitment to the emancipation and development of the Third World has reaped her handsome rewards. Internationally, her stature and prestige have increased dramatically; on the Middle East front, Arab attempts to isolate her have finally been circumvented, bringing about growing Afro-Asian pressure upon the Arab countries (in the U.N. and elsewhere) for a final negotiated peace in the region.[22] Perhaps the most cogent indication of Israel's new international prestige is the fact that, nominated by the many of the African states, Israel has been elected for the first time to a number of positions in the United Nations' committees and agencies as the official representative of the Afro-Asian bloc.[23]

But to no lesser an extent Israel's commitment to Afro-Asia has forced her to renounce certain previously-held orientations and postures. Thus, despite the fact that the Republic of South Africa was Israel's most important trade-partner in Africa (accounting for over 17% of all Afro-Israeli trade), and harbored a prosperous and influential Jewry, relations between Israel and the Republic deteriorated dramatically and nearly reached breaking point in 1964. The exigencies of her Afro-Asian policy led Israel to estrange a country traditionally favorably inclined toward her.

It is precisely in such instances that the strength of ideological factors in Israeli foreign policy can best be gauged. In the specific case at hand, Israel need not have necessarily estranged the Verwoerd regime. Even today, numerous countries (including Afro-Asian ones) pay lip-service to the ostracization of the racist regime in South Africa, but still find scope to maintain diplomatically "correct" relations with it. Israel in 1961, however, instructed her Mission to the United Nations to vote for the imposition of economic sanctions upon South Africa, when the anti-apartheid resolution was presented. Explaining this action to the public, Mrs. Meir stated that "...in this instance Israel's loyalty to a moral principle and considerations of political interest overcame considerations for the short-range interests of South African Jewry—Israel cannot allow itself to miss any opportunity to contribute to the removal of racialism." [25] Though certain very important pragmatic considerations were involved in the decision to vote for the harshest provisions against South Africa, the fact cannot be overlooked that a basic "raison d'etre" of Israel (protection of the status of world Jewry) had been compromised in the name of ideologism.

Possibly it might be appropriate to note one more messianic-ideological strand permeating some foreign policy-making in Israel. This concerns the notion of Israel serving as a bridge between the East and the West; between the developed and the developing nations of the world.

The origin of the concept that Israel may serve as a "bridge" between different socioeconomic systems has already been traced elsewhere in this paper to the early days of the State during which messianic fervour abounded. At the time it was felt that Israel could, through some unspecified means, bridge the gap between the two power conglomerations in the world. Though these expectations were rudely shattered within a short period of time, the "bridge" theory was, revived in the late 1950's. This time, however, Israel was to serve as a bridge between the developed and the developing nations of the world: a bridge serving to promote harmony and good will between the two groups of nations, as well as acting as the transfusion center for Western technology to the Third World. Abba Eban, opening the 1960 Colloquium on the Role of Science in the Developing Nations, summed up Israel's envisaged role when he stated that: "Israel is the meeting point for Western science and technology and the awakening countries in the modern world....in organizing the Colloquium in Rehovoth we wished to force upon scientists pangs of conscience regarding the Third World."[26]

Commenting on Israel's role in this sphere Eliahu Elath (then Israel's Ambassador to Great Britain) noted that "...the contribution Israel can make...will help to establish and preserve durable links between these African developing peoples and the family of nations, thereby promoting better understanding and cooperation between the peoples, and peace in world."[27]

The above brief outline should suffice to indicate the extent to which themes resting implicitly upon messianic considerations are prevalent in Israeli decision-making strata. This is not to imply, of course, that all, or even most, of foreign policy deliberations in Israel are garnished with messianic overtones. Indeed, in descending the administrative ladder one notes a radical diminution in such pronouncements. Many Israelis charged with executing their country's foreign policy tend to view the latter through excessively pragmatic-tinted tenses. Yet even the most ardent practitioner of *realpolitik* would likely admit that in the final analysis certain aspects of the nation's foreign policy are in some measure based upon non-pragmatic ideological-messianic grounds.

Such considerations are much more prevalent in intellectual and higher-echelon policy-making circles; and it is precisely at these levels that official ideologies and mystiques are most commonly born. Though the 1963 shuffle in Israel's leadership brought to the fore a slightly more managerial elite, its commitment to international cooperation is no less strong than its predecessors—though it appears less emotional in nature. On the other hand the *Mapai* alliance with the more leftist *Achdut Ha'avodah* (aimed at the eventual merger of these twin parties) guarantees that ideological discourses based upon the principle of proletarian internationalism are not to disappear from the Israeli scene in the foreseeable future.

Possibly the best way to categorize the contemporary messianic overtones of Israel's foreign policy is by viewing them as outcropping influences derived from Israel's cultural paternity, and hence inseparable from the "national character" of the state. Their effect upon future policy-formulation will vary with the kind of issues involved, the pragmatic considerations brought to bear upon them and the other "cultural" influences demanding their due. Even if in policy-formulation the weight accorded to the messianic influences is minimal, they provide at least a measure of legitimacy, rationale and historical continuity re-enforcing policies arrived at through more conventional deliberations.

FOOTNOTES

1. The terms "messianic influences" and "messianic features," as used in this paper, refer specifically to the more extended concepts linked with the prophetically-foreseen (Isaiah etc.,) visions of the post-Messianic era-to-come, and Israel's role in this Kingdom of Heaven on Earth. Thus defined, the Judaic "messianic yearning" refers to the desire for this biblically-promised global messianic mission (see the following paragraphs in the text), and the "messianic influences" (briefly sketched in this paper, so far as they impinge upon foreign policy) refer to some of the influences on policy-making, deriving from this entire sub-cultural stratum—the consciousness of an ordained and sanctioned messianic mission. Needless to say, the term "messianic" has several other meanings (usually theological.) An examination of their status and transmutation in modern Israel would be beyond both the scope and limitations, as well as primary focus, of this paper.

2. Walter Eytan, *The First Ten Years* (New York, 1958), p. 139.

3. According to then Foreign Minister Moshe Sharett, in a speech to the *Knesset* in 1950.

4. Cited in *Jerusalem Post*, July 23, 1957.

5. Pinhas Lavon "A Chosen Society and a Normal People," *New Outlook* (Tel Aviv), February 1962, p. 4.

6. *Ibid.*

7. Cited in *Israel Weekly News Bulletin*, May 16-22, 1962. Interestingly enough, Ben Gurion's views run parallel to those of Pinhas Lavon with whom he has bitterly clashed during the past six years. Lavon has in the past scathingly attacked the emerging Israeli pyramid of self-satisfied petty bourgeoisie, creating a "... new society which may be very good for the people living in it—they will work less, will eat well and enjoy themselves—but it will be a society without a god and even without idols of serious dimensions.

We shall become a completely "normal" society without any special charm and without any special attraction. We shall then be, in the last analysis, a Levantine country." (*Ibid*, p. 8.)

8. See, for example, Ben Gurion's comments in the *Israel Weekly News*

Bulletin, May 16-21, 1962, where he states, *inter-alia*, that, "Israel is not destined to be a world factor either in the military, the political or the economic field...but in the kingdom of the spirit we are capable of being an important factor, a by no means negligible force, not only vis-a-vis the Jewish people throughout the world, but even in the broad scene of international relations." This view has been reiterated by other members of the Israeli political elite.

9. Lavon, p. 6.

10. David Ben Gurion, *Israel Among The Nations* (Jerusalem, 1952), p. 12.

11. It would be instructive at this stage to recall that the Bible is in many respects a document on ethical standards. And though, as the scriptures relate, ancient Israel often succumbed to temptation, nevertheless the First Kingdom of Israel did incorporate many of the concepts of charity, relief for the disabled, poor and orphaned, social justice and other practices usually encompassed by the modern welfare state, yet so extremely rare in ancient societies.

The strong egalitarian influences, the variety of welfare and cooperative institutions, the stress on economic and social justice, that are to be found in modern Israel (even if some are in the process of withering away in face of the onslaught of the materialistic tendencies of economic prosperity) are to no small extent an indirect outgrowth of the heritage of the scriptural injunctions.

12. From an interview with Ben Gurion. See Gertrude Samuels "Israel at 13, Ben Gurion at 75," *The New York Times Magazine*, September 24, 1961.

13. See, for example, Julius Braunthal and J. B. Kripalani, *The Significance of Israeli Socialism* (London, 1958); Joseph Klatzmann, *Les Enseignements de l'experience Israelienne* (Paris, 1963); Elie Maissi "Israel et son example," *Cahiers Africains* (Paris), No. 2, 1961; Jules Moche, "Israel, Yugoslavie, Chine: Trois Methodes," *La Revue Socialiste* (Paris), May 1963, pp. 459-479; Mordechai Nessiahu, "Israel kegesher bein Haolam Hamefutach ve-Haolam Hamitpateach," (Israel as a bridge between the developed and the developing World) *Davar* (Tel Aviv), July 10, 1964; Robert O. Perlman, *Israel's Cooperation as the New Alternative to Communism Socialism and Capitalism* (Jerusalem, 1961.)

14. Cited in *Jeusalem Post*, August 17, 1962.

15. Ben Gurion to Gertrude Samuels. See *The New York Times Magazine*, September 24, 1961. 16 David-Ben Gurion "The Vision of Isaiah for Our Time," *The New York Times Magazine*, May 20, 1963.

17. David Ben Gurion, *Israel's Security and Her International Position Before and After the Sinai Campaign* (Jerusalem: Government Printer, 1960), p. 69.

18. *Israel Digest*, March 15, 1963, p. 3.

19. From Mrs. Meir's opening address in the special issue on Israel of *Afrique Nouvelle* (Dakar), November 22, 1961. Translated by the author.

20. Cited in *Abidjan-Matin* (Abidjan), June 10, 1961. Translated by the author.

21. On May 11, 1962, *Ha'aretz*, one of lsraei's few independent newspapers editorialized: "It is becoming more and more clear that the decision to nurture friendly relations with these countries in Africa was one of the most humane and wise decisions taken by our policy-makers in the past few years." Translated by the author.

22. See, for example, United Nations, General Assembly Official Records, #7th Session, Special Political Committee, Draft Resolution A/SPC/L.89 + Add. 1, December 9, 11, 1962, as well as the same Comittee's 18th session Draft Resolution A/SPC/L.100 + Add. 1, November 18, 20, 1963.

23. Three instances of this are the 1962 election of an Israeli to the Executive Board of the World Health Organization, the 1963 election of an Israeli Vice-President of the Fourth Committee of the U.N. General Assembly and the 1963 election of an Israeli to the Executive Board of UNICEF. These elections constitute significant breakthroughs for Israel, for in previous years the Arab powers and their allies were generally quite successful in blocking the nomination and election of Israeli candidates for most positions in the U.N. or its agencies.

24. *Ha'aretz*, December 22, 1961.

25. *Davar*, November 15, 1961. Translated by the author.

26. Cited in *Abidjan-Matin* (Abidjan), October 7, 1960. Translated by the author.

27. Cited in *The Ethiopia Herald* (Addis Ababa), September 26, 1959.

2 MESSIANIC INFLUENCES AND PRAGMATIC LIMITATIONS IN ISRAELI FOREIGN POLICY*

A country's foreign policy is generally based upon a complex amalgam of perceived national interests, ideological inclinations and international realities, stemming from the nation's historical, cultural, socio-economic and geopolitical parameters and colored—sometimes deeply affected—by the personality psycho-dynamics and predispositions of top policy-makers at the apex of the political power hierarchy.

The latter variable is especially relevant in any analysis of new states and their foreign policies, even though, paradoxically, it is these very countries that usually have the least luxury of maneuvrability on the international plane as a result of their neo-dependent status. Notwithstanding this, studies of central bureaucracies and patterns of decision-making in new political systems cogently underscore the degree to which policy-making is the province of small elites. Consequent to their role as founding fathers of the new polities, and to the paucity of trained personnel to staff their Foreign Offices and operating in an institutional vacuum, unrestrained by precedent or routinization of decision-making, such elites tend to impress their world-outlook upon their country's foreign policy.[1] And the slowly accumulating literature on the psychological bases of political behavior seems to indicate that it is essentially within such an unstructured and flexible context that systemic frustrations are translated through personalist or charismatic leaders into millennial dreams, messianic aspirations, mobilizing slogans or ideological frameworks.

Since the "personal element" in policy-making is but one of many vectors, some of which are external, the ideological component of weak states may be totally missing (as in much of French Africa), devoid of possibilities of its actualization (as with Congo-Brazzaville or Mali's neo-Marxist approach to development) or turned inwards towards domestic targets (as in Tanzania or, classically, the US "Manifest

*Originally published in M. Mushkat (ed.), *World Society*. The Hague: Mouton, 1974, pp. 373-382.

Destiny" in the 19th century.) As the political system develops and acquires greater institutional complexity and trained personnel, a process of bureaucratic routinization is often visible. In the absence of systemic traumas or discontinuities (e.g., the recession in pre-Hitler Germany) and buttressed by greater governmental efficacy in solving developmental problems, the personal weight in policy-making and its ideological components may well erode and decline in importance, as best manifested in post-1953 Russia. The purpose of this article is to point out a similar constellation of ideological and personal influences that played an important role in the formulation of Israeli foreign policy during the immediate post-independence period and the early 1960's before receding under the onslaught of economic prosperity, increased systemic goal-attainment and bureaucratic routinization of decision-making processes.

Israeli foreign policy is the inevitable end-product of a variety of inter-meshing factors and influences, pragmatic and ideological considerations, some of which are fixed or external and have a decisive effect on policy formulation. Among them may be noted the limitations imposed upon an "independent" foreign policy by the need for security, protection of world Jewry and domestic capital development in a world marked by scarcity of capital flows from developed to developing nations. Other variables which partake in moulding Israel's foreign policy are cultural and personal; they tend to linger in the background, coloring policy formulation and only occasionally assuming significant importance. Of this second kind are what may be called the "messianic" influences in Israeli foreign policy, especially as expounded by David Ben-Gurion during his period in office as Prime Minister.[2]

With an Israel born, as it was, in the midst of a dual struggle for self-determination—against the British Mandate and the Arab invasions attending its termination—and because of continuous Arab avowals of an impending "second round" that would end in the demise of the new state, security considerations have played the primary role in all formulations of foreign policy. The pragmatic dictates of Israel's original economic and military weakness, the erosion of initial Soviet and American support, and difficulties encountered in attaining international legitimacy via diplomatic recognition made even more imperative a pragmatic foreign policy aimed at securing the state, its territorial integrity and survival.

Yet all these factors could not quell deep cultural under-currents and personal visions of an Ideal State playing a global role that cried for public expression. The re-emergence of an independent Jewish state after an interregnum of two thousand years was a traumatic and momentous experience for world Jewry and for the Israeli settlers and their political leaders alike. The end-product of centuries of dreams and aspirations for the "Return to Zion", Israel became instantly the focus of attention of Jewish communities around the world and a source of spiritual leadership. The Law of Return, lodged in the very Proclamation of Independence itself, was a tangible reminder that Israel was not to be merely another newly independent political entity but that the new state had assumed certain world-wide responsibilities in the secular and religious spheres.

No sooner had the State been born, and the dust of its War of Independence had settled, than an acute debate was to emerge as to the nature of these responsibilities, the nature and purpose of the state, and its future role in the community of nations. In those heady days of euphoria at the miraculous national rebirth, national self- determination was too pedestrian a justification for the new polity: Israel had to have a more significant global role if it was to fulfil the prophetic vision contained in the Scriptures.

Imbedded in the Jewish collective consciousness, the biblical prophecy of a renascent Israel as spiritual leader of the world had survived throughout the ages. Embroidered by lore and legend, elevated to the status of a national mystique differentiating between the "Chosen People", who were to set an example for the world, and all other nations, it was to be a source of comfort in times of crisis and persecution. And the entire cultural heritage was to be transferred to modern Israel to perplex the country's leadership, secular as well as religious, once independence was achieved. For, with the attainment of national sovereignty, part of the biblical prophecy had been fulfilled; what was still unclear, however, was the nature of the "example" which Israel was expected to set.

Needless to say, not all in the Israeli leadership hierarchy of that era participated in the debate about Israel's modern purpose or role. Powerful voices were raised in support of Israel's becoming "a state like all states", distinguished possibly by its religious composition but without further pretensions to uniqueness or a world mission; a modern humanitarian welfare state, assuredly, along patterns developed during the Mandate era, but without an internally-imposed task to set the pace for mankind. Ranged against this viewpoint could be found others, headed by Ben-Gurion, deeply conscious of (as well as affected by) this momentous juncture in the history of the Jewish people, and the importance and world-wide significance of every one of their actions. It was largely on account of the kind of leadership that came to power in 1948 that the new state was to be infused with a strong dose of messianic idealism in its domestic as well as its foreign policies.

Attempts to define the nature, scope and direction of Israel's potential contributions to the human community (apart from serving as a haven for world Jewry) have vacillated among several options. Inevitably the self-imposed mission of 1948—when the state was economically weak, unsure of itself and still a pariah in much of the Third World—was to differ from that enunciated in the early 1960's, when the state was militarily secure, full of self-confidence and basking in the warmth of attention from the Third World. Almost equally inevitably, owing to the severe restrictions and counter-pressures exerted by external factors (especially in 1948-1956), and pragmatic considerations (during 1958-1962), the different formulations of Israel's messianic mission have tended to mesh precisely with the pragmatic necessities of the moment.

Conversely, in times of severe crisis—as in 1956—they have been eclipsed altogether. Of the various formulations of Israel's messianic mission, two will be noted in particular. The first sprang fully blown out of the euphoria of independence and the unique international circumstances that accompanied the creation of the state. Israel's first steps in the international arena were characterized by an attempt to chart a neutral course between the two main super-Powers whose amity and support appeared vital to her security and whose diplomatic and military support had helped her gain independence (Decalo, 1967b.)

Such a policy, it was felt, was only fitting a small country neither interested in getting involved in the East-West struggle, nor willing to alienate countries from which it had obtained part of its cultural and social ethos. Non-alignment, moreover, appeared to be congenial from the domestic point of view in the light of pockets of pro-Soviet sentiment that had coalesced and demanded an even-handed approach *vis-a-vis* East and West alike. The pragmatic considerations appeared, therefore, to argue for a neutral posture with respect to the global polarization.

To these considerations were added messianic-ideological ones. Non-alignment was viewed as "Israel's way of serving world peace, of making specific her contribution towards the bridging of the breach, and perhaps, within her restricted means, to narrow 'and heal the breach'". (Foreign Minister Moshe Sharett in a speech at the Knesset in 1950. See also Ben-Gurion, 1952, 1954, and Ben-Asher, 1954.) Israel's role was to lead in the actualization of the second part of the biblical prophecy—world peace; her birth had been aided by the American and Russian midwives—surely this was an auspicious sign of the constructive role that Israel was destined to play. The fact that lack of accommodations in the Tel Aviv of 1948 had resulted in the Russian and American delegations sharing hotel facilities with their flags flying side by side was viewed as further proof of Israel's unique ability to bring together the opposing powers. As Walter Eytan, Director-General of the Israeli Foreign Ministry, was to write in this context:

> .... there was a feeling that Israel had somehow brought East and West together. If they could act in concert, or at least in step, on Israel, why should they not come to agree on other things? The messianism latent in the Jewish soul, stimulated by the miracle of Israel's rebirth, was ready to embrace the whole world. With the fulfilment of the biblical prophecy, a new era of peace and goodwill could be dawning for all men (Eytan, 1958:39.)

The neutralist option was soon to be closed to Israel and with it were dashed the hopes for an Israeli contribution to a world entente. Increased Soviet hostility, the slow disengagement of the US from overt support of Israel, and the darkening military and security situation were to eclipse the early messianic zeal for a world mission, at least for several years.

Renewed debate about Israel's world mission was to emerge forcefully with the normalization of the power-balance in the Middle East and the recession of the Arab threat following the 1956 war. Once again the messianic-ideological influences intertwined with the perceived pragmatic requirement of post-1956 diplomacy; only this time the concept of Israel as a model for other states and a contributing factor to world peace was to be more solidly grounded in reality.

By 1957 profound changes had altered the socioeconomic infrastructure of Israel and impressive advances had been made in all
spheres. Israel's success in moulding a nation out of disparate social
elements with widely divergent cultural backgrounds; her communal
and cooperative structures, patterns of union organization and approaches to regional development (the Lachish project) had gained her
growing attention as a social laboratory and a developmental model of
great relevance to other new states (see, for example, Braunthal and
Kripalani, 1958; Klatzmann, 1963; Maissi, 1961; Moch, 1963.) Israel had
been "discovered" by the Third World (starting with Burma and then
the Gold Coast) and the impending independence of several African
territories already searching in Israel for relevant developmental guidelines presaged even greater interest in the Israeli experience.

The stream of delegations from the Third World (and especially
from Africa) began to assume the proportions of a minor deluge, as did
foreign acclaim for Israel's achievements. [3] The hitherto largely scorned
and isolated Israel appeared to have come of age and her "uniqueness"
was finally being recognized. It was, therefore, only a natural development that efforts to redefine the Israeli "mission" received a powerful
boost in the late 1950's and early 1960's. The psychological frustration
of the isolationist past, coupled with the arrival of long-awaited recognition of the relevance of the Israeli achievements, demanded an
ideological expression in the context of a society conditioned by
tradition and culture to regard itself as a moral pace-setter.

At the same time, powerful pragmatic reasons existed in 1956-57
for a major expansion of Israel's sources of international support. Its
former over-reliance upon the amity and support of the major Powers
had not paid out significant dividends. Isolated as it was from most of
Asia (only Turkey and Burma maintained relations with her in 1956),
there was the possibility that the countries soon to be independent
might also drift diplomatically into the Arab camp. Paradoxically, it
appeared that "only if Israel were independently powerful in the
diplomatic arena would she be able to obtain the greater support and
help that she needed from the West, and in particular from the USA.
A weak Israel was a diplomatic liability to a State Department frequently
swayed by global tactical considerations" (Jerusalem Post, 5 July 1956.) An
Israel more acceptable to the growing community of nations would be
able to receive greater consideration for her views and security needs
from Washington. Pragmatic reasons, therefore, urged a major multi-

faceted diplomatic assault on the Third World and especially Africa, still
a *tabula rasa* to Israel and the Arab countries alike (Decalo, 1967b:727-
733.) The dramatic expansion in Israel-Africa contacts and cooperation
that was to mark the post-1957 period meshed with the messianic
desire that had discovered in the Third World the outlet for its fulfilment.

"We cannot rest content with being an ordinary people of two
million people, living its life like every other nation," declared Histadrut
Secretary-General Pinhas Lavon in 1962. "Hardly a week passes without
our being given a lesson concerning our being a chosen people and our
obligation to be a light to the world. What does this mean? ... in what
way can Israel be a light?" (Lavon, 1962:4.) "Are we really able—is it
really our duty—to solve the problems of the human race, or to make
an important contribution to their solution?" queried Ben-Gurion
rhetorically, before giving a resounding affirmation of the messianic
aspiration:

> I have no sympathy with those clever people who regard messianic
> yearnings and the aim of the Hebrew prophecy as some kind of
> mysticism unfit for the attention of the modern man. Nor can I share
> the satisfaction of those sections which have already attained com-
> fort and tranquillity and believe that we are a people like all other
> peoples, and a state just like the rest (Cited in *Israel Weekly News Bulletin*,
> 16-22 May 1962.)

Israel's newly defined role in the early 1960's was seen as composed of
three parts: a) the conception, formulation and promotion of fundamental social values and mores applicable equally in relations between
nations as in relations between individuals; b) the building of a model
welfare state which could serve as inspiration to other societies; and c)
international assistance to the Third World in its efforts at socioeconomic development.

According to Lavon "We can be a light to the nations only to the
extent that we know how to create a people which will not be a copy
of other nations but one shaping a way of life and a regime morally,
socially and humanly expressing some redeeming idea for all mankind." (Lavon, 1962:6.) This is necessary since, according to Ben-Gurion
"... a model kind of civilization can emerge..." as a result of the Israeli
effort. (From an interview with Ben-Gurion; see Samuels, 1961.)

Israel-Third World cooperation is based on the moral concept of the inter-dependence of all nations and mutual responsibility for the security and well-being of each and every one of them. "It is a world cooperative commonwealth which we ought to aim at, built on freedom" (Samuels, 1961.) And again: "It is now the duty of the rich and the developed—for the sake of their own peace and liberty and future—to offer their devoted assistance to the backward peoples..." (Ben-Gurion, 1963), with Israel spear-heading this co-operative drive. For, once more according to Ben-Gurion, "Israel has been granted the great historical privilege—which is therefore also a duty—of assisting backward and primitive people to improve themselves, develop and advance, thus helping to solve the greatest problem of the 20th century" (Ben-Gurion, 1960:69.) Because of her unique achievements in the social and economic sphere, as well as her dedication to international cooperation, Israel could provide the bridge between the developing and the developed countries, a transfusion point for Western technology and science to the Third World.[4]

The moral duty of Israel to spur on and participate in the social and economic development of the Third World has been enunciated by a wide variety of leaders, secular as well as religious, and has not remained the philosophical province of a few prophetically inclined or inspired politicians.[5] The ideological vector of Israel's Third World policy in the 1960's, and the fact that it was enunciated and supported by some of the prominent leaders of the state, have given the Israeli programs of international cooperation consistency, legitimacy and priority.[6] The expansion of Israel's involvement with Africa and Asia has brought Israel immense practical benefits in terms of international support, increased prestige and greater consideration for her interests and views in the West. This has tended, in turn, to confirm the correctness of the original decision to stress links with the Third World and it has stimulated the further escalation of programs of cooperation with developing nations.

The debate about Israel's messianic role was at its peak during 1960-1964 only to decline dramatically in frequency and intensity in the following years. Undoubtedly a prime reason for this decline was the fact that Lavon, Ben-Gurion and several other top politicians of the Old Guard were to be displaced by the mid-1960's. A somewhat more pragmatic and managerial elite has slowly percolated into policy-making positions and the messianic dialectic has been one of several things to suffer as a consequence (especially with Abba Eban as Foreign Minister.)

It would be an error, however, to attribute the shift in political style in this area only to a partial shuffling of elites. Other societal variables have been at work all along, militating against the easy renewal of the dialogue and the poignant soul-searching of the past. Prime and foremost among these factors should be noted: a) further changes in the socioeconomic infrastructure of Israel; and b) increased institutional complexity and a routinization of decision-making in the Israeli Foreign Office.

The 1960's were, by all objective yardsticks, years during which the Israeli economy finally came of age and caught up with many of the West European states. By 1970 Israel's per capita income—a convenient though not a very satisfactory comparative statistic—placed her in twelfth rank in the world. Gone are the early days' self-doubts, insecurities and strivings for national fulfilment, swept away by the middle-class tendencies of a prospering society. Programs of international cooperation have not so much suffered from this as that their legitimation is no longer based (or needed) on ideological grounds. Pure humanitarian arguments, coupled with pragmatic considerations, sustain the programs in the 1970's with equal legitimacy and consistency.

The complexity and new social composition of the population have also changed the human infrastructure out of which ideologies spring or in which they take root. Native-born Israelis are moving into top administrative positions. Largely uninspired by the messianic prophecy which struck a responsive chord in the older generation owing to a variety of psychological factors, this new leadership group has been setting a very ideology-free pace for Israel. They have been joined by increased immigration from the West, traditionally suspicious of ideologies, and by immigration from North African and Middle Eastern communities, amenable to ideological appeals but not precisely of the kind sparked by the East European tradition. The latter elements are also much more concerned with finding their place in the sun than with philosophic deliberations regarding Israel's messianic mission.

Similar changes have been going on in the bureaucracy which has increased spectacularly in both size and complexity since the late 1950's. Bureaucratic routinization has set in as efficiency and administrative considerations have become more important. This style has had a powerful boost under Abba Eban's leadership, which has been singularly devoid of ideological or idealist strivings or goals. By reason of all these changes, it would be difficult today for a policy-maker to set the tone of the entire Ministry, even if only on the ideological plane. Indeed, even during the early 1960's, the second phase of ideological debate, a very definite schism existed between the top echelons of the decision-making process and the rank and file. Research conducted by the author in 1964 vividly underscored the extent to which those in the Foreign Ministry charged with the execution of their foreign policy viewed their task in straightforward pragmatic terms in contradistinction to the messianic overtones of their actions as articulated by the higher political echelons.

Curiously enough, many of the technical experts sent to the field in Third World countries tended to be midway between the two extremes. So that in all probability the cleavage, or, better still, the tension, between messianic-idealism and pragmatism was all along part and parcel of Israeli foreign policy, largely camouflaged in the early formative years of the state by the leadership style of the top policy-making hierarchy of those days. Whether or not messianic idealism will again become an important factor coloring Israeli foreign policy, messianic influences in the past have given it a legitimacy rationale and a sense of historical continuity that lent Israel's diplomacy the special vibrance and drive which allowed the state to establish itself firmly in the Third World and to consolidate its position in the wider community of nations.

FOOTNOTES

1. Analyses conducted by the author in 1963-64 at the UN brought to light the degree to which the African delegations had absolute freedom to vote on many issues in accord with their own estimates of the relevance of the resolutions to their countries' national interests. Several delegations also had blanket instructions to follow the lead of some of the bigger and better organized Missions (such as the Ivory Coast) or, later, the OAU caucusing bloc. Their general guidelines were laid down by the chief executives back home. This was true in the case both of authoritative systems (such as Uganda or the Central African Republic) and of the more flexible ones (such as Senegal or Togo.)

2. The analysis that follows relies to some extent upon the author's previous monograph (Decalo, 1967a.)

3. One of the first African leaders to visit Israel was John Tettegah, Secretary General of Ghana's Trade Union Congress, who exclaimed: "Israel has given me more in eight days than I could obtain from two years in a British University." *Jerusalem Post*, 23 July, 1967.)

4. See Abba Eban's and Eliahu's comments as reprinted in *Abidjan-Matin* (Abidjan), 7 October, 1960, and *Ethiopia Herald* (Addis Ababa), 26 September, 1959.

5. See, for example, Mrs. Meir's 1963 review of her Ministry (Foreign Affairs) at the *Knesset* in *Israel Digest*, 15 March, 1963, p. 3, as well as her opening address in the special issue on Israel in the then-influential *Afrique-Nouvelle* (Dakar), 22 November, 1961.

6. Despite its flaws the best single work on the Israeli effort is Kreinin (1964.) For a comprehensive bibliography of Israel-Africa relations, see Decalo (1967.)

REFERENCES

Ben-Asher, A.A., 1954. *Yachasei Hutz, 1948-1953* (Foreign Relations, 1948-1953.) Tel Aviv.

Ben-Gurion, David, 1952. *Israel Among the Nations.* Government Press, Jerusalem, 1954.

Ben-Gurion, David, 1954. *Medniyut Hutz* (Foreign policy.) Tel Aviv.

Ben-Gurion, David, 1960. *Israel's Security and the International Position before and after the Sinai Campaign.* Government Printer, Jerusalem.

Ben-Gurion,David, 1963. "The Vision of Isaiah for our Time". *New York Times Magazine*, 20 May, 1963.

Braunthal, Julius and J. B. Kripalani, 1958. *The Significance of Israeli Socialism.* London.

Decalo, Samuel, 1967a. *Messianic Influences in Israel Foreign Policy.* Occasional Papers in Political Science No. 2, University of Rhode Island.

Decalo, Samuel, 1967b. "Israel Foreign Policy and the Third World." *Orbis* (Fall): 724-745.

Decalo, Samuel, 1967c. "Israel and Africa: A Selected Bibliography". *Journal of Modern African Studies*, (3): 385-399.

Eytan, Walter, 1958. *The First Ten Years.* New York.

Klatzmann, Josepb, 1963. *Les enseignements de l'éxperience Israelienne*. Paris.

Kreinin, Mordechai, 1964. *Israel and Africa: A study in Technical Cooperation*. New York.

Lavon, Pinhas, 1962. "A Chosen Society and a Normal People". *New Outlook* (Tel Aviv), February.

Maissi, Ellie, 1962. "Israel et son exemple". *Cahiers Africains* (Bruxelles), No 2.

Moch, Jules, 1963. "Israel, Yugoslavie, Chine: trois methodes". *Revue social* (Paris), May.

Samuels, Gertrude, 1961. "Israel at 13, Ben Gurion at 75". *New York Times Magazine*, 24 September.

3 ISRAELI FOREIGN POLICY AND THE THIRD WORLD*

On Friday, June 17, 1966, President and Mrs Shazar of Israel and their entourage boarded an El Al jet at Lydda Airport on their way to a series of state visits in Latin America. Following the ceremonies the foreign envoys and Israeli dignitaries did not disperse immediately. Drifting in and out of the airport lounges, they waited to perform their second courtesy function of the day, greeting Prime Minister Eshkol, who was scheduled to arrive within a few hours after an extensive diplomatic tour of Africa. These two events, occurring on the same day, serve to point up Israel's diplomatic involvement with the Third World in the mid-1960's. The visits were important "firsts" for Israel. President Shazar's trip was the first Israeli state visit to Latin America and a tangible manifestation of the recent amplification of Israeli diplomacy in that continent. Eshkol's extensive crisscrossing of Africa was similarly the first such venture by an Israeli Premier.[1] In contrast with Shazar's visit, it emphasized the consolidated nature of Israel's position and influence in sub-Saharan Africa. With these twin events in mind, let us trace the course of Israel's involvement with the Third World.

Israel and the Third World Prior to Sinai

Born amid a dual struggle for self-determination—against the British mandate and the Arab invasions attending its termination—Israel has perforce given security considerations primacy in her decision-making processes. Since the successful war of independence (1948-1949) only assured the new state her immediate survival, and the Arab powers vowed a "second round" it is not surprising, that the quest for lasting security has been the theme underlying all Israeli foreign policy deliberations.

*Published originally in *Orbis*, vol.11 no. 3, Fall 1967, pp. 724-745.

Israel's first steps in the international arena sought to charter a strictly neutral course between the two world blocs whose amity and support were vital for her security. It was felt that such a policy befitted a young state neither interested in getting involved in what she considered to be remote issues of conflict, nor willing to alienate either of the two major powers. Non-identification, moreover, appeared to be an extremely congenial policy from the domestic point of view. Israel stressed pointedly, therefore, that part of her cultural and social ethos came as much from the East as from the West, and that her particular national interests were such as to preclude alignment with either.

The superimposition of the East-West struggle on the local Israel-Arab tug-of-war, with consistent Soviet espousal of the Arab cause shattered these early attempts at nonalignment. Massive deliveries of Czech and Soviet armaments for the Arab armies caused consternation in an Israel already strained by the Middle East arms race. This turned into frustration when the West joined in the courtship of the Arab powers, minimizing for this purpose its links with Israel. Israeli overtures regarding inclusion in the various regional defense associations then being proposed by the United States were quietly and indirectly rebuffed. Requests for heavy armaments were usually rejected with even less evasiveness. To support Israel openly was viewed by Washington as tantamount to inviting the complete alienation of the Arab Middle East and its "loss" to the Soviet Union.[2]

During the period 1949-1956 the Third World figured only tangentially in policy-making sessions of the Israeli Foreign Ministry. The bulk of the ministry's efforts centered around cultivation of close and amicable relations with Washington, Paris, London and Moscow. The creation of Israel's diplomatic corps was concentrated in these capitals and in the Mission to the United Nations. Though various drives had been mounted since independence to secure widespread diplomatic recognition from the community of nations, financial considerations ruled out the establishment of many Israeli missions abroad. As late as 1957 Israel maintained only seven embassies in the entire world, six of these in Europe and North America.[3]

In Latin America only three Israeli missions were to be found prior to 1956. Each of their heads was responsible for diplomatic relations and consular matters with up to four countries in his vicinity—this despite the crucial role Latin America had played in the United

Nations voting which preceded the establishment of the State of Israel. After independence Israeli interest in the continent diminished somewhat. Halfway around the globe, their foreign policies conditioned by the presence of their giant neighbor to the north, the Latin American countries appeared to offer few opportunities for Israeli diplomacy. Moreover, except in Mexico and Argentina, where trade prospects also seemed relatively bright, there were few sizeable Jewish communities requiring the attention and services of resident Israeli diplomats.

In sub-Saharan Africa, a *terra incognita* to the Israeli Foreign Ministry, only Liberia and Ethiopia were independent. Both were effectively isolated from Israel, Ethiopia by the Egyptian blockades of Suez and Sharm el-Sheik, and Liberia by sheer distance as well. Trade prospects with Liberia appeared nonexistent, those with Ethiopia meagre. And though both Haile Selassie and especially President Tubman had exhibited sympathy for Israel during the UN Partition Plan sessions and votes, they were nevertheless wary of establishing full relations with a country that seemed to have so many enemies. Thus, until 1956 not a single resident Israeli diplomat was to be found north of Johannesburg. A number of goodwill missions were dispatched from time to time; minuscule trade delegations occasionally explored the commercial possibilities of the continent, but it was not until 1956-1957 that the first breakthrough occurred in Ghana.

Of the three continents traditionally encompassed by the term "Third World," only in Asia did Israel mount consistent forays. Paradoxically, here in her own continent prospects were most bleak. It was only after Israeli efforts in Africa had been crowned by success that the Asian picture started to improve. When a leading Burmese newspaper noted that "though white men, Israelis consider themselves Asians,"[4] it unintentionally pinpointed one of the major psychological obstacles impeding the early acceptance of Israel as a kindred Asian political entity. The Asians' lack of familiarity with the Old Testament precluded their understanding the traditional Jewish longing for Israel as the ancient homeland. Without this background Zionism appeared in Asian eyes to be a largely alien "European" ideology and the return to Zion but a flimsy excuse for colonialist aspirations. Israel's then Prime Minister, David Ben-Gurion, complained as recently as 1962 that the Israeli struggle for self- determination and independence against Britain was the only national liberation movement in Asia not recognized as a genuinely anti-colonialist effort.[5]

Israelis on their part also exhibited abysmal ignorance at times in matters pertaining to Asian culture, society and religion. Lacking the familiarizing influences of common cultural background, tradition, history or prolonged contacts, Israel and Asia tended to see each other as worlds apart. The venomous anti-Israel propaganda emanating from Arab states did nothing to close the distance. To this day, despite many friendly contacts on the personal level between intellectuals, professionals, socialist and labor leaders, Israel has no diplomatic relations with Indonesia, Pakistan and Afghanistan. Communist China, recognized by Israel as early as January 1950, and host to a top-level Israeli goodwill mission in 1955, has adopted an increasingly hostile countenance. India has never consented to relations above the consular level, largely out of fear of provoking Arab support for Pakistan—despite sizeable and vocal sentiment to the contrary in the Congress and Praja Socialist parties, in the Bhoodan Movement and in certain sectors of the national press. Indeed, in 1965 India allowed the establishing in New Delhi of an Arab League Office, which became an anti-Israel propaganda center. Relations between the two countries were not improved when President Shazar, en route to Nepal on a state visit, was accorded curt and uncivil treatment during his brief stopover in India. [6] Budding Israel-Ceylon relations were crudely severed in 1956 by Mrs. Bandaranaika's capitulation to threats of an Arab economic boycott. With the notable exception of Burma, Israel's "key" to the Third World, formal relations with the other Asian states were not consolidated until after 1956.

Thus in her own continent Israel found herself regarded as an alien power. And although her Foreign Ministry endeavored to correct this picture, priority was always granted to diplomatic efforts in Western capitals. The two basic characteristics of Israeli diplomacy during this period were: (1) an emphasis on the creation of extensive and durable ties with the Western powers, arising from security considerations based on an exaggerated bipolar conception of the of the global power scene; and (2) an overly conservative budgetary and manpower policy, leading to gross underemphasis of relations with countries not regarded as likely to affect directly or alleviate Israel's security predicament.

During the years 1950-1956 Israel's international relations suffered several reversals. The Middle East had become an important pawn in the Cold War, and overall strategic considerations precluded the alleviation of the region's pressing problems by either of the major powers. Open Soviet hostility barred Israel from adopting a neutral stance, and the United States, itself then actively courting the Arab bloc, seemed to reject her as a major liability. As Walter Eytan, at the time Director General of the Israeli Foreign Ministry, wrote in 1958:

> All the great Powers have at various times in the past ten years expressed a desire, at least platonically, for peace between the Arab states and Israel. But their policies have, in practice, not worked for such a peace. In the opinion of many they have, if anything, worked against it. Israel-Arab peace, however desirable in itself, has never been the overriding interest of any of the Powers. They have never pursued it single-mindedly with all the means in their disposal, as they have pursued other objectives in the Middle East and elsewhere.[7]

Disowned and chided by East and West alike, Israel was diplomatically in a cul-de-sac, economically in the stranglehold of the Arab boycott and blockade of sea-lanes. The United Nations upon which Israeli leaders had pinned many of their hopes, had also shown its inability to calm the Middle East conflict. In fact in Israeli eyes the United Nations had consciously exacerbated the situation by not taking a stand against Arab intransigence and anti-Israel activities. The ease with which resolutions condemning Israeli military retaliations were passed, while those condemning corresponding Arab guerrilla provocations languished without support, was viewed by Israelis as indicative of a two-faced attitude on the part of the United Nations. By 1956 both major powers and the United Nations were commonly regarded in Israel as hypocritical and morally bankrupt."[8] Reliance upon international authority and the major powers appeared to have brought the young state to the brink of disaster. Indeed, Israel's very dependence upon international support seemed automatically to preclude her obtaining it. Paradoxically, one could conclude that only if Israel were independently powerful and influential in the international arena would she be able to secure the support she required. In 1956 an "agonizing reappraisal" of Israel's basic policy assumptions was undertaken "in order that in the future the State's foreign policy should be geared to facts, not hopes."[9] In the long run the reappraisal brought about powerful diplomatic drives upon Afro-Asia. In the short run it dictated a stiffening of Israel's policy vis-a-vis her neighbors, which led directly to the 1956 Sinai Campaign, designed to extricate her from the unendurable daily provocations and an adverse balance of power.

The failure of Israel's policy of reliance on the West and the United Nations should be viewed in conjunction with the trauma of Bandung. Probably no other event in its checkered diplomatic experience shook the Israeli Foreign Ministry as much as the 1955 Bandung Conference. The first augury of an impending "disaster" was the fact that Israel was not invited to attend the historic meeting. Even so, no Israeli truly expected the slur at her sovereignty contained in Section E, Article I of the conference's final communique.[10] Its effect upon the ministry was devastating. One high-ranking official described it to the author as follows: "Bandung was our greatest diplomatic setback. It was the greatest trauma we ever suffered. That two and one half billion people could be united in such a way against 1.8 million people in Israel was in itself soul-shattering to all of us in the Foreign Ministry."[11]

Officials in the ministry had been painfully aware that Israel's position in Asia was shaky—partly as a result of successful Arab propaganda in the Moslem nations, but also in part due to her tendency to concentrate diplomatic efforts in the West. It had taken six years and this diplomatic jolt to arouse Israeli policy-makers to the isolation facing Israel in Asia, and the exclusion was much harder to accept because of a similar isolation being felt in day-to-day relations with the West. The lesson was well-learned, however, especially since Israel's lone success in Burma pointed to the handsome dividends obtainable through careful and concentrated efforts.

Burma, it has been noted, was Israel's key to Asia. Burma was also Israel's key to Africa, for it was in Rangoon, during the first session of the Asian Socialist Conference in 1953, that Foreign Minister Sharett, representing his Socialist International linked Mapai, met and invited to Israel a number of participating Gold Coast trade union leaders. The reports on Israel presented by the latter on their return to Accra led to the close association of the labor movements of the two countries in the late 1950's. It was during the course of this conference that Burma and Israel agreed to establish diplomatic relations. Attempting to consolidate this lone foothold in Asia (at the time only Turkey, among Asian states, maintained relations with Israel), the Israeli government extended a modest offer of technical assistance. Within a short time Israeli technicians, doctors and military advisers were on their way to Rangoon. By 1957 Israeli officers were helping to reorganize Burma's

Northern Territories into kibbutz-style self-defense communities, while select Burmese Army servicemen underwent communal-life training in Israeli settlements. The Histadrut's (Trade Union Federation's) construction arm, Solel Boneh, started operations in Burma, and Zim (Israel's national shipping line) was requested to undertake the management of Burma's Five Stars Line. Moreover, arrangements were made to plant forty million acres of Burmese hill-country in wheat, destined to be exported later to Israel. And in 1955 U Nu granted Israel her first opportunity to play host to a visiting head of government.

Israel-Burma technical and cultural cooperation led to an increased awareness of the problems confronting the two countries. On the Burmese side, the relatively large number of individuals involved in these exchanges produced some sympathy for Israel's position in the Middle East. Burma was probably the only Asian state whose newspapers showed an understanding of the Arab provocations that led to Israel's Sinai Campaign. U Nu exercised his influence on a number of occasions in favor of Israel. He objected strongly, both prior to and during the Bandung Conference, to the fact that Israel had not been invited to that meeting. At the 1961 Belgrade Conference of nonaligned nations, to which Israel was again not invited, he blocked Arab attempts to castigate her. He had just offered to mediate the Israel-Arab dispute and help with normalizing Israel-China relations when he was deposed from office by General Ne Win.[12]

The lessons of the "Burma experiment" on the one hand, and Bandung on the other, were not lost on Israeli decision-makers. Throughout 1950-1956 a small but highly vocal group of officials pressed for closer Israel-Asia relations on the lines of the Burma model. Pointing out that Israel, an integral part of Asia, was for better or worse tied up with developments in the rest of the continent they urged greater attention to, and compassion for, Asian problems. Asia's potential good will, crucial to Israel in the long run, was being lost by default, they claimed, due to Israel's preoccupation with the major powers and Europe in general. Only the conscious integration of Israel in her continent could really solve her outstanding international problems.

The Transition Period: 1956-1957

Growing uneasiness in public and government circles over reverses suffered by Israel in the international field played an important role in the leadership shuffle that occurred in November 1955. Ben-Gurion, returning from his self-imposed seclusion in the Sde Boker kibbtutz, took over from Sharett as Prime Minister. In June 1956 Mrs. Meir, hitherto Minister of Labor, replaced Sharett in his second capacity as Foreign Minister. Sharett had been Israel's Foreign Minister since independence. Widely regarded as too "soft" in foreign affairs and overly inclined to rely on the United Nations and the great powers for the amelioration of Israel's security predicament[13], he was eased out of all governmental policymaking positions, though his party standing remained relatively unimpaired and his political acumen and experience were utilized in other spheres. The change in leadership was interpreted at home and abroad as signifying a stiffening of foreign policy and a more aggressive Israeli stand on all fronts.

One of the first foreign policy moves of the new leadership was a strong and extensive diplomatic thrust into Asia. On September 21, Sharett was dispatched on a long and delicate good-will mission prior to his representing Mapai at the second Asian Socialist Conference in Bombay. The official purpose of his trip was to create better understanding in Asia for Israel and her problems.[14] Sharett was empowered to establish, improve or expand all types of relations, diplomatic or economic, with the twelve countries he was scheduled to visit—Japan, Burma, the Philippines, Ceylon, Hong Kong, India, Nepal, Malaya, Thailand, Laos, Cambodia and Iran. Though the Sinai Campaign created some embarrassing moments in the middle of his mission, he made several important diplomatic advances. The Phillippines and Ceylon agreed to establish relations with Israel immediately; Thailand and Laos were to do so in a short time.[15]

The 1956 Sharett mission was, in a sense, a political follow-up to a previous Israeli economic initiative. In January of the same year the Ministry of Commerce and Industry had announced the government's decision to encourage, through direct grants, subsidies and loans, the formation of viable export companies aiming their activities at Afro-Asia. To assure the success of such companies, government-guaranteed minimum incomes were pledged to Israeli shipping lines establishing new routes to Afro-Asia. The political overtones of these moves were clear: increased economic contacts with Afro-Asia were now viewed as prerequisites for a rapprochement with the Third World. Moreover, their resultant two-way traffic was expected to generate stronger pressures against the Egyptian blockades by countries neutral in the disptite and standing to lose from their continuation.

Contacts with Africa were also expanded. Here the Israeli initiatives coincided with the "winds of change" that had begun to ruffle hitherto stable colonial empires, affording unique opportunities for the extension of new influences. A number of honorary and resident Israeli consuls were appointed both in independent Africa (Ethiopia, Liberia) and in territories not yet sovereign (Kenya, Gold Coast). Technical cooperation was pledged the Gold Coast, which was moving rapidly toward independence. In March 1957, when newly independent Ghana and Israel entered into diplomatic relations, the Israeli consulate in Accra (established only in November 1956) was promoted to the rank of embassy—the first such high-level Israeli representation in all of Afro-Asia.

Growing Israeli interest in the Third World, and especially in Africa, caused no sharp break from traditional postures and orientations. There was no corresponding de-emphasis of Israeli links with the colonial powers, or of Israel's efforts to extend her relations with the major powers. General Israeli disillusionment with the intentions and sincerity of the major powers and with the potentialities of the UN as an unbiased peace-promoting organization never went so far as to prompt moves toward dissociation. The amity and support of the West were still viewed as not expendable. Too many ties connected Israel with the West; and the alternative, non-alignment, was still denied her by Soviet hostility. Moreover, the United Nations—even if doublefaced, from Israel's point of view—merely mirrored Israel's international difficulties; it did not originate them. The fickleness of the West (swayed by shifting global strategic considerations) and the bias of the United Nations could be adequately compensated for, and eventually corrected, only if Israel strengthened her own international standing. Support from the West could not be expected until Israel became less of a diplomatic liability through forging for herself alternate bases of international support. A diplomatically strong Israel could hope not only to deter Arab intransigence and propaganda assaults, but also to have her own evaluations of the Middle East situation given more credence and attention during policy-formulation sessions in Washington and Moscow. The road to greater Israeli influence in these capitals passed through Accra, Rangoon, Abidjan and Manila.

Israel and the Third World Since Sinai

Israel's relations with the Third World since the Sinai Campaign fall into two sub-periods. From 1957 until roughly 1962 was a period of increasing involvement with the Third World and especially with Africa. The period since 1962 is marked by the consolidation of diplomatic gains and a recent amplification of effort in Latin America.

The breakthrough occurred in Ghana. Initial contacts had been made by the trade union movements of the two countries. Meeting their Israeli counterparts at sessions of the Socialist International, the Asian Socialist Conference, the International Labor Organization, and the International Confederation of Free Trade Unions, Ghanaian trade unionists were vividly impressed by accounts of the role of labor in Israel. When Ghanaian TUC Secretary General John Tettegah visited Israel in 1957 he exclaimed, "Israel has given me more in eight days than I could obtain from two years in a British University."[16] Soon Israeli unionists were invited to Ghana to help restructure the GTUC.[17]

The manner in which Ghana-Israel relations escalated between 1957 and 1960 has no parallel in Israel's diplomatic history. It was as if the Israeli Foreign Ministry, after wandering for years in the wilderness, had finally stumbled into the Promised Land. Under Ehud Avriel, an energetic ambassador with extensive powers, fully backed by Jerusalem, the Israeli Embassy in Accra rapidly became the most prestigious and influential of all the foreign missions, bar none. This was the "honeymoon" of Israel-Ghana relations, when the Israeli Ambassador was popularly credited with having immediate access to Nkrumah.[18] In Israeli eyes, during this period, nothing was too good or too much for Ghana. The cream of Zim's officers, Solel Boneh's and Tahal's engineers and foremen, and Hadassah's doctors began a mass pilgrimage to Accra, and the Israeli government mobilized further human resources to spur and staff Ghana's ambitious development projects. A number of joint companies, a joint merchant marine, an aviation school, a Builders' Brigade and many other enterprises were established with Israeli cooperation in what remains the most massive and concentrated instance of Israel's technical assistance programs. Concurrently, scores of Ghanaian cadres arrived in Israel to observe and assimilate the developmental experience of Ghana's newly found mentor.

The unexpected ease with which the Ghanaian foothold had been secured seemed to vindicate Israel's "turn to the Third World" approach in foreign policy, and the Israeli effort in Africa moved into high gear. Two new embassies were established in Monrovia and Conakry, in each instance with a pledge of extensive technical cooperation. In a complete reversal of previous policy, it now became an Israeli goal to try to place an embassy in every nation. Often Israeli ambassadors-to-be arrived in African capitals to present their letters of accreditation immediately following the representative of the ex-colonial power, thus acquiring at one stroke a measure of protocol priority and a ground swell of gratitude and good will for the prompt action.

The great emphasis Israel placed on the establishment of friendly Afro-Israeli relations was manifested when Foreign Minister Golda Meir made her first trip to Africa in 1958. In Liberia, Ghana, Senegal, Nigeria and the Ivory Coast Mrs. Meir had an early opportunity to meet some of the nationalist leaders of these countries. This visit was rapidly followed by numerous other high-level missions. Mrs. Meir herself was to revisit Africa four more times by 1965. By the end of 1965 over 6,600 African cadres from thirty-seven countries had been trained in Israel on Israeli scholarships, with hundreds more obtaining their training in Israeli courses or seminars organized in Africa. During the same period over 2,000 Israeli experts were sent to Africa in one capacity or another.[19]

There are many reasons for African—and Third World—interest in Israel. Suffice it to note here that her small size, non-aligned status and socialist inclinations, coupled with her original contributions in a variety of fields, have made her a socio-economic laboratory of great interest to developing nations facing similar problems. The mass adoption (by two dozen countries in Africa alone) of varieties of Israel's Nachal and Gadna youth organization structures; the wide-scale interest in, and imitation of aspects of Israel's kibbutz and *moshav* agricultural settlement systems, all attest to the close attention given to the Israeli developmental experience.

By 1966 Israel was represented in all of sub-Saharan Africa with the exception of Mauritania and Somalia.[20] The majority of African Heads of State have included Jerusalem at least once in their itineraries of state visits. In 1960-1961 seven such visits enlivened the hitherto parochial Israeli calendar of civic events with their colorful processions, fanfare and emotional joint declarations of "perpetual" amity. On the

Israeli side, in 1962 President Ben Zvi, though already seriously ailing, made a highly successful series of goodwill state visits to five African countries.[21]

In Asia, a reintensified Israeli effort was similarly to be capped with a measure of success, even though it was slower in manifesting itself. Pre-Sinai contacts were strengthened. The eventual recognition of Israel by Iran was a move that shocked the Arab world. Excellent relations were developed with Nepal, Singapore, Burma, Japan and the Philippines. Despite the important exceptions of Afghanistan, Pakistan, Indonesia, Communist China and Taiwan, Israel's position in Asia is today well established. Relations with the remaining Asian states are "proper" if not warm. More importantly, Israel's claim to be a legitimate Asian state is not widely or seriously challenged.

The problems confronting Israeli diplomats in the mid-fifties in Latin America were much simpler. As has been noted, the continent had in the past been sympathetic to Israel. This disposition toward amity was strengthened when the allocation of adequate manpower and financial resources made it possible for Israel to expand her representation throughout the region. Though trainees and cadres from Latin America had been dispatched to Israel from the inception of the latter's technical cooperation program, a marked step-up took place around 1962. The number of courses, programs and seminars specifically designed for Spanish-speaking students was greatly increased. Growing numbers of Israeli experts have been sent to Latin America, and by 1967 a number of states had set up joint companies and Gadna/Nachal structures with Israeli cooperation. President Shazar's June 1966 state visit to Latin America is viewed in Israeli circles as attesting to the dynamism of Israeli diplomacy in the "last frontier."

Israel's Policy Goals in the Third World

One of the prime considerations motivating Israel to expand her relations with the Third World was her fear of total isolation and need for supplementary bases of international support. From the purely pragmatic and immediate point of view every Israeli diplomatic gain in the Third World was also the elimination (or neutralization) of a potential source of support for the Arab countries. As one high-ranking Israeli Foreign Office official candidly confessed to the author, "Africa is a battleground between Israel and the Arabs. It is a fight of life or death for us." Viewed from this angle, minuscule states such as Gambia, Togo, Lesotho and Mauritius assume the proportions of major powers to be "won over" in the battle for influence in the Third World. "Our ties with the new nations will do more to strengthen our position in the world than anything else..." prophesied Ben-Gurion in a 1960 *Knesset* session.[22] The African countries are not powerful...but their voices are heard in the world, and their votes in international institutions are equal in value to those of more powerful nations," noted one of Israel's leading daily newspapers.[23]

The ultimate goal of Israeli policy-makers is to focus Third World support for Israel on the solution of her thorny problems in the Middle East. The Third World is regarded in Israel as a potentially powerful catalyst for effecting an Arab-Israel reconciliation. Friendly with both Israel and the Arab states, desirous of maintaining stable relations with both protagonists, basically unhampered by preconceptions or prejudices regarding either, and neutral in the dispute, Third World nations are seen in Jerusalem as a force which will provide moral backing for—indeed, will insist upon—the commencement of direct negotiations between the protagonists as a first stage toward conclusive peace agreements. The sympathy for Israel felt by many Third World leaders and their discomfiture at what they consider to be a fratricidal fight in the Middle East, reinforced by their desire to play a "global" role, has brought forth many personal mediation proposals and pressure for direct Israel-Arab negotiations.

While pragmatic political-diplomatic motivations impelled Israel to seek an *entente cordiale* with the Third World, strong ideological and emotional factors contributed to the formulation of Israel's policy of technical cooperation with the developing countries. As the *Manchester Guardian* pointed out "Israel's policy towards Black Africa should perhaps be seen in wider terms, and should be recognized to be not just part of its defense line against the Arab World, but also of a genuine desire to be of help. Africans respond because they recognize this."[24] This "genuine desire to be of help" rests partly upon psychological and partly upon ideological-messianic factors that are deeply imbedded in Israel's national consciousness and affect—albeit sometimes only marginally—the formulation of her foreign policy.[25] Indeed, only by fully realizing the significance of these factors can one understand why no other policy matter coming up before the *Knesset* Has evoked such remarkable unanimity among the various political parties as that of technical cooperation with the Third World.

The Israeli penetration of the Third World has not been achieved without opposition from a variety of sources. The Arab countries, of course, have attempted to block the expansion of Israeli influence. Arrayed against every Israeli ambassador abroad there are frequently as many as thirteen Arab ambassadors doing their utmost to negate his diplomatic efforts. In Europe and North and South America the Arab embassies have often aligned themselves with neo-Nazi or other anti-Semitic elements. In Africa and Asia the Arab powers have consistently attempted to block Israeli participation in various regional conferences and groupings. Islam has also been employed as a tool against Israel. The Sixth World Moslem Conference, meeting in Mogadiscio in 1964, proclaimed that henceforth Islamic preaching all over the world would include indoctrination on "the danger of Israel", and the need to unite against "Zionism."

Moreover, growing Israeli economic influence has at times antagonized local groups. Thus in Asia and Africa, Lebanese, Pakistani and Indian merchants and middlemen have objected to the introduction of Israel-made products and Israeli influence. On the broader international level Israel has been sharply denounced by both the Soviet Union and China. *Izvestiia* on December 12, 1960, for example, castigated Israel for "fulfilling the role of a Trojan Horse for the North Atlantic Treaty Organization in Africa." *Trud, Pravda* and the *Peking Review* have all carried similar denunciations from time to time.

There have been clashes of interest with some Western powers. Though French-Israeli differences have generally been settled amicably, reflecting their close cooperation on most levels and issues (at least prior to June 1967), Anglo-Israeli disagreements have on occasion been bitter. In West Africa established British economic interests resisted fiercely the intrusion of Israeli products and services in their traditional markets. In Ghana a serious clash developed in 1958-1959 over the economic, political and military implications of the Israel-staffed aviation school. Even a measure of American opposition has been encountered; the best known instance is the strenuous but unsuccessful effort of the United States to prevent the training of Congolese paratroopers in Israel in 1964-1965. In addition, Israeli diplomats in Latin America have felt that U.S. officials have responded with a certain resistance to the Israeli "intrusion" into the American "backyard."

The above comments notwithstanding, the Israeli effort has been generally successful. This has brought about a notable improvement in Israel's international standing. One of the attending benefits has been—as expected all along by policy-makers in Jerusalem—an increase in Israeli influence in Western capitals. Politically, Israeli evaluations of the Middle East and the developing countries are given far greater attention than was the case prior to 1957.[26] Significantly, the roster of Israeli diplomats attached to the embassy in Washington includes a Counsellor on the Developing Areas. Joint economic ventures with Israeli interests in Third World countries are actively pursued by American and other concerns, thanks to Israel's prestige in the developing areas. The relevance of Israeli methods of socioeconomic development to the Third World has been recognized at the highest international levels. The UN-sponsored Conference on the Application of Science and Technology for the Benefit of Less Developed Areas (1963) was convened at the request of U Thant under an Israeli Vice President and with the participation of twenty-three Israeli expects who delivered thirty-three papers. The conference itself was patterned on a series of similar international conferences held previously in Israel, and U Thant's personal scientific adviser was an Israeli.

The friendly relations forged between Israel and the developing world have been reflected also in the United Nations and its agencies. The UN, viewed several years earlier as a platform for anti-Israel vituperations, was utilized for the first time in 1961 as the forum for a powerful Israeli drive for a negotiated peace in the Middle East. Sixteen nations, nine of them African, supported and guided by Israel, presented a motion calling for immediate direct negotiations between Israel and the Arab states. When this was defeated by an alliance of the Arab states, the United States and the Soviet bloc—each opposed to it for different reasons—an identical motion was presented in 1962, this time sponsored by twenty-one states, twelve of which were African. Similar drafts presented to subsequent sessions have not been allowed to go to a vote because of insufficient support, but the fact that the Arab states are now under increasing pressure to negotiate their differences with Israel is indicative of Israel's improved standing in the Third World. Moreover, the Arabs have suffered several reversals when, in a number of elections for executive positions in UN agencies and other organs, Israel has been chosen to represent the entire Afro-Asian bloc, including the Arab states.

Reciprocally, because of her more intimate association with the Third World, Israel has had to respond to Afro-Asian pressure and bring her foreign policy into closer accord with the interests of the developing countries. Possibly the clearest manifestation of this was Israel's commitment in 1961 and 1962 to vote for the imposition of economic sanctions on the South African government, thereby alienating a country traditionally friendly toward her and a major trading partner in Africa. On a variety of other issues she has cautiously edged closer to the position of the moderate nonaligned countries, bearing out the *Israel Economist* statement as early as September 1960 that "the basic line underlying Israel's policies today is complete integration with Afro-Asia." In part pragmatic, this shift in orientation nevertheless conforms with basic Israeli inclinations and outlooks. It has been made possible in large part by the growing multipolar nature of the global scene. An independent and nonaligned position was out of the question for an isolated and threatened Israel in the 1950's—when, moreover, non-alignment was regarded by both major powers as "immoral." In the 1960's it has been achieved by a diplomatically stronger and more influential Israel amid a multitude of new nations professing one variety or another of nonalignment. Thus Israel's foreign policy seems to have completed a full circle since the early days of 1949-1950.

Third World Reactions to the Middle East War

The recent war in the Middle East and the UN deliberations attending its conclusion provide an opportunity for a tangible, tentative, evaluation of Israel's standing within the Third World.[27] Any such analysis must, however, take into consideration that a UN vote is not necessarily a reliable indicator of a country's amity or enmity toward another country whose, actions are in question. During the June-July emergency sessions a variety of powerful cross-pressures was brought to bear upon the UN delegations, and some of the votes registered were in contradiction to known national orientations. By the time the General Assembly had convened, the Arab-Israeli conflict was no longer the only or even the main issue; the major powers were now deeply involved, and the Sino-Soviet schism had even been introduced via the Albanian resolution.[28]

The two major resolutions presented to the General Assembly were the Yugoslav ("nonaligned") resolution calling for a unilateral Israeli withdrawal from all occupied territory, and the Latin American resolution which linked Israeli withdrawals with an end to the Arab state of belligerency and the start of negotiations aimed at the total liquidation of the Middle East dispute. For all practical purposes a vote for the latter may be interpreted as a pro-Israel gesture (as it was considered by the militant and pro-Arab states), and a vote for the former—especially if unequivocal—as a pro-Arab gesture. Neither was regarded with great favor by Israel, even though the Latin American resolution, in Israeli eyes, was the more realistic of the two. Israel had had experience with the worthlessness of international guarantees and was aware of the strength of her position; she stood fast in her demand for a directly negotiated peace aimed at settling all outstanding issues in the Middle East. During the voting she abstained on the Latin American resolution and rejected the Yugoslav draft.

Latin America was by and large solidly behind Israel, both prior to and following the June hostilities. During the UN deliberations Colombia's delegate, Julio C. T. Ayala, told the Assembly [Israel's] non-recognition was a hostile act. Not the creation of the State of Israel constituted the problem, but the obstinate and futile denial of its existence."[29] Other Latin American delegates stressed that the General Assembly had not met to allocate blame or responsibility for the war, but to create the infrastructure for a true and lasting peace. Their vote was cohesive, 22 nations backing the group's own resolution and the same 22 rejecting the Yugoslav alternative. Haiti did not participate in the voting; Cuba voted for the Yugoslav resolution with other members of the communist bloc.

The reaction of sub-Saharan Africa was mixed, 17 of the 32 non-Arab states favoring the Latin American resolution as opposed to 14 for the Yugoslav. France's support for the Yugoslav resolution, termed by Israel's Foreign Minister, Abba Eban, as "identical in purpose and effect" to the one proposed by the Soviet Union, created a measure of confusion among the African delegations, especially those from French-speaking Africa. Franco-Israeli amity and cooperation in the decade since 1956 had been crucial factor in facilitating unhindered Israeli access to this area of the continent. Whether or not de Gaulle had pledged to round up French Africa's support for the Yugoslav resolution, the French stand dismayed delegations not wishing to vote at variance with France.

On the broader plane, there were pressures for "continental solidarity" in African voting. Most of the leaders of sub-Saharan Africa rejected the Somali-Guinean request for an emergency meeting of the Organization of African Unity (OAU) to discuss the implications of the war, on the grounds that the Arab-Israeli conflict was not an African issue, yet they no doubt also wanted to avoid the harsh continental split along radical-moderate lines that such a meeting might have produced.

Ten countries opted for a stronger anti-Israel stand for a variety of reasons not always connected with the problem at hand.[30] Guinea was by far the most radical in this group. Rupturing diplomatic relations and expelling all Israeli experts, the *Parti Démocratique Guinéene* even toyed with the idea of declaring war on Israel and dispatching troops to the UAR. Besides calling for an emergency meeting of the OAU, Guinea also had harsh words for the moderate states that did not see fit to support the Yugoslav resolution.

The magnitude of the Arab defeat elicited a burst of sympathy for the losers from some African leaders. As President Leopold Senghor of Senegal expressed it (although this was certainly not the only reason for the Senegalese vote) "We are on the side of the Arabs; they have been humiliated three times and they need us."[31] Religious sentiment was also mobilized in support of the Arabs, and there were suggestions for the internationalization of Israel's capital, Jerusalem.

Though Israeli leaders had anticipated much stronger support from Africa and were inclined to be disillusioned with the attitude of the Third World as a whole, the backing Africa gave the Latin American resolution cannot be regarded as negligible. In view of the fact that the complexity of counter-pressures was especially felt in this continent, it had more significance than the actual vote tally would indicate.

The Asian reactions reflected strong pro-Arab and Pan-Moslem sentiments buttressed by nineteen years of Arab propaganda not fully dissipated by Israeli diplomacy. The support Israel obtained from this group of nations was minimal. Only the Philippines voted against the Yugoslav resolution, though four states—Taiwan, Japan, Thailand and the Philippines—voted for the Latin American draft. Even such staunch allies as Burma and Nepal deserted Israel, though Burma qualified her vote somewhat by abstaining on the Latin American resolution, and

Table 1: THE UN GENERAL ASSEMBLY VOTE ON THE YUGOSLAV AND LATIN AMERICAN RESOLUTIONS

Country	Yugoslav Resolution	Latin American Resolution	Country	Yugoslav Resolution	Latin American Resolution
LATIN AMERICA			AFRICA		
Argentina	n	y	Botswana	n	y
Barbados	n	y	Burundi	y	n
Bolivia	n	y	Cameroon	y	y
Brazil	n	y	Central African Republic	a	y
Chile	n	y	Chad	a	y
Colombia	n	y	Congo/Brazzaville	y	n
Costa Rica	n	y	Congo/Kinshasa	y	y
Cuba	y	n	Dahomey	a	y
Dominican Republic	n	y	Ethiopia	a	y
Ecuador	n	y	Gabon	y	a
El Salvador	n	y	Gambia	n	y
Guatemala	n	y	Ghana	y	n
Guyana	n	y	Guinea	y	n
Haiti	—	—	Ivory Coast	a	y
Honduras	n	y	Kenya	a	a
Jamaica	n	y	Lesotho	n	y
Mexico	n	y	Liberia	n	y
Nicaragua	n	y	Malagasy Republic	n	y
Panama	n	y	Malawi	n	y
Paraguay	n	y	Mali	y	n
Peru	n	y	Mauritania	y	n
Trinidad and Tobago	n	y	Niger	a	a
Uruguay	n	y	Nigeria	y	a
Venezuela	n	y	Rwanda	a	a
Totals	*1 yes*	*22 yes*	Senegal	y	n
	22 no	*1 no*	Sierra Leone	a	y
ASIA			Somalia	y	n
Afghanistan	y	n	Togo	n	y
Burma	y	a	Uganda	y	n
Cambodia	y	a	Tanzania	y	n
Ceylon	y	n	Upper Volta	a	y
China	a	y	Zambia	y	n
Cyprus	y	n	*Totals*	*14 yes*	*17 yes*
India	y	n		*8 no*	*10 no*
Indonesia	y	n		*10 abstain*	*5 abstain*
Iran	y	a	ARAB STATES		
Japan	y	y	Algeria	y	n
Laos	a	a	Iraq	y	n
Malaysia	y	n	Jordan	y	n
Maldive Islands	—	—	Kuwait	y	n
Nepal	y	n	Lebanon	y	n
Pakistan	y	n	Libya	y	n
Philippines	n	y	Morocco	y	n
Singapore	a	a	Saudi Arabia	y	n
Thailand	a	y	Sudan	y	n
Turkey	y	a	Syria	y	n
Totals	13 yes	4 yes	Tunisia	y	n
	1 no	8 no	UAR	y	n
	4 abstain	6 abstain	Yemen	y	n
			Totals	13 yes	13 no

Nepal's delegate, Major General Padma Bahadur Khatri, delivered a balanced speech prior to the voting. Among all the factors that figured in this adverse reaction in Asia, the most important may have been the almost pathological Asian sensitivity to anything open to interpretation as an act of aggression.

On the other hand, public opinion in some of the countries, backing the Yugoslav resolution—and not only those of the Third World—was markedly pro-Israel. French popular opinion, for example, was overwhelmingly on the side of Israel, and even on the cabinet level there was disagreement over France's vote. In Nigeria, which voted for the Yugoslav resolution and abstained on the Latin American one, public sentiment, even in some Moslem circles, appears to have leaned toward Israel. Separatist non-Arab, elements in Southern Sudan voiced support for Israel, and there were stirrings of discontent among the non-Moors in Mauritania over that country's strong pro-Arab line. In India, which continued in her traditional anti-Israel orientation, opposition to Mrs Gandhi's policy was evident in some sectors of the press, the Lok Sabha and the politicized elites[32]. Amazingly, by September it was apparent that even in Eastern Europe there existed a measure of sympathy for Israel, especially in Rumania. In conclusion, a compilation of the voting data reveals that the pro-Arab Yugoslav resolution failed to obtain even a simple majority from the nations of the Third World—if the Arab bloc of 13 unanimous votes for it is excluded. The non-Arab tally was 28 yeas, 31 nays and 14 abstentions. Members of this group preferred the Latin American resolution by a majority of more than two to one—43 yeas, 20 nays, 11 abstentions. Though these figures must take into account the bloc of 22 pro-Israeli Latin American votes, the fact remains that Israel's position among the nations of the Third World was sufficiently strong to ward off one-sided denunciations in the United Nations despite the somewhat embarrassing situation in which she found herself in the summer of 1967.

It is of no small significance that an Arab-Israeli "balance of power" appears to have established itself in the General Assembly. No longer can that organ be regarded as an automatic converter of Arab military defeats into political triumphs, as in 1956. The immediate consequence of this development is that, if only for their own territorial and economic normalization, the defeated Arab states must deal with Israel in a more realistic manner. Several moves in this direction have already been undertaken, the "free" produce traffic across the

Jordan River possibly being the best example. Given proper Third World prodding and the continuation of the Arab-Israeli stalemate in the UN, such dealings may shift to weightier issues and assume a permanent and institutionalized status. Even if this development turns out to be the only tangible result of Israel's improved stature within the Third World, then her reliance upon the Third World's peace-promoting capabilities will have been largely vindicated.

FOOTNOTES

1. The late President Ben Zvi had, however paid brief visits in 1962 to Congo, the Central African Republic, Congo/Brazzaville, Congo/Kinshasa, Liberia, and Senegal.

2. According to the *Jerusalem Post* correspondent in Washington, "The State Department is taking the position that it is not in America's security interest to be more closely identified with Israel, since such identification might further propel the Moslems towards the East." *Jerusalem Post*, July 5, 1956.

3. In France, Canada, Italy, Argentina, the Soviet Union, the United Kingdom and the United States. In contrast, by 1964 Israel was represented in 87 countries. Of these representations, 75 were at the ambassadorial level. Israel's diplomatic network today is surpassed only by those of the United States, the United Kingdom and France.

4. Cited in *Jerusalem Post*, March 25, 1956.

5. See *Israel Weekly News Bulletin* (Jerusalem), May 16-22, 1962.

6. Possibly the best example of the latent sympathy for Israel in certain sectors of the Indian polity was the outcry in the *Lok Sabha* and the Indian press to this obvious snub by the Indian Foreign Ministry. See Joseph B. Schechtman, "India and Israel," *Midstream*, August-September 1966, pp. 48-61.

7. Walter Eytan, *The First Ten Years* (New York: Simon and Schuster), 1958, p. 152.

8. See, for example, the results of the public opinion survey undertaken by a Hebrew University study group: Carnegie Endowment for International Peace, *Israel and the United Nations* (New York: Manhattan Publishing Company 1956), pp. 289, 293.

9. *Jerusalem Post*, June 7, 1956.

10. For the full text see the Appendix in George M. Kahin, *The Asian-African Asian-African conference* (Ithaca: Cornell University Press, 1956.)

11. In an interview at the Israeli Foreign Ministry in Jerusalem on August 13, 1964.

12. Ne Win—highly regarded in Israel—initially pledged the continuation of Israel-Burma cooperation even as he moved to eliminate all other foreign influences in the country. Only recently has he requested the termination of a number of Israel's programs of technical assistance.

13. Foreign Minister Abba Eban is now being regarded in a similar way in some Israeli circles.

14. *Jerusalem Post*, September 21, 1956.

15. Israel-Ceylon relations were to be ruptured shortly afterward. Illustrative of the concern over Israel's diplomatic isolation at the time is the following *Jerusalem Post* comment (January 4, 1957) with regard to the possible establishment of relations with Laos: "Laos, though small [sic!] and weak, cannot be overlooked by Israel in her quest for such friendly relationships."

16. Cited in *Jerusalem Post*, July 23, 1957.

17. For some of the changes in the organization of the Ghanaian TUC—not all initiated or relished by the Israeli advisers—see T. O. Elias, *The British Commonwealth: The Development of Their Laws and Constitutions, Vol. X, Ghana and Sierra Leone* (London: Stevens & Sons, 1962), pp. 211 ff. For the eventual subordination of the GTUC to the CPP see the issues of *West Africa* (London) for February 1 and August 29, 1958; January 17, 27 and November 1, 1959.

18. See, for example, John B. Oakes, *The Edge of Freedom* (New York: Harper & Brothers, 1961), p. 45. Something similar occurred in the Central African Republic during 1961-1963. There the Israeli Ambassador and & President Dacko became fast friends, the latter frequently visiting the ambassador in his residence for a respite from official duties.

19. The equivalent data for the rest of the Third World for this period add up to 5,000 cadres trained and 850 experts dispatched. On a per capita basis, Israel's technical assistance program is one of the most extensive in the world.

20. In both states strong Pan-Moslem and Pan-Arab sentiment precluded the establishment of stable relations. It should be noted, however, that while Somalia has been openly hostile to Israel, Mauritania has been much less so. In the latter country there is a certain friendship for Israel among the Bantu elements as opposed to the ruling Moorish majority.

21. See note 1 supra.

22. Israel, *Divrei HaKnesset*, October 24-26, 1960, p. 12. As the *Israel Economist* noted in its July 1961 issue (p. 115), "Israel's future may in no small part be determined by her success in gaining the confidence and sympathy of the newly independent states of Afro-Asia." See also Emil Lengyel, "Israel's Campaign in Africa," *The Reporter*, February 4, 1960, pp. 23-24.

23. *Ha'aretz*, August 19, 1962, p. 24.

24. Quoted in *Jerusalem Post*, August 17, 1962.

25. For a brief analysis of some of these factors, see the author's "Messianic Influences in Israeli Foreign Policy" University of Rhode Island, Occasional Papers in Political Science, No. 2, 1967.

26. Note the difference in the attitude and policy of the United States toward Israel during and following the 1967 Middle East war as compared with the US position in the 1956 crisis. Though these events are not strictly comparable,

Washington in 1967 paid immeasurably more attention to Israeli policy evaluations and demands than it did in 1956.

27. For two good reviews of the conflict and its repercussions, see Walter Laqueur, "Israel, the Arabs, and World Opinion," and Theodore Draper, "Israel and World Politics, both in *Commentary*, August 1967, pp. 49-59 and 19-48, respectively.

28. The Albanian resolution, which was defeated by a large margin, condemned the United States and the United Kingdom as well as Israel. In sponsoring and calling for its passage, Albania specifically blamed the USSR for "valuable assistance" granted to Britain and the United States both prior to and during their "attack" on the Arab states. (*UN Monthly Chronicle*, July 1967, p. 53.)

29. Paraphrased in *ibid*, pp. 58-59.

30. For a more detailed analysis of the African reactions, see the author's "Africa the Mid-Eastern War," *Africa Report*, October 1967, pp. 57-61.

31. *West Africa*, August 5, 1967.

32. Public opinion surveys have indicated that a sizeable section of the population was sympathetic to Israel in the recent conflict. See, for example, issue No. 142, 1967) of the *Monthly Public Opinion of the Indian Institute of Public Opinion*, New Delhi.)

4 AFRICA AND THE MID-EASTERN WAR*

The Six-Day war between Israel and the Arab states, and the attendant debates in the UN General Assembly in June and July, confronted African delegates with a series of resolutions on ways to restore peace in the Middle East. Because it tested their interests and sympathies on both sides of the conflict, the General Assembly session can be used as a laboratory for assessing Israel's standing with the African countries; and though the results allow only tentative judgments, the voting patterns suggest that 10 years of Israeli effort have borne fruit.

Laying the Groundwork

No observer of the African scene could fail to be impressed by the determined emphasis Israel has placed on the creation of extensive and amicable relations with sub-Saharan Africa. After an early but significant tour of Africa in 1958, Foreign Minister Golda Meir was to visit the continent four more times by 1964. In 1962, despite his illness, President Ben Zvi undertook a strenuous trip through West Africa, and in 1966 Prime Minister Levi Eshkol crisscrossed the continent to cement relations further. And there was travel in the opposite direction. By 1967, a large number of African heads of state had included Israel at least once in their itineraries of state visits.

To consolidate these high-level political contacts, Israel has built an edifice of technical cooperation programs which on a per capita base is one of the most ambitious in the world. From 1957 to 1965, over 11,600 cadremen from the Third,World, of whom roughly 60 percent were from Africa, were trained in Israel. During the same period, approximately 2,500 Israeli experts were sent to countries as far apart as Nepal and Chad. In 20-odd states in Africa alone, youth-mobilizing

*Originally published in *Africa Report*, October 1967, pp. 57-61.

and/or agrarian-centered movements have been established along Israeli lines. More than 30 Afro-Israeli joint stock companies have been formed, for Israeli public and private interests have also joined in the "rush" to the Third World, and especially to Africa, so visible since 1957. By 1965 Israel trailed only the US, Britain, and France in the number of diplomatic missions it had established throughout the world. In sub-Saharan Africa, where Arab diplomacy has sought to discourage relations between Israel and the newly independent countries, Israel maintains embassies in every country but two, Somalia and Mauritania; and six of the eight African ambassadors resident in Israel have their chanceries not in Tel Aviv but Jerusalem, the capital for which Israel seeks wider, international recognition.

It would exceed the scope of this brief article to examine the political and ideological considerations that impelled Israel to forge with Africa what *Newsweek* has rather extravagantly called "one of the strangest unofficial alliances in the world." Yet in order to place the analysis that follows in perspective, we must note one cardinal fact. Beyond the ideological, messianic, and more obvious pragmatic considerations involved, Israeli policymakers have consistently viewed Africa as a potentially important catalyst for the negotiation of a settlement in the Middle East. Such a view was enunciated by Prime Minister Ben Gurion as early as 1956, and it has since been reaffirmed in much the same terms. In Israeli eyes, Africa has many qualifications for the role: friendship for both Israel and the Arab states, freedom from preconceptions or prejudice, psychological discomfiture at the "fratricidal struggle" in the Middle East, and a desire for a global mission. Africa is conceived as a source of moral backing for—indeed, insistence upon—direct negotiations between the contenders.

Several mediation proposals have been made by African leaders, including Kwame Nkrumah, but they have all come to nothing. The most tangible initiative was taken in the UN in 1961, when a number of Afro-Asian and Latin American states friendly with Israel sponsored a resolution calling *inter alia* for direct negotiations between the Arab states and Israel. It was, defeated. Similar drafts were formulated in subsequent sessions, with increasing Third World support, but they never reached a vote. By 1967, nevertheless, a growing sentiment in favor of a negotiated settlement in the Middle East had been mobilized in the UN. It was buttressed by the apparent unwillingness of most African states to chose sides in the controversy—or even to discuss it—during sessions of the Organization of African Unity, when the topic was inevitably introduced by one or another of the North African heads of state. Indeed, persistent Arab efforts to introduce the dispute with Israel into African organizations have aroused a good deal of resentment in countries that consider the conflict a Middle Eastern issue, not an African problem, and wish to keep good relations with both sides. In non-governmental Third World forums, Arab diplomacy has had more success. The Afro-Asian People's Solidarity Conference held in Tanganyika in 1963 condemned "Zionist infiltration" into Africa, and a 47-nation nonaligned conference held in Cairo in 1964 endorsed "full restoration of the rights of the Arab people of Palestine to their homeland." To the latter resolution, however, the spokesmen from Ethiopia, Chad, Liberia, Nigeria, Senegal, Tanganyika, and Togo reportedly expressed reservations.

The Test Approaches

In the summer of 1967, initial African reactions to the deepening crisis and to war itself were, with a few predictable exceptions, largely sympathetic to Israel. Before the shooting started, senior officials of Ethiopia, Nigeria, Liberia, Togo, Kenya, and Cameroun joined Dahomey's Foreign Minister, Dr. Emile Zinsou, in supporting freedom of navigation in the Strait of Tiran; others, including Emperor Haile Selassie, recognized the explosive potential of the situation and urged caution and self-restraint. Much of the African press deplored the UAR blockade, and a number of sub-Saharan newspapers anticipated Israel's military counter-move.

When it finally erupted, the war raised such grave concern that it moderated the public statements of African leaders. Most African officials adopted a detached position as they appealed for a quick end to hostilities. The press and public opinion groups did not remain so neutral, however. In Ghana, the press overwhelmingly favored Israel and ridiculed the Arab charge of Anglo-American air support to the Israeli forces. Among other papers, Accra's *Daily Graphic* drew a parallel between Nasser and Nkrumah and castigated both of them for their "subversive and interventionist" policies. Public opinion in Nigeria (even in some Moslem circles) was also sympathetic to Israel, despite the officially neutral stance of the government. In Francophone Africa, much of the press leaned toward the Israeli side despite the severity of President De Gaulle's oral strictures; and when the war was over, francophone leaders joined the majority of African statesmen in rejecting initiatives for a special meeting of the OAU on the Middle Eastern situation. There were some outspoken exceptions to the general pattern of partiality to Israel, starting, with Guinea. During the Gulf of Aqaba crisis, President Sekou Toure declared unequivocal support for Nasser in a communique quoted in *Horoya* on May 28: "You may rest assured of our complete solidarity and, if necessary, of our desire to give military cooperation." There was talk in Conakry of declaring war on Israel and despatching Guinean troops to the UAR, but the Political Bureau of the ruling *Parti Democratique de Guinea* decided only to break relations with Israel and expel Israeli technicians. Afterward, Guinea was a major proponent of an extraordinary meeting of the OAU to investigate the "relationship between foreign interventions in the Congo and the imperialist plan of conquest of Africa through the Middle East."

The governments of Mali, Mauritania, and Somalia also issued strongly pro-Arab statements before and after the war. Mauritania broke with the UK and US, and began collecting an emergency fund for the defeated UAR Army. Somalia, pursuing a rapprochement with the Arab world begun in the spring of 1966, denounced Israel on African Solidarity Day (May 25), and followed through with a series of pro-Arab declarations and with support for a special meeting of the OAU. (From London, *West Africa* reported on September 23 that the Middle East was "unexpectedly" discussed at the OAU heads of state conference in Kinshasa. A resolution was passed expressing sympathy for the UAR, but the African states agreed only to work through the UN to help the UAR to recover parts of its occupied territories. (Israel was referred to merely as "a foreign power," without condemnation.)

Of all the African reactions to the conflict, the most distressing to Israeli policymakers was probably Tanzania's. Until the crisis, Israeli-Tanzanian relations were warmly amicable, and Israeli assistance in the fields of medicine, youth, labor, and the cooperative movement was among the most extensive in Africa. Yet even before hostilities began, President Julius Nyerere sent a cable to President Nasser offering aid "in defense of your rights against imperialism." Tanzania followed a correspondingly pro-Arab line in the General Assembly debates following the war; it did not, however, break relations or expel Israeli technicians.

When the UN General Assembly met in mid-June in the special session convened at the request of the Soviet Union, the African positions began shifting amid the new cross-pressures that were brought to bear. The issue was no longer a clear cut Arab-Israeli conflict: it now involved the US and the Soviet Union, each exerting its influence in an effort to line up support for the resolutions it favored. France's attitude created a measure of confusion among the franco-phone states. Franco-Israeli amity, given concrete and forceful expression in the decade since 1956, had been a most influential factor in facilitating unhindered Israeli entry into French-speaking Africa. Now France was at odds with Israel to the extent of supporting the Yugoslav resolution, termed by the Israeli Foreign Minister as "identical in purpose and effect" to the one proposed by the USSR.

A number of other factors should be taken into account in analyzing the African vote. Since neither the Arab states nor Israel could, as parties to the dispute, introduce resolutions of their own, the General Assembly voted on third-party motions reflecting the interests of the contenders in varying degrees. None of them offered a clear choice between the Arab and Israeli positions, and one—the Albanian motion condemning Israel, the US, and the UK—carried overtones of the Sino-Soviet conflict that many African states preferred to avoid. The so-called Latin American resolution was the mildest and most "pro-Israel," and the so-called nonaligned resolution presented by Yugoslavia was the most "pro-Arab." Pressures for continental solidarity behind one or the other of these resolutions were exerted among the African delegations, but did not bring about a unified African position.

Another factor was the sheer magnitude of the Arab defeat. Knowledge of the scale and completeness of Israel's victory triggered a measure of sympathy for the underdog that may have modified some African positions that were initially favorable to Israel. As one African delegate told the author, there was a feeling among some delegations that the military victory was "too perfect, too total," and the Arab humiliation too huge, to win much sympathy for Israel. There was the image of a powerful "European" state crushing a group of non-Western states—and indeed, the first shot did appear to have been fired by Israel.

Finally, it should be recalled that a number of African delegates have wide discretion in deciding how to cast their votes at the United

SUBSAHARAN AFRICAN VOTES
on the
TWO MAJOR UN RESOLUTIONS
ON THE ARAB-ISRAELI WAR
July 1967

Group One.
Voted "yes" on Latin American, "no" on Yugoslav resolution. (Total: 8)

Botswana	Liberia
Gambia	Malagasy Republic
Ghana	Malawi
Lesotho	Togo

Group Two.
Supported Latin American resolution, but equivocally. (Total: 12)

Voted "yes on Latin American, abstained on Yugoslav resolution:	Same vote on both Latin American and Yugoslav resolutions.
C. A. R.	Congo-Kinshasa
Chad	Cameroun
Dahomey	Kenya
Ethiopia	Niger
Ivory Coast	Rwanda
Sierra Leone	
Upper Volta	

Group Three.
Supported Yugoslav resolution, but equivocally. Voted "yes" on Yugoslav, abstained on Latin American resolution. (Total. 2)

Nigeria
Gabon

Group Four.
Voted "yes" on Yugoslav, "no" on Latin American resolution. (Total: 10)

Burundi	Senegal
Congo-Brazzaville	Somali Republic
Guinea	Uganda
Mali	Zambia
Mauritania	Tanzania

Nations. While presidents' offices in Africa are often sympathetic to Israel, this is not always true of foreign ministries and UN delegations that are in daily contact with their Arab counterparts.

How They Voted

If we take the Latin American resolution as the one most in accord with Israeli interests and the Yugoslav resolution as representative of Arab interests, a fourfold breakdown of the vote indicates the degree of African support or opposition to the Israeli position (see table).

In group one are eight states that voted no to the Yugoslav motion and yes to the Latin American, indicating a clear preference for Israel. Here are found some of Israel's staunchest friends—Gambia, Liberia, the Malagasy Republic, and Togo (which once issued a set of postage stamps commemorating Togo-Israeli friendship)—as well as Ghana, whose presence in the group probably reflects in part a penalization of the UAR for its support of former President Nkrumah.

In group two are 12 states that gave what may be termed equivocal support to the Latin American resolution. They voted yes to the resolution and abstained on the Yugoslav motion, voted yes to both resolutions, or abstained from both. The two members of group three gave equivocal support to the Yugoslav resolution. The motives behind some of these votes are probably not fully related to the merits of either proposal, and presumably included such factors as a desire to keep one foot in each African grouping (Congo-Kinshasa and Cameroun voted yes to both resolutions), or a wish to avoid voting at complete variance with France, which came down openly on the Arab side. Some may have sought to mollify pro-Arab Moslem minorities.

The fourth category includes states traditionally hostile to Israel (Mauritania and Somalia) and some with which Israel has consistently had difficult relations (Mali and Guinea, and Burundi and Congo-Brazzaville since the ousters of the Mwami and former President Fulbert Youlou). Some of these states espouse "revolutionary" pan-African policies that incline them toward the Arab position, and two of them (Mali and Guinea) were charter members of the "Casablanca group" that included the UAR, Algeria, and Morocco. Five have Moslem majorities that identified closely with the Arab cause. Though some urban elites felt obliged to identify with the progressive forces in Algeria and the UAR, this factor probably counted for less than religion among the people as a whole. In Senegal, the attraction may have been magnified by President Senghor's interest in bringing Africans and Arabs together in an Arab-Berber-Negro community and, closer to home, in consolidating the regional river basin group comprising Senegal, Guinea, Mali, and Mauritania. More difficult to explain is the contingent from East Africa. The votes of Uganda and Tanzania may reflect, each in its way, the quest for a "revolutionary," anti-imperialist image.

A vote in the UN is often not the most reliable indicator of a nation's amity or enmity, and it would be foolish to seek hard and fast conclusions on the results of Israeli diplomacy in Africa. Nevertheless, a tabulation of the countries that fully or equivocally supported the Latin American resolution yields a total of 20 of the 32 sub-Saharan states. Taking into account the cross-pressures brought to bear on all delegations during the emergency session, and the aversion of small powers to any act that smacks of aggression, the amount of African support for the Latin American resolution is impressive. To the extent that diplomatic success is measurable, Israeli diplomacy appears to have paid off.

5 AFRICA AND THE MIDDLE EAST *

The history of political contacts between the Middle East and sub-Saharan ("Black") Africa is marked by ebbs and flows, major discontinuities and long periods of stagnation and mutual neglect. Despite centuries of economic and cultural interaction, the attention of the Arab states in the Middle East was never directed at Africa except tangentially during the early days of Islamic proselytizing and the slave trade. The early explorations of Arab traders and scholars in Africa, and the participation of many of the latter in medieval African centers of learning (such as Timbuktu-today in Mali) did not result in a mutuality of interests and stronger contacts between the two regions in the modern era.[1] Likewise, the re-integration of Jews in their ancient homeland hardly evoked much curiosity about the lands to the southwest. For both the Arab states and Israel, Africa was of only peripheral interest: their major cultural, economic and political concerns lay outside sub-Saharan Africa. That this was to change in the mid-fifties only attests to the ebb and flow of international relations and the shifting nature of foreign policy objectives. With hindsight, the past decade and a half may well be seen as the high tide of interaction between the Middle East and Africa: already there has been a noticeable decline in interest in Africa on the part of the major Middle East powers that are currently both disillusioned with their African record and preoccupied with other regional and global concerns.

Though nearly every country in the Middle East has, at one time or another, exhibited a half-hearted interest in expanding its contacts with Africa, the major actors in the continent have been Israel and the UAR—for political, economic and ideological reasons—and Lebanon, with thousands of nationals who are merchants, traders and middlemen in West Africa. Algeria's desire to play a major role largely died with Ben Bellah's demise in 1965, as did Morocco's, when its dispute with Mauritania was settled, obviating the need to recruit African allies. Recently, oil-rich Libya under the mercurial Qaddafi, has made a strong bid for the leadership of the radical group of African and Asian states,

* Originally published in *Middle East Information Series*, no. 22, February 1973,pp. 2-7.

intervening in Africa especially in Chad[2] and Uganda.[3] For all practical purposes, however, the major diplomatic onslaughts in Africa have come from Israel and the U.A.R.

The Israeli Entry into Africa

Paradoxically, it was Israel, recently established, and with hardly any economic, cultural or historic links with Africa, that initiated the first major thrust into that continent. Until 1956, Africa was very much a *tabula rasa* to the Israeli Foreign Ministry and diplomatic efforts in Asia had also been spotty. The bulk of the Ministry's efforts centered around the cultivation of close relations with the Western powers. Financially hard-pressed and diplomatically riveted to the actions and reactions of the major powers and the U.N., Israel established few diplomatic missions outside the nerve centers of the world, and then usually in countries with sizeable Jewish minorities.[4] The failure of Israel's early policy of over-reliance upon the West and the U.N. for its security objectives, coupled with her growing isolation from the newly emerging forces of Afro-Asia, best exemplified by the trauma of Bandung,[5] led to a re-assessment of Israel's global position and a sustained diplomatic assault on Africa and Asia.

While pragmatic political-diplomatic motivations impelled Israel to expand her contacts and seek allies in Africa, strong ideological and emotional factors cemented and gave supplementary sustenance to this drive. Indeed, no analysis of at least the formative years of Israel's "African" foreign policy can be complete without recognition of the complementarity of these two factors that gave the Israeli effort in Africa much of its uniqueness.

From the pragmatic point of view, Israel's entry into Africa was an attempt to gain allies vis-a-vis the Arab world, or at least to secure the neutrality of these new states in the Arab-Israeli disputes. Though in foreign policy there are usually "maximum" and "minimum" goals, in both instances, in the case of Israel, it was felt that the end result would be the same, namely, bolstering Israel's international position, blocking the by-now automatic reversals at the U.N. and the use of friendly Third World nations as a pressure upon the Arab countries for a negotiated peace in the Middle East.[6] The first two objective were rapidly to materialize, as best exemplified by the 1967 U.N. vote (following the war) when a majority of the non-Arab Third World backed the moderate Latin American resolution.[7] The last and most important objective, however, eluded Israeli policy-makers.

The pragmatic rationale for greater involvement with Africa led to a proliferation of technical cooperation programs that established Israel (at least up to 1964) as a major donor-nation comparable to Great Britain and France.[8] These programs received a powerful boost from the socialist political culture of Israel and from deeply imbedded psychological-cultural aspirations for an international role, a modern day fulfilment of the biblical prophecy of Israel as a model state and a "light to all nations."[9] It is this factor, and its pervasive influence upon many of the kibbutz-originating experts sent to Africa, that led the *Manchester Guardian* to comment: "lsrael's policy towards Black Africa should perhaps be seen in wider terms, and should be recognized to be not just part of its defense line against the Arab World, but also of a genuine desire to be of help. Africans respond because they recognize this."[10]

The Arab Counter-Reaction

Egypt's traditional foreign policy interests reside squarely in the Arab Middle East, including the Maghreb, and in Sudan. Globally, her ambitions were (as set by Nasser) to assume an important leadership role in the anti-imperialist camp. On both counts the U.A.R. was to encounter a measure of suspicion and opposition once her foreign policy scope expanded to include sub-Saharan Africa. For many of the newly independent countries, dependent as they were upon the former metropolitan powers, adopted relatively conservative postures; and the U.A.R.'s preoccupation with purely Arab and Middle Eastern matters (e.g. the Arab-Israeli conflict), even at the expense of pan-African unity, raised the question of the U.A.R.'s "African" credentials."[11] Indeed, in practically all instances where the U.A.R.'s African interests ran counter to her Middle East objectives, the clash was resolved in favor of the latter.[12]

In essence, the goals and motivations of the U.A.R. in sub-Saharan Africa were not very different from Israel's *albeit* minus the latter's messianic-ideological features. Africa was to be denied to Israel as part of the global efforts to isolate her diplomatically and economically; and African support was to be obtained for the U.A.R.'s anti-imperialist leadership claim, which was to bolster the U.A.R.'s international standing. These goals (as was the case with Israel's political objectives in

Africa) were not to be attained in their entirety. Though Nasser enjoyed a measure of popularity in sub-Saharan Africa, his claim for continental leadership was blocked by the conservative states, many of which also refused to break with Israel and by the existence of competing claims to the throne (Nkrumah, Touré, Haile Selassie.) Indeed part of the disillusionment with Africa—both on the part of Israel and the U.A.R.—was consequent to their operating on the assumption that the African states were available for mobilization by either one or the other of the contestants, would not develop independent orientations or be pressured by the real powers in Africa—France, Great Britain and to a lesser extent the U.S.[13]

Nasser's *The Philosophy of the Revolution*[14] stipulated an important U.A.R. role in Africa, and a high-level Committee was given the task of making specific policy recommendations.[15] The first major concrete expression of the U.A.R.'s interest in Africa took the form of support for radical African liberation movements, which were frequently in opposition to both the colonial powers and the rump of the indigenous nationalist movements.[16] These groups were invited to Cairo, where they set up their respective "National Bureaus." Among them one could note the radical wing of Cameroon's U.P.C., the leaders of Niger's Sawaba party and other opposition elements from Ivory Coast, Chad, Guinea, Nigeria, Kenya and Uganda. Since, in the majority of cases, independence brought to power moderate groups, the continuing presence in Cairo (in several instances up to 1964) of radical elements frequently banned in their home country, created serious pinpricks in the normalization of U.A.R. relations with several African states.

Indeed, until 1963-64, the U.A.R. diplomatic effort in Africa, apart from a small number of key countries, was minimal, this at a time when Israel was zealously pursuing a total reversal of her pre-1957 policy and establishing Embassies with every country in Africa.[17] Moreover, early U.A.R. inexperience with African sensitivities resulted in several fiascos in Liberia, Nigeria and Sierra Leone, which further exacerbated U.A.R.-Africa relations.

The Arab-Israeli Competition in Perspective

The expansion of the Arab-Israeli conflict into sub-Saharan Africa and the Israeli successes and failures in the region have already been extensively documented elsewhere[18] and hence only warrant a broad overview at this stage.

First, the greater involvement of Israel in Africa has brought about Israeli entanglement in African domestic conflicts. Thus, for example, for both very pragmatic as well as emotional-ideological reasons the lbo cause in Nigeria struck a responsive chord in the Israeli body-politic. Many of East Nigeria's leaders had visited Israel numerous times and had formed the backbone of the "Israel lobby" in Lagos. Moreover, Israel had an important cooperation program in East Nigeria, where, also, Israeli economic interests were deeply involved. When civil war enveloped the country these mutual links could not be shelved in favor of neutrality and, overnight, Israel and the U.A.R. found themselves supporting different sides in the civil war.

In a somewhat more calculating manner Israel became drawn into the Sudanese civil war. While reliable documentation on this involvement is simply non-existent, Israeli sources in East Africa and Jerusalem do not deny rumors and reports about arms supplies and personnel training for the Anyanya troops in South Sudan. The potential advantage of a black Southern Sudanese political entity as a "buffer state" for East Africa was denied to Israel consequent to the recent peace treaty, which gave the region only a measure of autonomy. In like manner, the victory of the Federal forces in the Nigerian civil war has prevented the birth of a strongly pro-Israel Biafran state; on the other hand the training and support provided to General Mobutu and his troops, even before his clear-cut ascendance in Zaire, did pay off handsome dividends. In general, however, Israeli policy makers have tried to steer clear of domestic conflicts which in light of the volatility of African politics can bring her sharp diplomatic reverses.

Secondly, the early period of frenzied Afro-lsraeli contacts, bilateral cooperation programs and Israeli diplomatic successes had largely petered out by the late 1960's, with a concomitant reduction in Israel's stature on the continent. This has been the result of a number of interlinked factors, all of which have quantitatively diluted Israel's potential importance to Africa. Among these one can note the growing recognition of the inapplicability (without drastic modifications) of many of Israel's developmental models;[19] the proliferation of more sources of foreign aid for African states; greater resiliency and competitiveness of expatriate (French or British) companies vis-d-vis Israeli enterprises in some parts of Africa; the cooling off of Franco-Israeli relations, which has had its direct reverberations in some African capitals; the downfall of several political leaders who had been especially linked with Israel (Dacko in the Central African Republic, Youlou in Congo/ Brazzaville and a large number of East Nigerian politicians among others) and the growing awareness of other African leaders of the complexities of the Middle East clash and the potential pitfalls—to their own national interests—of over-identification, for whatever reason, with either one of the contestants. One should hasten to add that politically, economically and diplomatically, Israel of the 1970's is vastly stronger and more solidly imbedded in the community of nations than was the Israel of the mid-fifties; consequently the relative utility to Israel of weak international allies has declined proportionately.

Thirdly, with the shift in U.A.R. diplomacy from exclusive support of radical movements and regimes to the expansion of contacts with the more conservative African states, an Arab-Israeli "balance of power" was established in Africa. This has been accompanied by a less dogmatic soft-sell of the Arab position, which has had greater success than the previous inflexible, adamant U.A.R. approach towards Afro-Israeli relations. The balance of power is a dynamic one in the sense that many African states have moved to a posture midway between the two contestants while, at the same time, radical swings do occur (e.g., Uganda.) The balance of power is tipping, however, in favor of the Arab states, as evidenced in 1971-72 by the increase in the number of anti-Israel resolutions passed at the U.N. with broad African support.[20] Undoubtedly, some of this African support is due less to anti-Israel feelings than to the desire to present the image of pan-African unity. Such was indeed the case with many of the anti-Israel resolutions that were passed in the mid-1960's at the Organization for African Unity (OAU), and which were immediately followed by verbal assurances that the vote would have no practical implications for Afro-Israel relations. Nevertheless, Israel recently has suffered several objective reversals in its grasp of the allegiances of some of its staunchest allies in Africa.[21] This has deepened the Israeli malaise regarding the trustworthiness of its erstwhile African allies and has shifted Israeli attention back to the major centers of international power.

In many respects the same process has occurred in the U.A.R., where there is greater awareness that mere lopsided anti-Israel votes at the O.A.U. or U.N. are not likely, by themselves, to attain the withdrawal of Israeli forces from areas occupied in the 1967 war.[22] In a sense, the circle has been completed, especially for Israel: from gross neglect of the Third World prior to 1956-57, through the long trek via Africa, which at least marginally solidified her international sources of support, and back to the ultimate guarantors of power and stability in the Middle East.

FOOTNOTES

1. For a brief account of early Arab-African contacts see Jacques Baulin, *The Arab Role in Africa*, Penguin, 1962.

2. See for example *Africa Research Bulletin*, Political, Social and Cultural Series, September 1971.

3. *The New York Times*, April 10, 1972; *Jerusalem Post*, March 27, 1972.

4. Samuel Decalo, "Israeli Foreign Policy and the Third World," *Orbis*, Fall 1967, pp. 724-745. As late as 1957 Israel maintained only seven Embassies in the entire world, six of these in Europe and North America. By 1964 Israel was represented in 87 countries, 75 of which were served by an Embassy. Israel's diplomatic network is surpassed today only by that of the U.S., U.K., and France.

5. In an interview in Jerusalem on August 13, 1964, a high-ranking Foreign Ministry official referred to the 1955 Bandung Conference's anti-Israel communique as follows: "Bandung was our greatest diplomatic setback. It was the greatest trauma we ever suffered. That two and one half billion people could be united in such a way against 1.8 million people in Israel was in itself soul-shattering to all of us in the Foreign Ministry." For the full text of the communique see George M. Kahin, *The Asian-African Conference*, Cornell University Press, 1956.

6. See Ben Gurion's speech at the *Knesset*. Israel, *Divrei Haknesset*, October 24-26, 1960, p. 12. Also *Israel Economist*, July 1961, p. 115; Emil Lengyel, "Israel's Campaign in Africa," *The Reporter*, February 4, 1960, and *Ha'aretz*, August 19, 1962.

7. *U.N. Monthly Chronicle*, July 1967, p. 53. For a detailed analysis of the African reactions to the war see Samuel Decalo, "Africa and the Mid-Eastern War," *Africa Report*, October 1967, pp. 57-61. For world-wide repercussions see especially Walter Laqueur, "Israel, the Arabs, and World Opinion" and Theodore Draper, "Israel and World Politics," both in *Commentary*, August 1967, pp. 49-59, and 19-48 respectively.

8. A description of these programs is contained in Leopold Laufer, *Israel and the Developing Countries*, Twentieth Century Fund, 1967, and Mor-

dechai Kreinin, *Israel and Africa: A Study in Technical Cooperation*, Praeger, 1965. For an annotated bibliography of much of the literature on Israel's relations with Africa see Samuel Decalo, "Israel and Africa: A Selected Bibliography," in *Journal of Modern African Studies*, 1967, vol. 5, No. 3, pp. 385-399.

9. Pinhas Lavon, "A Chosen Society and a Normal People," *New Outlook* (Tel Aviv), February 1962; Ben Gurion's discourse on the same theme in *Israel Weekly News Bulletin* (Tel Aviv), May 16-22, 1962; David Ben Gurion, *Israel Among the Nations*, Jerusalem, 1952, p. 12; Gertrude Samuels, "Israel at 13, Ben Gurion at 75," *New York Times Magazine*, September 24, 1961 and David Ben Gurion, "The Vision of Isaiah for Our Time," *New York Times Magazine*, May 20, 1963.

For an analysis of the "messianic" theme see Samuel Decalo, "Messianic Influences in Israeli Foreign Policy," Occasional Papers in Political Science No. 2, University of Rhode Island, 1967 and Samuel Decalo, "Messianic Influences and Pragmatic Limitations on Israeli Foreign Policy" in Mushkat, M. (ed), *World Society: Changing Structures and Laws*, Mouton Co., 1973.

10. Quoted in *Jerusalem Post*, August 17, 1962.

11. At the 1960 Addis Ababa Conference of Independent African States an unyielding U.A.R. attempt to ram through a resolution calling for sanctions on Israel caused significant annoyance among many delegations. See *New York Times*, June 25, 1960. Likewise, plans to set up Arab League offices in West Africa were resisted by several countries. Sierra Leone's Foreign Minister, Dr.John Karefa-Smart, retorted that "African members of the League will have to decide soon where they stand. Are they in the Middle East or in Africa?" *Arab Observer*, March 9, 1964.

12. Tareq Y. Ismael, *The U.A.R. in Africa*, Northwestern University Press, 1971, p. 70.

13. See for example Tamar Golan's article in *Ma'ariv* (Tel Aviv), June 1, 1972.

14. Published in 1954 in Cairo by the National Publication House.

15. Published as "An African Policy for Egypt" in the semi-official *Egyptian Economic and Political Review*, August 1956. Interestingly, Nasser's "The Egyptian Revolution," *Foreign Affairs*, January 1955, hardly mentions Africa.

16. Ismael, p. 37.

17. Actually, two countries refused to establish relations: Somalia and Mauritania. In 1967, in solidarity with the U.A.R. over the Middle East War, Guinea broke her relations with Israel. This was followed in 1972 by the widely reported Uganda-Israel rift. Currently, Israeli relations with several other classically "difficult" states, are quite strained-notably with Congo/Brazzaville and Mali.

18. For a guide to the literature see the author's bibliographical article in *Journal of Modern African Studies*, 1967, vol. 5, No. 3, as well as two recent Ph.D. dissertations in this field, available on microfilm or in xerox form from University Microfilms, Arm Arbor, Michigan: T. S. Rodin, "Political Aspects of Israeli Foreign Aid in Africa," University of Nebraska, 1969 and S. Decalo, "Israel and Africa: A Study of Foreign Policy and Technical Assistance," University of Pennsylvania, 1970.

19. Many of the Gadna-Nahal youth structures had to be radically restructured until in many countries they do not serve as supplemental tools for national unification. The kibbutz concept was never widely experimented and even the *moshav* model had to be repatterned to suit specific African settings.

20. For one recent example see *New York Times*, December 9, 1972.

21. In the second half of 1972 neutral or pro-Arab positions have been voiced, for example, by Dahomey, Togo and Upper Volta.

22. Moreover, the financial resources of the U.A.R. are stretched very thinly and cannot continue sustaining at the same level foreign policy goals in the Third World. See Ismael, p. 232, inter alia.

6 AFRO-ISRAELI TECHNICAL COOPERATION: SUCCESSES AND SETBACKS*

The Israeli program of technical cooperation with Africa has had its fair Share of successes and setbacks since its inception in the late 1950's. In common with other programs of technical assistance, the Israeli projects started off with unrealistically high goals and expectations, a great deal of zeal and ambition which had to be tempered in due time by the reality of Africa's socioeconomic and political context. It in now possible, after more than a decade of joint effort, to draw the outlines of the generic causes of the successes, and failures of some of these programs.

For analytic purposes it is useful to distinguish between programs aiming at social change and development and those involving the transfer of technical skills and the bolstering of the service and industrial sectors of African economics. The distinction is not totally satisfactory since many Afro-Israeli projects aim at development in both spheres and, moreover, the boundary lines between social development, institution-building,and enskilling populations are blurry. Nevertheless the distinction in crucial for it in essentially in the first category of projects that powerful and resilient obstacles arise, rooted in traditional values and preventing rapid meaningful social change.

The various *Nachal*-type programs and projects of agricultural training and resettlement that have been established in over twenty African states with Israeli cooperation are examples of programs of social change. Implicitly and explicitly they aim at human resources development with all that this entails in the realm of modernization of styles of life, attitudinal, value and culture changes, and shifts in perceptions of the world and the role of the self within it. By definition advances in these directions lead to the meet meaningful kind of social and economic development; equally obvious is the fact that therein lie the most complex and resilient aspects of the developmental syndrome.

---

*Address delivered (by invitation) at the Arden House Conference, March 24, 1973.

The Israeli programs have frequently had to retreat from original goals in face of the non-malleability of the African reality, namely traditionalism and tribalism. Programs set up to foster civic- consciousness and a sense of common nationality had to be modified so that the intake of recruits came from only one ethnic group or region. Projects to siphon off unemployed youth from urban to rural areas following training saw their new trainees desert back to the cities. And the agrarian modernization "spill-over" effect which was supposed to transform traditional agriculture following the implantation in villages of newly trained farmers often worked in the reverse direction as the traditional socioeconomic ethos overwhelmed the agents of modernization. Moreover, the modest scale of the programs, dictated by the economic non-viability of young African states, and attempts by political elites to view the new structures as patronage outlets and sources of personal political support, further undermined their potentialities an agents of modernization.

The record of Afro-Israeli efforts in this sphere must be placed in proper perspective, however. If unrealistic original goals were not attained significant inroads have been made which will pay handsome dividends, even if only in the distant future. Moreover, the modification of many of the programs, which are now better suited to the African reality, assures more speedy progress even if on a more limited front. Since many of these cooperative ventures are only a decade old and their hybrids were established only 4-6 years ago, more time will have to pass before a full evaluation in possible.

It in essentially when one moves to an examination of the second category of Afro-Israeli programs that the record of success in more clearly visible. Paradoxically these programs which include transfer of technical skills through training of African personnel, joint companies in a wide array of fields and Israeli aid to clinics, hospitals, educational establishments, and military hierarchies, are highly visible since they exist In coastal areas, yet are comparatively ignored. Undoubtedly part of the reason for this is that technical enskilling and the bolstering of service and industrial sectors is less glamorous than bold programs of social transformation. Yet the development of Africa's economic infrastructure and the training of her technical and administrative personnel are equally important prerequisites of entry into the modern world of nations. And in this area cultural factors carry less weight, and profitability, non-wastage of resources are important considerations to African states despite the occasional attempt at patronage political interference and bureaucratic haggling. The activities of Solel Boneh and Tahal in Africa are no doubt familiar to all. There are other mutual enterprises of equal merit. Indeed, an excellent example of a particular successful joint company that has contributed significantly to the development of Ivory Coast is *Motoragri*. This large company, set up in 1966, engages in mechanized clearing of bush and forest land contracted by the central government, local authorities or private landowners that wish to open up new land for agricultural production. Other activities include construction of roads and irrigation, earth dams and other related areas connected with preparing bush and forest land for modern use. The success of *Motoragri* in Ivory Coast has led to requests of other states for Afro-Israeli companies of the same kind, and must be compared with the dismal record of a similar enterprise net up with Soviet aid in Ghana.

In sum, the Israeli activities In Africa have had their ups and downs as would be expected from any program of technical assistance. The programs that have encountered the meet difficulties are not surprisingly those which tried to come to grips with the core issue of changing attitudes and life-styles. By definition such projects require a longer span of time before they can be properly evaluated. Even if the early overly-ambitious goals are not attained in their entirety the record of Afro-Israeli effort in this domain leaves nothing to be ashamed of. In other areas, Afro-Israeli cooperation has resulted in a large number of joint companies which have contributed significantly to the transformation of the infrastructure of Africa, and a growing pool of Israeli-trained personnel who are even new moving up the administrative ladders of their countries.

7 AFRO-ISRAELI TECHNICAL COOPERATION: PATTERNS OF SETBACKS AND SUCCESSES*

Few events in the field of international cooperation stirred as much attention and interest as the rapid escalation in Afro-Israeli technical cooperation in the late 1950's and early 1960's. From very modest roots and origins, mutual contacts and exchange of personnel and cadres mushroomed into what *Newsweek* somewhat exaggeratedly called "one of the strangest unofficial alliances in the world."[1] By 1963 the Israeli aid program had become an established fact in over a dozen African states, and hundreds of experts had been dispatched on a variety of consultative or developmental missions. Streaming in the reverse direction came thousands of Africans preparing to undertake training in Israel in a multitude of technical and cooperative fields. Israel's isolation in the world arena, vividly felt even before the 1956 war, appeared to have been irrevocably shattered. Its importance as a major laboratory for socioeconomic experimentation had finally been fully recognized as further underscored by the procession of foreign dignitaries and heads of state that made a visit to Jerusalem a *sine qua non* of their international itineraries.[2]

Israel's involvement with Africa sparked a deluge of articles in the scholarly and popular press, in Europe as well as in the United States. Israel had always shared the distinction, together with only a handful of other countries, of being a "newsworthy" country; its entry into Africa (and the Third World in general) only heightened editorial interest and the proclivities of writers and scholars.[3] Yet by the late 1960's the outpouring dried to a trickle, and the main sources of data on Afro-Israeli cooperation were reduced to specialized research bulletins.

*Originally published in Michael Curtis and Susan Aurelia Gitelson (eds.)., *Israel and the Third World*, Transaction Press, 1974, pp. 81-99.

There are several reasons for this dramatic decline in world interest in the Israeli effort in Africa. For one, the novelty had rapidly worn off, consequent to its early "overexposure." Israeli aid—crucial and dominant as it may have been in the early hectic days following Africa's independence[4]—began to tell its qualitative limitations as other assistance programs that took longer to set up began to overshadow what has always been a modest Israeli presence in the continent, and a financially limited assistance program.[5] More important was the growing gap between excessively heightened expectations of achievement of unrealistic goals with Israeli aid and the cruel reality of the resilience of poverty and the traditional socioeconomic order to anything, short of sustained and comprehensive developmental assaults spearheaded by sincere and dedicated political elites commanding adequate financial and technical resources. In the absence of such dedication and resources in most African states, perception of the chasm between aspirations and realities became poignantly clear, accompanied by the belated realization that the Israeli effort in Africa, with all its dedication and ingenious developmental models and approaches was not the overnight panacea that many in Africa and Israel had so ardently sought. The problems of transferring, cross-culturally to traditional, status quo oriented extended-family societies in tropical Africa, techniques for rapid socioeconomic change developed in other socio-cultural settings, was immensely more complicated than originally assumed, especially when African political hierarchies themselves were not often prepared to accept the burdens of a sustained drive in that direction.

Afro-Israeli cooperation in certain domains proceeded very smoothly and resulted in a variety of striking achievements of considerable value to the modernization and developmental aspirations of African states, negating prophecies of perpetual stagnation of these societies. In a sense the composite picture that emerges of fifteen years of Afro-Israeli cooperation is an intricate mosaic of advances and reverses, successes in some fields and setbacks in others, with attempts to adjust projects to better accommodate the lessons of past experience and the demands of a differently perceived reality. The multitude of Afro-Israeli programs of cooperation have been discussed at great length elsewhere:[6] The purpose of this chapter is to pinpoint several generic causes of success and failure.

Programs of Social Development and the African Context

When attempting to evaluate Israel's technical assistance to Africa it is useful to distinguish for analytic purposes between programs aiming at social and agrarian development and those oriented at the importation of strictly technical skills and the creation of services and economic infrastructures. The distinction is somewhat arbitrary and superficial, and the boundary lines between the two are frequently blurred. Many programs mesh social development and the implantation of new skills and techniques. Yet the distinction is nevertheless crucial for any understanding of the nature of problems facing Israeli programs of social change in Africa. Programs of this nature are implicitly or explicitly aiming at a transformation of the social ethos, reorganizing social patterns of interaction, modernizing life-styles and reshaping perceptions of the world and the role of the self within it. Cultural change and psychological shifts in perceptions and attitudes are the bedrock of such programs. It is change of this kind which leads eventually to meaningful systemic change, and is an inevitable process on the road to economic takeoff. By the same token programs in this area will face the greatest difficulties and the stubborn resistance of ingrained and still largely functional traditional values to the trumpets heralding the appearance of the new order. Herein lies the first cluster of factors which interacts with the various Israeli programs in Africa.

A second set of considerations that has to be taken into account, both in planning programs and in their evaluation, is the economic and political background of recipient countries. The two most important factors here are the political and economic fragility of many African states, which may lead to hasty erection of programs with ambitious goals that are doomed in advance to remain empty shells, testimonials to good intentions but empty state coffers. The success or failure of a program frequently depends on whether the two partners in the venture have similar or different intentions regarding use of the final product. For example, various African varieties of the *Nahal* concept are often viewed by African elites as supplementary sources of political support for their shaky thrones, and as ideal forms of patronage, rather than as nation-building structures and agents for social and agrarian change. Joint commercial ventures and state farms, where profitability (or at least non-wastage of resources) is an important

consideration, may turn into dumping grounds for political appointees leading to gross overstaffing and economic loss.[7]

The Traditional Setting

A large number of Israel's programs in Africa have to do with social
development. Agrarian reorganization and resettlement (along whatever lines) aims not only at implanting new administrative and
agricultural skills, but at the creation of upwardly mobile, individual-
istic and profit-inclined attitudes in the economic sphere, within
boundaries of mutual cooperation. Model and state farms aim at
creating a tangible visible example of what can be achieved with the
right implements, fertilizers and seeds; through the spillover (or multiplier) effect other neighboring farmers, it is assumed, will attempt a
replication of these new agricultural procedures—obviously, on a more
modest scale—leading to a transformation of the agrarian sector.

Finally, *Nahal* programs aim at eradication of tribalism, the
inculcation of civic consciousness, new modern values and a zest for
manual labor preparatory to resettlement on the land. The cultural
background of these bold experiments, however, is hostile to rapid
change. Even assuming successful completion of a training and resettlement project, new pioneers are both part of, and at the mercy, of
the traditional host culture which surrounds them. Pierre Alexandre,
former French Colonial Service administrator and distinguished
scholar, vividly described traditional African society and values when
he wrote:

> Seen from the angle of the individual's relationship with the group
> these societies were...*collectivist, status-bound and absolutely functional*. Their
> collectivism ... embraces every activity of the individual including
> the physical life. It can even be said that there was strictly speaking,
> no individual behavior or action but only fractional aspects of the
> collective life of the group. Moreover, any member who tended
> towards individualism should theoretically become divorced from
> the group and be outlawed as a social outcast. The individual, in
> order to remain integrated into the group had to conform. Noncon-
> formism was to be condemned since, as has been seen, any ques-
> tioning of the social order compromised the whole order of the
> cosmos...The development of each individual's existence depended

then, not so much on his own intrinsic qualities or his personal or individual peculiarities as on external factors which had little to do with his own efforts and which determined his status: sex, affiliation rank in the order of births, etc.[8]

These parameters are still very much part and parcel of the social context of much of Africa. There is wide variation, as in areas with a history prolonged contact with European and modern influences (coastal regions where traditional values have been partly broken down consequent to decades of sustained socioeconomic development (Ivory Coast, Gabon and parts of Kenya and Ghana) or in areas where traditional hierarchy was not powerful to start with (as in Southern Nigeria and especially among the Ibo). Yet even in these areas ethnic exclusiveness may still be high for it is now becoming evident that there is no necessary unilinear correlation between modernity and the growth of inter-ethnic linkages.[9]

The practical implications of the traditional and ethnic nature of Africa society for programs of social change such as Israel's are obvious. In Dahomey, Togo and Ivory Coast, to cite but three instances, agrarian resettlement and *Nahal*-type projects have had to abandon a former *sine qua non*—the fusion of different ethnic elements into cohesive "national" groups. The nation-building aspects of the *Nahal* concept, so much an integral and core part of the rationale of these programs and the *raison d'etre* of their implantation in Africa, proved totally unmanageable within the context of acute regionalism and historic ethnic animosities and suspicions—even when the subjects were, as at the outset, urban unemployed "transitionals" and not rural elements.[10] Continuous tension, friction and overt hostility among opposing ethnic elements not only broke discipline and prevented the growth of national consciousness, but also contributed to high levels of desertion from the formations (up to 60 percent). In like manner ethnic tensions were marked also in the training of the Ivory Coast's women's auxiliary corps in Bouaké by officers of Israel's *Chen* (women's army), and in Sierra Leone where Mende-Temne friction was intense. With the shift from recruitment of disparate tribal elements to training and resettlement of socially and ethnically cohesive units in their own regions (again, a major deviation from original plans for national integration that called for the interspersing of such units all over the country), a reduction of this form of friction was accomplished though desertion still remained high.

The basic values of African traditional life have similarly created obstacles to programs of socioeconomic change. As Alexandre has noted, an individual's social status is largely determined by factors outside his immediate control; attempts at social and economic amelioration through individual efforts and new techniques (unless one moves to urban areas) may lead to ostracism of the individual concerned and his entire kinship group. In light of the importance to Africans in the traditional sector of their ties to their extended family—without which one has little influence or social status in a village community—Israeli-trained farmers returning to their native villages have often shied away from actions that might bring upon their heads the wrath of village elders and the social pressures of their kinfolk.

Coexistence is often difficult (though this is slowly changing) between a traditional ethos that stresses egalitarianism in consumption and wealth, subordination of certain activities to dictates of ritual, and immemorial tradition and age as criteria for wisdom or status—and young farmers with new concepts and methods and an ethic that does not subordinate the product of their extra labor and knowledge to the aggregate needs of the village. Since the elders are not only the repository of accumulated wisdom but also the link between the ever-watchful lineage ancestors and their offspring, both living and yet unborn, acts of insubordination are seen as directly threatening the dependency linkages between the dead, the living and the yet unborn, with dire results for all. Quite apart from the social tensions inherent in a situation where the elders are not given their customary deference, nor are they any longer the prime repositories of wealth or knowledge, pressures from relatives of newly trained farmers for a distribution of their increased crops can rend villages asunder.[11] The social security framework of traditional society simply cannot tolerate individuals who wish to partake of its psychological comforts without subordination to its socio-economic dictates.[12]

It is consequent to the factors noted above that resettlement of farmers trained in *Nahal* units or in other institutional frameworks has been marked by difficulties experienced in their native villages. Even resettlement a mile or two away may cause tensions and strife in social relationships as it has on several occasions in Dahomey and Ghana. This problem was so acute in Upper Volta that newly trained formers have occasionally been allocated land in areas far away from their native villages. While this may appear as one possible way to break the social obligations expected of more successful farmers by their village kinsfolk, the psychological deprivation many of the former feel may lead to the collapse of the new settlement as "pioneer" settlers drift back to their native villages forsaking their newly gained knowledge that had poisoned their social relations. This approach is only feasible in a few countries such as Upper Volta, where poor soil conditions, soil erosion, population pressure, pest invasions and frequent droughts have traditionally forced groups of villagers to found new settlements away from their native villages, or to migrate to the Ivory Coast in search of salaried work.[13]

It is also-important to examine the motivations of those who are recruited into new agricultural programs. The *Nahal*-type formations, which existed in over twenty states in Africa alone, were originally aimed at soaking up unemployed youth in urban areas (where a 25-30 percent unemployed rate is common) recently arrived from the countryside.[14] Many of the original operative guidelines of these structures were not overly successful due to high desertion rates and lack of motivation or inclination for manual and agricultural labor on the part of urban recruits who were not suitable for cooperative work.[15] These youths had after all moved away from rural areas in order to escape both the social oppressiveness of traditional life and the drudgery of agricultural work. Inculcation of the zeal for manual work in Israel was a very unique process with strong emotional and ideological overtones which were already in existence as part of the country's political culture. The effort to acculturate African urban youth with this mystique in the absence of the sustaining cultural values that existed in Israel often resulted in failure. Even African governments trying to impose upon high school or university students a one or two-year period of national service in the countryside (not necessarily manual work) have faced virtual revolts from this segment of society which is for all practical purposes the future elite of the country.[16] After the largely unsatisfactory conclusion of several agricultural training programs, new directives were issued in many African countries to start recruiting uneducated, rural youth, and a certain improvement in the attrition rate was clearly visible. Even now, however, a significant percentage of ex-trainees, as in the Ivory Coast, for example, where many flatly refuse to join their villages, promptly move to urban areas with their newly acquired agricultural expertise. As one Israeli official in Abidjan noted, completion of a course of instruction in agricultural

training camps is viewed by some recruits as an educational qualifica-
tion—incongruous as it may be—for clerical work in the cities.[17]

Political and Economic Setting

The previous considerations which so obviously affect the nature and
success of Israeli programs of social and agrarian development in Africa
are rooted in the cultural milieu of African states. The economic and
political background of these programs also affect their operation and
chances of success.

The most important aspect of the economic setting, is the
scarcity of budgetary and developmental resources in most African
states. This leads among other things to the erection of programs
without any hope of successful completion due to financial considerations. In general Israeli experts in the field have been able to cope with
this problem through improvisation, which has given the programs
an added distinction and attraction. Occasionally, this is impossible,
as when the Tadzewu cattle ranch was set up in Ghana in 1962 with
an anticipated investment budget of $490,000 for superior cattle from
Mali and machinery from Europe. Ghana's shortage of foreign funds
delayed the project, which eventually commenced its activities with
cannibalized machinery from various state farms and one-tenth of its
anticipated herd of two thousand, largely inferior stock hastily culled
from other Ghanaian sources. This inauspicious beginning together
with political interference, immeasurable bureaucratic haggling between various Ghanaian ministries, lack of accounting and established
administrative procedures, created a variety of problems to an inher-
ently sound and eminently feasible project.

Shortage of funds, despite Israeli estimates which has been
approved in advance, caused a temporary stalemate in the program to
establish a Nahal-type formation in the Central African Republic (called
Jeunesse Pionnière Nationale, or JPN) in 1962. Criticism and opposition to it
rapidly built up in the National Assembly consequent to the fact that
the JPN had been allocated a modest budget, yet still larger than that
of several ministries including the presidency itself.[18] Largely consequent to President Dacko's excellent relations with Israel, and the
latter's interest in maintaining its presence in the Central African
Republic, relevant treaties were renegotiated with Israel assuming a

larger share of the financial burden. Similar parliamentary opposition arose in West Nigeria over the regional government's plan to allocate funds for the erection of five farm institutes to train school leavers who would be resettled with government loans of approximately six thousand dollars per family. Chief Akin Deko envisaged that through the spillover effect levels of productivity throughout the region would rise; the opposition argued that few farmers would be able to amass the financial resources needed to emulate the trainees, and that in terms of cost-benefits the program was totally irresponsible. [19] As an example of the relatively large cost of providing for a rural resettlement program one can note that Ivory Coast's two new villages set up in 1956 consumed over 55 percent of the entire budget of the Community Service. In like manner the Gadna-type *Jeunesse et Travail* program in Ivory Coast was greatly hampered by a low budget and a very high ratio of recruits per instructor (1 to 260)—both of which prevented the fuifillment of even an approximation of the program's goals.

A number of other projects in Africa have suffered either through criticism of their (relative) cost or more frequently consequent to financial overextension of African governments. This has inevitably delayed or truncated programs with adverse effects on productivity (in the case of State Farms, as in Ghana, where profitability was important), emulation effect (in the case of Model Farms, as in Upper Volta, Dahomey, the Central African Republic) and recruits (in the case of *Nahal* or cooperative projects in many countries). Budgetary limitations in Dahomey, for example, has meant that the central *Service Civique* training camp at Ouassa (near Bohicon) accommodated trainees in dilapidated dormitories with straw mats on the floor and few other facilities, while food and operating funds arrived very irregularly. On a few occasions when conditions were especially bad, trainees have had to fend for themselves, many deserting for good. And this in a program administered by the Dahomean army (the *Service Civique* was set up as a separate branch in 1971 under a senior officer) with which both the Israeli Embassy and the Israeli Military Training Mission had the best possible relations (at least until the 1972 coup). These harsh financial conditions have existed to some extent in the civil service as well; assembling the monetary outlay and meeting the deadline of each payday has been a never-ending part of the harrowing nightmares of most officials in the Finance Ministry. Its effect upon the *Service Civique* was an important contributing factor to the heavy desertion rate of recruits whose numbers have tended to drop from a high of two hundred at the outset of the nine-month course to a graduating class of approximately sixty. Training was frequently disrupted when recruits simply melted into the bush for various periods of time whenever their help was needed in their own native villages.[20]

Financial problems plagued the creation of the Central African Republic's *Nahal* program and they continued even after the program was officially set up. The budget stipulated a monthly outlay per recruit of CFA Fr 4,500 ($16.66) of which $2.00 per month constituted pocket money. Delays in the transmission of these funds caused heavy resentment among recruits who had been asked to volunteer for the nation-building effort. In Tanzania poor pre-planning and lack of resources prevented the deployment and resettlement in 1965 of national service units, despite the significant outlay of funds and efforts in creating and training them.[21] Such programs have also suffered from serious interministerial haggling over responsibilities and budgets, lack of accounting and bookkeeping procedures, red tape, overstaffing consequent to political appointments, overt attempts to transform them into personal political and patronage machines, and even an occasional embezzlement of funds.[22] The degree to which programs have been affected negatively has depended upon the extent of interference and the firmness, tact and improvisational abilities of Israeli experts in the host country. One of the best known examples of political penetration and interference occurred in the case of Ghana's Workers' Brigades. These, which in their heyday included over fifteen thousand Ghanaians, chaotically organized for poorly defined and continuously shifting developmental tasks,[23] served functionally as a patronage machine for the Nkrumah regime. With unemployment in most cities fluctuating between 25 and 30 percent, the removal off the streets of restless young elements and their integration into fon-nations which at least provide for their sustenance becomes an action of considerable political importance.

In like manner the former Tanzanian minister, Oscar Kambona, attempted to spread his wings over the National Service units; and, in the Central African Republic there was competition between the head of the army, Bokassa (currently the president) and Izamo, head of the police, over ultimate control of the units. Even in the Ivory Coast, which rapidly became the crowning jewel of Israel's multifaceted assistance program, there has been at least one instance of political interference and a recent trend to transform Civic Service units into a personal patronage machine and power source for the presidency.[24] One 1971 semi-restricted Israeli report that evaluated the Israeli programs of social and agrarian change in the Ivory Coast warned that the Ghanaian pattern may be repeating itself again since the regime appeared to be more concerned with short-run solutions to political unrest than long-range social and agrarian transformation. Several Israeli officers in the country have suggested an Israeli pullout as more advisable than countenancing a repeat of the Ghanaian experience. Most probably here too, political considerations will assure continued Israeli participation in programs in this key state, just as political considerations impelled Israel to continue "showing the flag" even in the darkest days of Nkrumah's rule.

The above points should suffice to indicate the wide range of problems that programs of social and agrarian change face in Africa. All this is not to imply that every or most Israeli efforts in this domain have been unsuccessful or beset with problems that drastically curtailed their effectiveness. Such an interpretation would be far from the truth since many programs of agrarian training and settlement have been highly successful. However, a sizable number of Israeli programs in this specific area of technical cooperation, and especially in West Africa, have encountered the problems previously noted, resulting from the cultural, political and economic context within which they are established. Several of the same factors also exist in Asia and Latin America, where Israel has extensive programs of cooperation. There the cultural framework is quite different, and important progress has been achieved especially with Latin American peasantry. Some of the more important obstacles to successful social change are unique to Africa and do not allow for comparison with other regions.

Despite the above analysis of the state of some programs and their problems it is hard to reach any meaningful conclusions. It is extremely difficult to set criteria for the evaluation of programs aiming at social change, since some of the variables involved cannot be quantified. It is not simply a matter of counting the number of cadres trained and remaining on their farms, or the number of new settlements established; nor does it involve attempts to measure increased productivity and the application of new techniques of farming in villages where trained cadres have been implanted. Evaluating social change, which many of Israel's programs in Africa aim at, is a much

more complex process than mere assessment of tangible manifesta-
tions of agrarian modernization and productivity. Success and failure
are relative. The span of time over which programs have been operative
is an important consideration. And though some of Israel's programs
in this domain have been in existence for over ten years, their hybrids,
established after years of experimentation, and currently more attuned
to the limitations imposed by African conditions, have been operative
in many cases for only five to six years, a far too short period of time
to allow for valid generalizations beyond those already attempted.

It is safe to conclude that the limited scope of these programs—dictated by African budgetary considerations—greatly curtails
their potential benefits; at the most—even taking into account the
multiplier effect—they can only produce limited pockets of modernization which will have to be carefully nurtured by the host country
lest they be drowned and overwhelmed by the surrounding traditional
ethos. On the basis of past experience it can be argued that meaningful
long-lasting change depends upon the dedication and commitment of
political elites. To date, with the one clear exception of Tanzania, and
possibly a handful of other states, this has been sadly lacking in Africa.

Transfer of Skills and Erection of
Service Infrastructures

It is when one moves to an examination of Israeli programs which
involve transfer of technical skills to Africa and the creation of joint
companies and/or service infrastructures, that one encounters the
most clear-cut successes of Afro-Israeli joint efforts. This is because the
cultural variables noted previously are only marginally important, so
that Israeli selection standards and quality control can be adhered to
and hence Israeli control and influence are more marked. The profitability, or at least nonwastage of resources of the joint companies is of
some importance to African political elites who might otherwise have
to foot the bill. Paradoxically, training programs in Israel and Afro-Israeli joint companies usually based in urban areas, have earned less
attention despite their importance and visibility. Technical training
and joint companies in the construction area are less glamorous forms
of international cooperation than programs of rural agrarian and social
development. Though modernization of agriculture and the forging of

a nation out of ethnically diverse elements is a key stage on the road to socioeconomic development, so is the process of expanding the service, technical and administrative sectors of an underdeveloped country.

Afro-lsraeli cooperation in this field falls into three separate categories: transfer of technical and other skills through training programs (including those for *Nahal* leaders and agrarian cadres), short or long-term loans of Israeli experts, and the creation of joint companies or transfer of managerial skills to African enterprises. Tables 1-4 indicate the magnitude of the Israeli training programs and the number of Israeli experts serving in Africa. In 1970, the last year for which full statistics are available, 246 Israeli experts served in Africa a total of 1,495 man/months—36.8 percent of the latter figure devoted to *Nahal*-Gadna activities, 26.6 percent to agricultural guidance and 13.8 percent to managerial and public service assistance. During the same year a total of 434 Africans came to Israel for 1,724 study months: 120 studied agriculture, 99 cooperation activities and 59 community development.[25] The striking fact about Table 3 and projections through 1973 is that some 8,000 Africans have been directly exposed to Israel and its developmental concepts and approaches in a continent where urban and rural modern or modernizing sectors are relatively small. This has important side benefits to Israel from the political standpoint, 26 and adds much needed middle-range technical and administrative personnel to Africa's pool of cadres involved in the developmental process.

TABLE 1: Israeli Experts Abroad 1958-1970

Africa	2,483
Latin America & Caribbean	530
Mediterranean Area	504
Asia	431
Total	3,948

Source: *Israel's Programme of International Cooperation*, (Israel: Ministry for Foreign Affairs, 1971), p. 57.

TABLE 2 Israeli Experts Abroad by Specialization 1959-1967

Agriculture	916
Youth organization	354
Health	262
Education	238
Others	566
Total	2,582

Source: *Israel's Programme of International Cooperation*, (Israel: Ministry for Foreign Affairs, 1971), p. 57.

Enthusiasm and satisfaction with training courses in Israel has been high judging by figures cited by Yannay based on a 1963 survey, despite pockets of criticism regarding length of courses and insufficient time devoted to practical work (see Table 5.) Subsequent courses took into account these criticisms which stemmed, according to Israeli instructors, from the greater need of Africans for visual aids and/or more extensive practical demonstrations. Complaints have also been voiced by financially pressed African governments about the high cost of travel to Israel for training purposes (courses have been offered in Africa but this is not possible in many fields and the impact is enhanced by direct exposure to the Israeli context), or the considerable expenditures required to host and pay Israeli experts. Despite the fact that the latter are relatively cheaper than comparable non-Israeli experts (in fields where they are available), the Israeli government has at times quietly picked up the tab for expenses normally covered by recipients of such assistance.

TABLE 3: Trainees in Israel 1958-1970

Africa	6,623
Asia	2,510
Mediterranean Area & Others	2,476
Latin America & Caribbean	2,181
Total	13,790

Source: *Israel's Programme of International Cooperation,*
(Israel: Ministry for Foreign Affairs, 1971), p. 57.

TABLE 4: Trainees in Israel by Field 1958-1968

Agriculture	2,747
Study tours & seminars	1,582
Cooperative & labor studies	1,246
Community development	1,007
Academic, including medicine	729
Youth leadership	567
Vocational training	538
Individual trainees & miscellaneous	2,153
Total	10,569

Source: *Israel's Programme of International Cooperation,*
(Israel: Ministry for Foreign Affairs, 1971), p. 57.

On the Israeli side there have been some grumblings about occasional African students sent out to Israel on junkets consequent to their connections in various ministries, or of inadequate screening of prospective trainees who arrive without the barest of qualifications. Greater Israeli control over intake of trainees, exercised by Israeli embassies in Africa, has reduced the number of such cases. A more difficult problem to solve was the decline in the late 1960s of the number of experts available for work abroad. The gradual retirement of many older personnel sent in earlier years and the end of the brief recession in the Israeli economy dried up many sources of recruitment. Some of the "experts" recently sent abroad have been fresh young university graduates not all of whom were fired with the same zeal or possessed the same professional skills and experience so manifest in experts sent to Africa in earlier years. Agricultural experts in particular have had to cope with a variety of problems in the field not the least of which were soil conditions, pests and crops that they had not encountered before. Their adjustment to tropical conditions and crops has been remarkably smooth. The quality of Israeli personnel in Africa has in general been high.

TABLE 5: Evaluations of Israeli-Trained Cadres

Question	% Yes	% No
Are you employed in the field in which you got training?	78	22
Has the training helped you in your work?	95	5
Have you been promoted since your return home?	48	52
Was the course well planned?	90	10
Were the lectures effective and was the level of theory adequate?	90	10
Was the practical work sufficient?	65	35
Was the course long enough?	41	59
Was there satisfactory written material to accompany the course?	74	26

Source: Y. Yannay, "Technical Cooperation between Israel and the Developing World," International Development Review, vol. 6, no. 3 (1964), p. 10-15.

Joint Companies

Of all Afro-lsraeli joint ventures established since 1958 those formed
by Solel Boneh with African public capital are probably best known
abroad. Five such construction companies were established in Ghana
(GNCC), Western Nigeria (Nigersol), Eastern Nigeria (ENCC), Sierra
Leone (NCC) and Ivory Coast (Sonitra.) Of these only Sonitra remains
as a de facto joint company, the others having been turned over to full
African control. Altogether, up to the point when the Israeli connection
was broken (and in the case of Sonitra up to 1970), a total of $107
million in works have been executed. Nine Solel Boneh branches,
operating as expatriate construction companies, were also established
in eight countries (two in Nigeria)[27] of which six are still operative
today. Their total of works executed by 1970 amounted to $71 million.
These operations of Solel Boneh cannot be considered technical cooperation. Several other Afro-lsraeli joint companies have been established involving, on the Israeli side, Tahal and Water Resources
Development International, a subsidiary of Mekorot. Also notable are
the activities of private Israeli capital and management concerns such
as the Federman group and the Mayer brothers.

   While most joint companies have been successful financial
ventures that have also contributed significantly to the development
of Africa's infrastructure (roads, building complexes, dams, airports),
there has been a trend among Israeli public companies not to get overly
involved in new enterprises of this kind. With the new economic
pickup in Israel, construction companies have sufficient work to
occupy them at home and this in turn translates into a paucity of
skilled personnel available for missions abroad. Managerial fees and
the share of profits that the Israeli partner gets in a joint company are
quite low. Risks on the other hand are potentially high, whether
consequent to political turmoil, as occurred in the regional government of West Nigeria with Nigersol caught in the middle, or as a result
of premature and underhanded dissolution of the joint enterprise, as
occurred in Ghana with GNCC. Joint companies have to contend with
a variety of political pressures, interministerial bog-downs, cumber-
some and tardy procedures for payments for services rendered to the
government, and a host of intrigues sponsored by anti-Israeli
groups—whether they be Lebanese, Syrian, French or British expatriate
economic interests. The above points not-withstanding, Afro-lsraeli

joint companies have been ideal mechanisms for the transfer of technical, managerial and administrative skills, and useful devices for breaking the monopoly metropolitan companies possess in Africa.

To better illustrate both the kinds of problems Afro-Israeli joint companies have faced and their contributions to the transformation of the host country's landscape, the operations of Motoragri in Ivory Coast might be instructive—even though Motoragri is not a joint company in the strict sense of the term. Motoragri was set up in April 1966 following a survey conducted by Agridev[28] experts at President Houphouet-Boigny's request, to ascertain the best way to utilize some $4 million worth of agricultural machinery attained through an AID loan and already being unloaded at Abidjan's docks. Following the survey Agridev signed a managerial contract specifying an annual fee of $140,000 (in 1969 reduced to $85,000) in exchange for which it recruited Israeli managerial, technical, administrative and training, personnel (at the outset twenty-four for the new company in the Ivory Coast.[29] Motoragri was given considerable autonomy in its activities, though it was ultimately responsible to a super-board of directors (in which French interests were indirectly represented) which included delegates of all ministries, the National Assembly and even the private sector. Motoragri's prime task was to engage in large-scale mechanized clearing of tropical forest and bush land for new agricultural or other use, under contracts from central and local authorities, village communities or private landowners. Other activities included construction of roads and irrigation of earth dams, clearing of projected village sites, and plowing and subsoiling existing plots.

The company faced from the outset the opposition of entrenched interests (Ivoirien as well as French) and inherited a wide assortment of incompatible new machinery since Houphouet-Boigny had allocated his AID loan purchases equally among the the main American manufacturers of machinery equipment. There was also a very acute shortage of skilled labor, foremen, tractor drivers and mechanists which necessitated an immediate crash training program. Other complications arose when the best applicants for jobs consistently turned out to be diligent and honest Mossi emigrants from Upper Volta, a fact which caused some resentment because it reduced the number of openings available to native Ivoirien. There were also the usual attempts of local notables and politicians to exert influence upon Motoragri to recruit personnel from their own regions or to give priority to projects of personal interest to them.[30]

The Israeli team rapidly commenced activities with a headquarters, repair shop and spare parts manufacturing workhouses in Abidjan, and seven regional centers where the actual machinery and staff were concentrated. Tight control was exerted on the precise location of all equipment and its regular maintenance and repair—a fact which was commented upon favorably in the press[31] and which can be contrasted with the poor administration and maintenance of a larger (2000 machines) but similar Soviet venture in Ghana. Different price lists were calculated to assure amortization of equipment and capital on a nonprofit basis while allowing enterprising villages and/or medium landowners to avail themselves of Motoragri's services. While most of the work was contracted for by various ministries as part of their development plans, a significant number of projects were completed for local communities and individuals.[32] The initial April 1966 staff of 85 greatly expanded as the training programs—of extremely high standards[33]—churned out the skilled manpower needed. By the end of that year the staff numbered 250, and it more than doubled in 1967 to a total of 650 native employees and 31 Israelis. In 1969 further expansion commenced consequent to the addition of a new and big regional center and the acquisition of new machinery.

By 1971 Motoragri had completed contracts worth $16 million, including over 2,170 miles of roads of all kinds and had cleared 17,500 hectares (43 million acres) of land. Its impact upon the development of Ivory Coast's infrastructure and its contributions in the field of expanding the size of available agricultural land have been immense. Through its training programs Motoragri has also created a sizable pool of skilled and semiskilled labor. Though the Africanization process has been slow an Ivoirien was promoted to the post of managing director in 1969 and most Israeli personnel had practically from the outset Ivoirien assistants who were being prepared to take over responsibilities once Israeli presence was no longer deemed necessary. The unqualified success of Motoragri in the Ivory Coast has led to several requests by other African states for similar joint ventures, even if on a more modest scale. Agridev (and Solel Boneh) has been hesitant to respond affirmatively to these invitations for reasons previously noted. Though Agridev's political vistas in Ivory Coast have been minimal, this has not been entirely the case with Sonitra (the Ivory Coast-Solel Boneh construction company) and Agridev's financial incentive

($85,000 a year) has been very small.[34]

There are a variety of other aspects of the Afro-lsraeli history of technical cooperation that cannot be dealt with due to space-limitations: military and internal security personnel training, loans of Israeli staff to African ministries, hospitals, national lotteries, etc. 35 In terms of scope and variety Afro-lsraeli cooperation has been both unique and one of the most significant examples of international cooperation. Despite various problems that have afflicted several of these efforts, and despite intense international pressures by Arab states against overly close Afro-Israeli relations, these programs of cooperation have not altered and are continuing to contribute their share to social and economic development of the continent.

FOOTNOTES

1. "A Surplus of Brains," *Newsweek*, August 20, 1962.

2. These state visits not only shattered the hitherto parochial nature of Israeli civic events, but more than anything attested to Israel's coming of age. Prior to these African state visits (in 1960-61 alone there were seven) only one leader had deigned to visit Israel. For a discussion of the evolution of Israeli foreign policy vis-a-vis the Third World see Samuel Decalo, "Israeli Foreign Policy and the Third World," *Orbis* (Fall 1967): 724-45.

3. For a review of some of the literature see Samuel Decalo,"lsrael and Africa: A Selected Bibliography," *Journal of Modern African Studies*, vol 5, no. 3 (1967): 385-99.

4. In the "honeymoon" period of Ghanaian-lsraeli relations (1967-62) the Israeli Embassy in Accra and the Israeli technical assistance in Ghana were the most prestigious and influential bar none. The Israeli Ambassador was credited with having immediate access to Nkrumah at all times. The same was true in the Central African Republic (under Dacko) and in a couple of other states. See, for example, John B. Oakes, *The Edge of Freedom* (New York: Harper & Brothers, 1961), p. 45.

5. Among other external factors that worked to diminish lsrael's role in Africa can be noted the Franco-Israeli break, which had significant repercussions in French Africa; the Arab-Soviet propaganda drive against Israel's activities in Africa; and, more recently, the Libyan financial juggernaut assault on several African states.

6. Mordechai Kreinin, *lsrael and Africa: A Study in Technical Cooperation* (New York: Praeger, 1964); and Leopold Laufer, *Israel and the Developing Countries: New Approaches to Cooperation* (New York: Twentieth Century Fund, 1967.)

7. See among others Victor Uchendu, "Socioeconomic and Cultural Determinants of Rural Change in East and West Africa," *Food Research Institute Studies*, no. 3 (1968): 225-42; Howard Schuman, "Economic Development and Individual Change: A Social-Psychological Study of the Comilla Experiment in Pakistan," *Occasional Papers in International Affairs*, no. 15 (Cambridge: Harvard University Center for International Affairs, 1967); Philip Porter, "Environmental Potentials and Economic Opportunities, Background for Cultural Adaptation," *American Anthropologist* (April 1965): 409-20; Arthur Nichoff, "Peasant Fatalism and Socio-Economic Innovation," *Human Organization* (Winter 1966): 273-83; Philip Hauser, "Cultural and Personal Obstacles to Economic Development in Less Developed Areas," *Human Organization* (Summer 1959): pp. 78-94; and Development of Smallholder Agriculture in Eastern Nigeria," *Economic Development and Cultural Change* (April 1965): 278-92.

8. Pierre Alexandre, "The Problems of Chieftancies in French Speaking Africa," In *West African Chiefs*, ed., Michael Crowder and Obaro lkime (Ile-Ife, Nigeria: University of Ife Press, 1970), p. 28.

9. See among others Robert Melson and Howard Wolpe, "Modernization and the Politics of Communalism: A Theoretical Perspective," *American Political Science Review* (December 1970): 1112-30; and idem, *Nigeria: Modernization and the Politics of Communalism* (East Lansing: Michigan State University Press, 1974.)

10. From interviews in Dahomey and Togo, 1971 and 1972. For the background and contemporary setting of these tensions see Samuel Decalo, "Regionalism, Politics and the Military in Dahomey," *Journal of Developing Areas* (April 1973): 1-41; and idem, "The Politics of Military Rule in Togo," *Geneve-Afrique* (January 1974.)

11. For an example in a different geographical area see the illuminating article by Vaiao and Fay Ala'ilima, "Samoan Values and Economic Development," *East-West Center Review*, vol. 1, no. 3 (February 1965): 3-18.

12. See also the pessimistic view of the possibilities of cooperative efforts in Africa contained in Xavier A. Flores, "Institutional Problems in the Modernization of African Agriculture," in *A Review of Rural Cooperation in Developing Areas* (Geneva: United Nations Research Institute for Social Development, 1969.)

13. See Peter B. Hammond, *Yatenga: Technology in the Culture of a West African Kingdom* (New York: The Free Press, 1966); and Elliott P. Skinner, *The Mossi of Upper Volta* (Stanford: Stanford University Press, 1964.)

14. See for example Walter Elkan, "Out of School Education and Training for Primary-School Leavers in Rural Kenya, "*International Labour Review*, (September 1971): 205-16.

15. See Moshe Dayan's comments on Central African Republic's *Nahal* in "West African Diary, IV," *Jerusalem Post*, November 26, 1963.

16. For a recent example of this in Nigeria, see *West Africa*, March 12, 1973.

17. From interviews in Abidjan. See also Laufer, *Israel and the Developing Countries*, p. 117.

18. *Marchés Tropicaux et Méditerrannées*, January 5, 1963.

19. See M. Kreinin, "The Introduction of Israel's Land Settlement Plan to Nigeria," *Journal of Farm Economics* (August 1963): 535-46; idem, "Cooperative Farming: West Nigeria's Exciting 20 million Scheme," *Africa Trade and Development* (September 1961): 12-13; idem, "Farm settlement schemes in Nigeria," *Nigerian Trade Journal* (January-March 1962): 2-6; and idem, *West Africa*, February 24, 1962.

20. Interviews in Cotonou and Ouassa, July-August 1971. For further background on Dahomey's economy see Samuel Decalo," The Politics of Instability in Dahomey," *Geneve-Afrique*, 7, no. 2 (1,968): 5-32.

21. Laufer, *Israel and the Developing Countries*, p. 116.

22. An interesting case cropped up in the State Lottery of Dahomey, which was a different form of technical assistance than the one currently being discussed. There a ranking officer presented to the lottery a patently forged winning ticket. Despite representations of the Israeli director, the military junta then in power ordered payment of the prize.

23. In 1964 the brigades were separated into two sections, one for agricultural work and the other for construction. Though it is undeniable that the units performed some important work, productivity was low, discipline and control were lax and many members regarded their entry into the brigades as official sinecures.

24. Interviews in Jerusalem, Abidjan and Ouagadougou, June-August 1972.

25. Figures from Dan V. Segre, "The Philosophy and Practice of Israel's International Cooperation."

26. On several occasions in different countries a measure of pro-Israeli sentiment was visible even when the official governmental posture was neutral or hostile. This occurred, for example, in Nigeria following the 1967 war and in Mali during the Munich 1972 murders. In the latter instance the author was witness to several personal expressions of regret at the incident by civilians and soldiers who approached the Israeli Embassy in Bamako, at a time when the government-controlled press was taking a positive view of the incident. See *L'Essor* (Bamako), September 6, 1972.

27. In Ivory Coast, Kenya, Nigeria, Tanzania and Afar and Issa Territory, where they still operate, and formerly in Ethiopia, Zambia and Uganda.

28. Agridev is a subsidiary of Water Resources Development which

in turn is a subsidiary of Mekorot, and had hitherto operated mostly in the Far East.

29. Hence Motoragri is different from the Ivory Coast-Solel Boneh joint company SONITRA, insofar that in the latter the Israeli partner has a financial stake in the form of 45 percent of the shares.

30. Thus Motoragri acquiesced to rush certain work in Yamous-soukro, Houphouet-Boigny's native town and site of his country residence.

31. See issues of *Fraternité* (Abidjan) for December 7, 1966, March 31, 1967 and April 7, 1967; and *L'Observateur Africain* (Dakar) April 1968.

32. From interviews in Abidjan, August 1972.

33. Of 4,000 applicants in 1966-67 only 650 were admitted and a further 40 percent of those were found unsuitable by the end of the training period. See *Fraternité*, December 7, 1966.

34. Its overheads have also been low, but according to sources in Abidjan much more agreeable terms are available practically anywhere else.

35. Israel has set up or helped reorganize the state lotteries of Cameroon, Dahomey, Togo, Sierra Leone and Ghana.

8 LIBYA'S QADDAFI: BEDOUIN PRODUCT OF THE SPACE AGE*

On September 1, 1969 Colonel Muammar el-Qaddafi, the forceful twenty-nine-year-old leader of a youthful officer clique that toppled the world's newest monarchy, became the ruler of Libya. Today, his personal imprint on the politics of the region is so great that it is difficult to remember the Arab world prior to his meteoric rise.

ABedouin product of the space age, the awesomely austere and puritanical Qaddafi has outflanked King Faisal of Saudi Arabia in religious fundamentalism. As a social revolutionary, he has put to mock Algeria's Boumediene credentials. And his utter rejection of Israel's right to exist makes the anti-Israel militancy of Syria's and Iraq's leaders pale by comparison.

Since the coup, which made Qaddafi chairman of the Revolutionary Command Council—effectively, head of state—he and Libya's other young leaders have attracted frequent and unaccustomed world attention to that vast area of desert and oil. Their domestic and foreign policies are as fascinating to observe as they are enigmatic to assess. Domestically they have put the country on a course of xenophobic Islamic fundamentalism and radical social experimentation. Externally, they follow a policy of intransigent militancy aimed at a renascence of a "dar-el-lslam" coequal with major world powers in terms of strength, prestige and respect. And, in the current "haves/have-nots" tug-of-war, Libya has been a pacesetter in wringing unheard-of concessions and steadily escalating prices from the world oil monopolies. Practically every one of Qaddafi's policy decisions, marathon discourses and idiosyncracies sends shockwaves to world capitals. In Cairo, Sadat is barely able to restrain his annoyance with the impetuous young upstart. In Beirut and Damascus, Palestinian guerilla movements that have profited from Qaddafi's largess try to reconcile their benefactor's rabid anti-Communism with their own neo-Marxist beliefs. In Gibraltar, British authorities keep track of Ireland-bound boats

*Originally published in *Present Tense* (New York), vol. 1 no. 2, Winter 1974, pp. 50-54.

that might have loaded arms in Tripoli, while the Philippines tries to curb gun-running to its Moslem minority in the south. And the Israelis, confronting the cresting diplomatic tide against them, wish that this most dangerous adversary had never been born.

Important as Qaddafi's multifaceted challenge to the Middle East establishment seems to be today, it is not easy to assess his potential long-run impact on the Arab world. In this region, tradition and the passage of time have often negated the efforts of similarly zealous crusaders. Yet Qaddafi is more than merely another ephemeral figure in Islam's tradition of revivalist movements and reformist upheavals. In his highly distinctive way, he represents some of the deep frustrations and psychological dislocations of transitional Arab societies. Indeed, in order to understand this relentlessly dogmatic visionary, one must be aware of the socio-cultural bedrock from which his beliefs sprang.

Africa's fourth largest country, Libya combines a thin, fertile coastal strip with the vast reaches of the Sahara desert. The state was formed in 1951 under United Nations auspices, when a quasi-federal merger was imposed upon its three historically distinct regions (Cyrenaica, Tripolitania and Fezzan) under the rule of the former Senusi Brotherhood Emir of Cyrenaica. Culturally and geographically located between Egypt and the Maghreb to the West, the kingdom's three regions never quite meshed, retaining their individual peculiarities. Tripolitania has always been the modern, urbane business center, while highly traditional Cyrenaica, the base of Senusi power, dominated political life. Tripolitania's rejection of the Senusi brand of Islam (favoring, instead, Tunisia's brotherhoods) and the different reactions of the two regions to Italian colonialism (which the Senusi unyieldingly resisted) further extended the cleavage between them. Fezzan, deep in the Sahara and conditioned by its isolation, developed its own garrison outpost mentality.

Until the early 1960s, Libya was one of the least developed countries in the world. Exploitable resources were few, and far from the coast. Agricultural potential was restricted by the paucity of arable land and the semi-nomadic nature of much of the population-estimated, at independence, at just over one million. Miniscule national budgets allowed for little social or economic expansion. This typically backward desert kingdom was completely changed by the discovery and exploitation of Libya's vast oil deposits in the early 1960s. Almost overnight the country was catapulted into the era of technology and the vortex of Middle East politics and Western influences. Heavy urban-rural migration led to the shattering of social norms and traditional moorings. A similar process has occurred elsewhere in the world, but rarely has it been as rapid, thorough or visible. Poor but proud Libyan peasants and nomads were transformed in to poor, lumpen-proletariat shanty-dwellers as the gap between them and a rapidly growing elite widened. The psychological dislocation attending this complex process was but one of the social costs of rapid change.

By the late 1960s, the nation's socioeconomic parameters were dramatically different from those of the 1950s. In 1951 the total budget was less than twenty million; in 1969 the government spent over $1.1 billion on a single housing project. During this period, traditional elites and wily entrepreneurs close to the throne reaped windfall profits. Libya's predominantly rural population became eighty-five per cent urbanized. The cities—where inflation had put the cost of living among the world's highest—became choked with recent immigrants from the countryside and with free-spending, pleasure-seeking expatriates.

Despite the monarchy's conservative bias, the rudiments of a modern welfare state—including free schools and clinics—sprouted in most parts of the country. And while illiteracy was still high, eighty-five per cent of school-age children began to benefit from free primary and secondary education. The state bureaucracy rapidly expanded, largely through patronage; an anti-manual labor ethic, common in transitional societies, became widespread. Even the military—warily kept at arm's length in Tripolitania—benefited from Libya's boom; in 1968 the regime ordered a $500 million air defense system from Great Britain, clearly as a deterrent against Egypt's increasing interest in her oil-rich neighbor. Yet even as the Libyan society began to be transformed with funds from oil royalties, the pace of change was slow and controlled, with the throne boarding massive funds in British banks.

Meanwhile, in Benghazi, capital of Cyrenaica, the aging and heirless King ldris ruled over this booming kingdom in the benign style of a tribal sheikh. Arrayed behind the throne were the Cyrenaican Defense Force and most of Cyrenaica's tribal clan leaders, whose loyalties were to the King as leader of the Senusi religious order. The Defense Force had traditionally been the monarchy's power base, and dwarfed the Army in terms of manpower and material. Political parties and trade unions were banned by law. Libya's elections, replete with "irregularities," were contests between representatives of various clans and extended families, many beholden to the King. Incessant cabinet shuffles and revolving-door prime ministers became Idris' particular penchant. By the time of the coup in 1969, Libya had had twelve different governments (and 200 ministers) with an average life span of eighteen months.

Born in a Bedouin tent in the desert between Tripolitania and Cyrenaica, Qaddafi was inculcated with traditional Bedouin values—austerity, moral rigidity and directness. He was weaned on horror stories about the Italian invasion and occupation of Libya, which may explain his expulsion of Italian expatriates shortly after he came to power. (Interestingly, while expelled Italians were stripped of their possessions, Libya's Jews were permitted to take their property when they were forced to leave.) Much of Qaddafi's early schooling was in the backwaters of Fezzan, where his world outlook developed in the parochialism of a stagnant, austere and hostile environment. As he matured, he observed Libya's inherent contradictions as the nation became caught up in rapid social and economic change.

A veritable mythology has developed around Qaddafi's formative years and his early political beliefs. Extreme frugality characterized his childhood and does so to this day. His colleagues maintain that, as early as his primary school years, Qaddafi was disenchanted with King Idris' hedonistic and corrupt regime, and urged his classmates to join the Army to acquire a power base from which to topple the monarch. More important is the fact that young Qaddafi became one of Nasser's most ardent admirers.

A member of the generation of Arab youth which grew up with ears glued to Cairo's virulently anti-Israel and anti-Western radio "Voice of the Arabs," Qaddafi was affected for life by the speeches of the fire-breathing champion of Pan-Arab nationalism. It is impossible to exaggerate the transcendental fixation Qaddafi developed towards his Egyptian mentor, or the crucial influence of Nasser's early radical rhetoric and invective upon the formation of his young mind. One of Qaddafi's most deeply cherished memories is his encounter with Nasser after the Libyan coup, when, after he had energetically expressed his views on the problems of the Arab world, Nasser wryly smiled and said, "You remind me of my youth." Today Nasser's memory lives on in Libya, with radios incessantly blaring old tapes of his exhortations and Nasser posters plastered everywhere.

Qaddafi attended the University of Libya, where he obtained a License in Arab history and joined the Army in 1963. By this time oil royalties were flowing freely into the Libyan treasury, and the austere young officer observed at first hand the growth of urban slums and the material decadence of the *nouveau riche*. On his visits home he lamented the breakdown of traditional values of life in the countryside. He was also offended by the monarchy's pro-Western orientation, its servility to foreign oil and military interests and the arrogance of expatriate technicians in Libya. He was imbued with Nasserite visions of the resurrection of past Islamic splendors and the renascence of the contemporary Arab world.

Even before the 1956 debacle in the Sinai, Qaddafi's hatred of Israel and his opinions on the rights and wrongs of the Arab-Israel conflict were well established in his mind. He reacted to the humiliating Arab defeat at the hands of Israel in 1967 as to a personal blow. It symbolized much more than Israel's overwhelming military might, for which he developed a deep, if somewhat naive, appreciation. To him it underscored the helplessness, decadence and disunity of the Arab world, which, he felt, had resulted from misplaced values and the dilution of spirit that materialism and Western-inspired obsessions had brought about. Revenge for the 1967 defeat and rectification of the 1948 "betrayal of the Palestinian people"—to be achieved via the complete dismantling of Israel—became for Qaddafi a vital necessity to restore Arab national spirit.

Driven by a consuming drive to shatter the old order and join hands with his Egyptian surrogate father in re-creating a glorious Islamic Commonwealth, he was perhaps inspired by Nasser's words in *The Philosophy of the Revolution*:

> I do not know why I always imagine that in this region there is a role wandering about in search of an actor to play it. And I do not know why this role, tired of roaming about in this vast region, should at last settle down, exhausted and weary, on our frontiers, beckoning us to assume it as nobody else can do so....It is a role of interaction and experimentation with all these factors, a role for us to harness the powerful energy latent in every part of this vast region....

Grasping the role, Qaddafi patterned his future coup on Nasserite lines. From the day he entered Benghazi's Military Academy he assiduously cultivated like-minded classmates and forged them into an austere and dedicated "Free Officers" clique which became the core of the Revolutionary Command Council after the coup. The cohesion of Libya's military regime is to no small extent an outcome of the conspiratorial bonds established during the coup's long gestation, when reformist planks and policies were hammered out. After the upheaval, Libya's "Neguibs" (the senior officers) were retained in office for a while. The Cyrenaican Defense Force, neutralized in the first hours of the coup, was restructured and absorbed into the expanded armed forces. In a further effort to popularize the "revolution," the Revolutionary Command Council reduced all rents for civil servants and announced an across-the-board salary hike for everybody, which made the Libyan army the highest-paid armed force in the world.

Qaddafi's world outlook is anchored by three core points of reference: the need for a fundamentalist back-to-origins Islamic renascence, pan-Arab unity and a populist socialist revolution. The first is the binding thread that runs though all three and gives coherence to many o contemporary Libya's often bizarre domestic and foreign policies. Its importance in understanding Qaddafi's Libya cannot be exaggerated.

The three concepts are Nasserite in origin, although their relative importance has been shifted and their specific policy implications twisted beyond recognition. The young Nasser's uncompromising revolutionary world outlook still strongly inspires, Qaddafi, though the Egyptian leader's early militancy gave way to the mellowness of middle age and disillusionment. Qaddafi truly believes, as he solemnly declared to a jaded Egyptian audience after the coup, that "the Libyan revolution began where yours ended and is a continuation of Gamal Abdel Nasser's revolution."

To Qaddafi, the spiritual rebirth of the Moslem world requires a return to the fundamental precepts of Islam. In his words, "Islam exists to organize all aspects of life and society." It is a comprehensive cultural system with sets of values and codes of behavior ordained by God and immutable over time. It cannot be modified to mesh with the temporal needs of a modern society.

The Koran and *Sharia* law (literally the path") affect all political, social, economic and religious matters. The *Sharia* acts as private, public and international law. All aspects of life are regulated by specific prescriptions and injunctions and the *raison d'etre* of the State—according to the Koran—is to administer *Sharia* law and propagate the faith.

Many of Qaddafi's policies aim at transforming Libyan society into a pure, orthodox Islamic community, much to the growing uneasiness of the country's middle and secular classes. Alcoholic beverages are no longer available; casinos and women's hairdressing shops have been closed, miniskirts banned and urban areas cleared of prostitutes. Foreigners living in Libya are barred entry unless their passports carry Arab script (thirty-six states have so far complied) and European-language signs have been virtually nonexistent except in oil installations.

Flogging for adultery (100 lashes) has been introduced under the provisions of a detailed decree (e.g., pregnant women may be flogged only two months after they give birth). Amputation of the arms of habitual thieves has also been authorized. Qaddafi himself periodically swoops down, in uniform or disguise, to verify implementation of the regulations. As one uneasy Libyan aptly put it, "He is turning all of Libya into a mosque".

Religious precepts are also anchor points for Qaddafi's foreign policy. He has linked Libya's international stance toward Jordan, Lebanon, Israel and India directly with specific Koranic injunctions. As protector of the faith, who also fortunately controls vast oil revenues, Qaddafi has come to the aid of Moslem interests around the globe—supporting Chad's Moslem Toubbous in their rebellion against the Fort Lamy (Christian-led) government, the Eritrean Liberation Front against Ethiopia and southern Philippine Moslem guerrilla groups against their government. Libyan-transshipped guns have been sent to the Irish Republican Army because the British bad "to be taught a lesson" after a Persian Gulf dispute. Several grants have been made for the construction of mosques in Africa and a $3-million-dollar loan has gone to the Black Muslims in Chicago.

Qaddafi has also at various times called for the assassination of King Hussein, who traces his descent from the Prophet, because of the King's crackdown on the Palestinian guerrilla movement. In a *New York Times Magazine* interview with Edward Sheehan, Qaddafi vehemently denounced Hussein's action in religious terms:

> Hussein has deviated from the right path....As far as Islam is concerned, he is in a state of excommunication. He's disobedient. He's an outlaw. The Prophet Mohammed—may God bestow His blessings on him!—denounces Hussein's actions.

Indeed, at one recent Arab summit meeting Qaddafi nearly threatened Hussein with the pistol he habitually carries.

The mercurial Libyan leader has not hesitated to espouse his religious fundamentalism and abhorrence of the moral "decadence" of the contemporary Arab world even when this has worked to the detriment of secular projects dear to his heart. During meetings to consolidate the projected Arab Union, he frequently embarrassed and offended his Cairo hosts. Unable to curb his tongue, he has publicly expressed total contempt for Egyptian society and its nightclubs, liquor consumption and *bon vivant* orientation. He has categorized Egyptians as lazy and drunkards, and has berated Sadat's regime for its corruption, nepotism, pervasive secret police and political oppression. He has argued that Egypt is ripe for a Libyan-style cultural revolution. It would be dangerous, however, to pigeonhole Qaddafi as a religious fanatic. Certainly he is a totally committed fundamentalist who tends to view the world through pre-tinted lenses.

Most scholars, journalists and diplomats who have talked with Qaddafi are unanimous about his utter sincerity and simplicity, as well as his undiplomatic honesty and directness. Yet he is also crafty and calculating, capable of shifting gears and sacrificing previously held positions when he considers it necessary. Thus after consistently aggravating Sadat with his adamant anti-Soviet positions, he made a total about-face in inviting Soviet technical assistants to replace Western petroleum experts. Likewise, Libya's assistance for Chad's "gallant Moslem heroes" promptly dried up when Fort Lamy indicated that for a small consideration it would be willing to break off relations with Israel. Finally, English-language warning signs were permitted in oil installations despite the regime's early insistence that all posters, public and street signs be exclusively in Arabic.

Pan-Arab unity is to Qaddafi a *sine qua non* for the creation of an ideal Islamic Commonwealth, and he has demonstrated that he would go to great lengths to achieve it—but always on his own terms. He has shown no interest in the structural mechanics or technical and administrative details of such union, nor has he expressed any ambition to be its leader. Yet his impetuous style and harsh line on major substantive issues tend to work against the consummation of any Arab union with Libya.

On another level, Qaddafi has long been urging Sadat to move faster in the direction of a total merger of Libya and Egypt as the only conceivable base for a wider federation. Sadat, still sensitive about the Syria-Egypt federation that collapsed more than a decade ago, is acutely aware that Qaddafi would be an extremely difficult partner to live with. The two leaders are as different in terms of personality, style and beliefs as their respective countries. And few Egyptians are attracted to Qaddafi's argument that the total economy and the efforts of every citizen must be geared to one gigantic battle (to include nuclear weapons if available) to annihilate Israel, nor to his thesis that when victory is achieved Egypt must undergo a social cleansing and a cultural revolution.

The unpopularity of Qaddafi's views in Egypt as elsewhere and his felt rejection by the leaders of his adopted spiritual homeland have deeply frustrated him and led to rumors that he has suffered nervous breakdowns. His direct pressure tactics, including a procession Of 50,000 unity demonstrators sent from Libya into Egypt, have not sparked much response among Egypt's masses. And the cessation of the 1973 Arab-Israel hostilities, instead of "fighting from the caves for twenty years if necessary," as he urged, has been his final disillusionment. He expressed his anguish when he wrote to Sadat: "I cannot sleep because of what is happening at Kilometer 101, or perhaps I am asleep and it is a terrible and peculiar nightmare." Finally, in total exasperation, Libya temporarily closed her Embassy in Cairo on December 1, 1973, warning that more than 100,000 Egyptian technicians currently in Libya may be expelled and—baring his financial claws—subsidies to the Egyptian war effort cancelled.

The "popular revolution" Qaddafi officially unleashed in April 1973 is aimed at involving the largely apathetic masses in the tasks of socialist and Islamic reconstruction. Ideologically, the "revolution" is a curious blend of extreme Left populism and xenophobic Arab nationalism. "Peoples' Committees" set up all over the country are enjoined to purify and revolutionize Libya's social fiber. They can petition for repeal of existing legislation and enactment of new laws more in conformity with Islam or the needs of the masses. Originally, the committees were to be armed, but this has been only selectively done. In less than eight months they denounced and purged some 1,000 atheists, Communists, "deviationists" and Moslem Brotherhood Members, ostensibly by "popular demand," and several administrators were promoted spontaneously. The generally easygoing and swollen civil service has been put on notice that incompetence and arrogance can now lead to dismissal in the name of the revolution. (As early as 1972, Qaddafi shook up the bureaucracy by removing chairs in government offices to prevent social gatherings during office hours, an ingrained custom in Libya.) On the other hand, books not supportive of Islam, Arabism and Socialism have been burned in only a few instances, despite a particularly animated Qaddafi speech urging their total destruction. Several other activities such as proposing new laws, originally declared as within the scope of the committees, have been similarly soft-pedaled.

Despite its potential for systemic chaos and anarchy, the "popular revolution" has been tightly controlled by the regime. Some observers believe that the discongruity between the stated goals of the "popular revolution" and its smothering controls attest to an ideological cover-up for a general purge of opposition elements. In light of Qaddafi's contradictory political style, however, it can also be seen as an example of, for want of a better term, "pragmatic idealism."

Any effort to assess Qaddafi's long-range impact upon Libya and the Arab world in general must underscore that, though he rules supreme in Tripoli, he has bad to drag and cajole the population toward its goals. It can be assumed that the predictable pattern of Libya's social and economic evolution in the future will act as a powerful brake on easy implementation of many of Qaddafi's domestic policies. He is personally popular in some student and religious circles, but neither his orthodox fundamentalism nor his burning ambition for unification with Egypt are in much favor among the urban masses, who dislike the prospect of giving up decadent lifestyles before they can be fully savored, and resent the ubiquitous Egyptian presence in Libya.

While reports of serious opposition to Qaddafi within the Revolutionary Command Council are exaggerated, the daily frustrations of a healer leading a people who do not wish to be healed have several times led Qaddafi to threaten to resign. He has developed a martyr complex and frequently acts less as head of state and more as an opposition crusader. Opposition to his reforms may spur him to more drastic social policies in the future.

Internationally, Qaddafi's success has been somewhat limited despite his role in helping to double world oil prices, goading the oil powers toward a united stance vis-a-vis the West, and swinging the diplomatic balance in the Third World against Israel. His fundamentalist religious beliefs, sharp clashes with many Arab leaders, and concept of a purifying "popular revolution" militate against the attainment of his paramount goals. Paradoxically, a somewhat more flexible or mellow Qaddafi might well be the kind of charismatic leader who could comfortably don Nasser's shoes and give the Arab world a major galvanizing thrust toward a semblance of cohesion.

It would be difficult, however, to conceive of Qaddafi mellowing with time and adjusting some goals to make them more compatible with the domestic or the world situation. Any such alteration in world outlook is highly unlikely for a person with his dynamics and, if it occurred, would signify basic personality changes that could spark intolerable tensions and strains.

What seems more probable is that—since to true believers moral issues rarely allow for compromise—Qaddafi's views will remain rooted in his religious convictions and fervor. How much longer he can attempt to rule Libya on his own anachronistic terms is another question. But whatever his personal future, Qaddafi's impact on his country and his region is certain to be remembered for a very long time.

9 AFRICA AND THE U.N. ANTI-ZIONISM RESOLUTION: ROOTS AND CAUSES*

In the evening of November 10, 1975, as hundreds of thousands of American viewers followed the bizarre events over a few television stations, the United Nations voted to sanctify an anti-Semitic and rabidly anti-Israel resolution classifying Zionism as a form of racism. The resolution, one in a series of increasingly sharp Israeli reverses in the international arena, was passed by seventy-two votes to thirty-five, with thirty-two abstentions. The very next day the Soviet Union and a few other states began using the now U.N.-approved prefix "racist-Zionist" when referring to Israel. What has been called "the [Hitlerian] technique of the Big Lie"[1] had succeeded at the U.N. and the Soviet-Arab bloc was clearly pressing its advantage in a prelude to an attempt to oust Israel from the international forum.

The passage of the resolution evoked strong condemnations from various delegates including the eloquently outraged U.S. Ambassador Daniel Moynihan (whose sincere and impassioned speech immediately gained him a political constituency should he wish one), and General Assembly President—and Luxembourg Premier—Gaston Thorn. The American Congress hinted at budgetary cuts for the U.N. while some of its more incensed members even talked of a possible U.S. withdrawal from the international organization. American academics and nobel laureates mobilized anti-U.N. petitions while among the wider public a massive boycott developed of travel to, and purchases from, states that had endorsed the anti-Zionism resolution.[2] Within a month the latter campaign had so seriously crippled the tourist industry in a few countries, especially Mexico but increasingly Brazil, that the former's Foreign Minister Emilio Rabasa found it necessary to fly to Israel to "explain" his country's vote (he was shortly to be replaced)[3] while Miguel Aleman, former President of Mexico and

*Published in *Cultures et Développement* (Louvain), vol. 8 no. 1, 1976, pp. 89-117.

current head of the National Tourist Council did likewise to Jewish and non-Jewish boycott organizers in New York.[4]

The anti-Zionism resolution can be regarded as Israel's single worst international reversal since the 1955 Bandung Conference.[5] Because of the numerical weight of Africa in forging the final majority against Israel, November 10 also cannot but mark a clearcut, definitive and unequivocal turning point in Afro-Israeli relations, so warm and friendly in the decade and a half since 1958. For while between the 1973 Yom Kippur War (when most of Africa reluctantly broke diplomatic relations with Israel) and the 1975 anti-Zionism vote a few diehard Israeli optimists (encouraged by Africa's disenchantment with the miserly Arab fiscal support) still hoped for an eventual Afro-Israeli rapprochement, the trauma of November 10th may never be truly healed by any possible byzantine diplomatic doubletalk such as Mexico's. In 1973 the mass desertion of Israel by her erstwhile African friends had triggered off a hard-nosed *real-politik* reassessment in Jerusalem of the value of the fickle Third World: a reassessment that called for the dismantling of the huge edifice of Israel's technical cooperation program[6], and an Israeli disengagement from all but a very few proven allies (such as Ivory Coast, Liberia, Kenya—among the last and most unwilling to break with Israel). While such a course of action was indeed commenced, it was done only half-heartedly due to Israeli nostalgia for the days when the country was a major developmental mentor for the Third World and an important dispenser of socioeconomic and agrarian technical assistance. Now, following the November 10th vote all hope of a return to the former Afro-Israeli entente is dead; the former sympathy for the aspirations of the Third World are buried beneath the Israeli leaders' day-to-day preoccupation with wording off the most serious Soviet-Arab challenge to the state's legitimacy.[7] The certainty that the future will bring further anti-Israel resolutions and attempts to expel Israel from the various international organizations[8] with wide African backing may yet relegate, in Israeli eyes, the entire 1958-1973 era of Afro-Israeli cooperation to the realm of irrelevant prehistory.

The purpose of this article is to briefly trace Afro-Israeli relations since their inception and to highlight some of the roots and causes of the coalescence of an African anti-Israel majority in the United Nations. The emergence of this majority has usually been explained in terms of the political clout of Arab petrodollars on fiscally beleaguered African mini-states. Such a unicausal explanation, while to a significant extent valid, nevertheless belies the complexity of the matter that needs to be brought into sharper focus.

The Afro-Israeli Honeymoon

The origins and early evolution of Afro-Israeli relations hardly require more than a cursory summary in light of the large amount of literature already published on this topic.[9] Essentially a *tabula rasa* to the Israeli Foreign Ministry in the early 1950's, Africa became, if hardly a cornerstone, a major pillar of Israeli diplomacy in the late fifties and early sixties.[10] Casual early contacts in 1953-1955 (mostly between union leaders at the Socialist International and Asian Socialist Conference) opened Israeli eyes both to the potential diplomatic possibilities of the continent soon to become independent, and to its vast need for developmental assistance of the kind Israel could readily share. Until then quite parsimonious in its foreign representation via full-fledged embassies, Africa's importance to Israel was attested to in 1957 when Israel's eighth embassy was erected in Accra. (All previous Israeli embassies had been located in Europe or the Americas[11]. Shortly later a policy of establishing embassies in every country that would welcome an Israeli Ambassador resulted by 1964 in the world's fourth largest diplomatic network, surpassed only by the U.S., U.K. and France.[12]

A wide variety of considerations, pragmatic as well as ideological, impelled Israel to place such a stress on her budding relation with the Third World, and Africa in particular. From the pragmatic point of view, of course, Africa was but another extension—and with the proliferation in independent states, a growingly important extension—of the global diplomatic tug-of-war between Israel and the Arab world. In the simplistic mathematical world of the U.N. where all votes carry equal weight, growing African sympathy and support for Israel was an important balance to the Soviet-Arab axis. The formation of an Afro-Israeli informal *entente*—"one of the strangest unofficial alliances in the world"[13]—dramatically catapulted Israel out of her diplomatic isolation in the 1960's. As Israel's Ben Gurion so accurately prophesied in a 1960 *Knesset* session "Our ties with the new nations will do more to strengthen our position in the world than anything else."[14] This theme, that Israel's security and diplomatic problems in the Middle

East could be greatly eased via Israel's forging new sources of support in the Third World became one key leitmotif for the Israeli effort in Africa. The original very modest goal—breaking out of the diplomatic isolation of the mid-1950's—was very rapidly attained thanks to the alacrity with which diplomatic, economic and technical cooperation links were established with all but two (Somalia, Mauritania) of the new Black African states. As the *New York Times* pointed out, "From a scribbled word in a black notebook the Israeli government has built an aid to Africa program that has broken some political barriers and made the Israelis possibly the most welcome strangers in Africa."[15] Indeed, in 1960-61 seven African Heads of State visited Israel; in the entire preceding twelve years of independence only one other leader of similar caliber had visited Israel.

The ease with which the Arab diplomatic boycott had been vaulted in Africa and the incredibly fast amelioration of Israel's sub-sequent international position led to an Israeli diplomatic effort in 1961-63 to force the Arab powers to the negotiating table for the final resolution of the Middle East dispute. This move took the form of U.N. resolutions calling for direct negotiations between Israel and the Arab powers. [16] Though not successful, the presentation of such resolutions calling for direct peace-talks—anathema to the Arabs—was a powerful symbol of the collapse of the Arab efforts to isolate her in the international community; shortly later, again with strong African backing, Israelis began to be elected for the first time in the UN's history to executive-administrative posts as representatives of all of Afro-Asia. [17]

The very important pragmatic considerations that impelled the Israeli entry into Africa should not cloud, however, the equally important ideological factors that played a role. By now we have become jaded, perhaps, by the "birth" of some ninety new states in the world. Yet, as one of the very first of these, and a nation-state at that whose cultural origins stretch to biblical days and whose future national resurrection is specifically referred to in the scriptures, many in Israel—and not only the religiously observant—were not content with mere independence from British colonial rule but sought a deeper meaning, or national purpose, in Israel's rebirth in the modem era. These messianic aspirations[18] and this quest for a global spiritual and inspirational leadership, found scope for its actualization in the opening horizons of Israel's technical cooperation programs. Midway at the time on most indicators between the developed and the developing world, and increasingly lauded by the latter's statesmen for her developmental patterns and approaches[19] Israeli leaders began to see their country's role as a bridge between the "haves" and "have-nots", and a catalyst for socio-economic modernization.

It was this paradoxical combination of pragmatic foreign policy goals and ideological-cum-messianic considerations that gave Israeli diplomacy in the Third World in the 1960's its vibrance and zeal so refreshing to many African leaders when compared to the "blase" attitude of the metropole. Needless to say, as the Old Guard, or the Founding Fathers, died or retired, and as the state matured and developed with an inevitable routinization and bureaucratization of foreign policy, the messianic factor receded or became blurred with humanitarian goals. Yet the existence of this vector in the early formulation of Israeli foreign policy has contributed to the contemporary inability of many Israelis to accept philosophically the African "betrayal" (as it is popularly called) at the U.N.; Africa was much more than a mere battle ground for U.N. votes. And the bitterness felt by many Israelis today is a function of the high standards of conduct expected from friends rather than simply political allies.

By the mid-1960's Israel was one of the most sought-after donors of technical assistance. Requests for training scholarships and for the dispatch of experts far outstripped the country's resources. Already in 1962 Israel had distributed scholarships amounting to 38% of those offered by France—despite the latter's residual responsibilities in Africa and much wider and stronger economic base.[20] Only the coming of age of several economic sectors in Israel (freeing personnel for overseas duties) and the local recession in the mid-1960's allowed highly qualified Israeli personnel to be siphoned off in increasing numbers for projects in Africa. The raw figures are in themselves highly revealing. In 1972 alone, as the technical cooperation program began to grind to a halt, Israel dispatched 254 experts to Africa (out of a total of 541 to the Third World) and received 402 trainees (of a total of 1,094). Indeed, in the fifteen years between 1958 (when the program was initiated in Africa) and 1972, fully 3,017 Israeli experts served abroad on short or long-term missions in Africa (out of 4,882 sent to all areas of the Third World), while 7,199 African trainees were hosted by Israel (of a total of 16,352) with several thousands more trained by Israeli experts in Africa.[21] If these figures are placed in proper perspective (i.e. taking into account Israel's size, population, resources etc., compared to that of other major donors) the immensity of the Israeli contribution comes into much sharper focus. Indeed, it might substantiate the point made to the author by an Israeli Ambassador in Africa "There is hardly an Israeli who either has not had a member of his family or a friend serve overseas in one capacity or another,"[22] or Sylvia Kaiwff's stunning conclusion that Israel's aid effort in 1962 was (on a per capita basis) comparable to the U.S. granting one million free scholarships for that year or sending out 360,000 experts to all corners of the Third World![23]

The evolution of the Afro-Israeli entente of the early 1960's was not without its ups and downs. Again, this is hardly the place to discuss these vicissitudes at any length; suffice it to note that idiosyncratic events, changes in leadership and, in a few areas, local Moslem opposition took its toll. Moreover, the Franco-Israeli estrangement of 1967 made the Israeli task in Francophone Africa more difficult though in reality French expatriates with few exceptions had all along resisted the entry of Israeli influence in their private (and monopolistic) preserves. (So did British firms that fought bitter and highly "un-British" price wars against Israeli firms in Anglophone Africa). And while the Soviet Union lost no opportunity to castigate Israel for "fulfilling the role of a Trojan Horse for N.A.T.O. in Africa,"[24] neither was the U.S. always happy with specific Israeli successes in the continent, as in the case of Zaire opting to have Israel create, staff and provide the training in her Paratroop Training School.

The extension of Israeli influence in Africa was also contested by the Arab states, yet these counter-efforts were only minimally successful until the 1970's. Even though in a few capitals the Israeli efforts were undermined by as many as four or five Arab Ambassadors, early Arab diplomacy in Africa was in general incredibly naive and unsophisticated, ineffective (at times positively counterproductive) and quite uncoordinated.[25] Moreover, caught between conflicting pressures to support Arab anti-Israel resolutions (thus "proving" pan-African solidarity) and genuine pro-Israel sentiments, many African statesmen resented the continuous intrusion of Middle Eastern issues in essentially African forums with the inevitable polarization this evoked. In due time the "golden mean" was discovered: the passage of mild anti-Israel resolutions at the O.A.U. and elsewhere, followed by an immediate reassurance to Israel that the resolution meant nothing and would have no practical import.[26] And most Arab attempts during the early and mid-1960's to have O.A.U. ostracise Israel in more than symbolic terms led to African outcries that the Arab states were trying to exploit the African organs for non-African purposes.[27]

In light of all this, how can one account for the quite rapid and total collapse of the Israeli position and influence in the continent? Why was the collapse so complete? While certainly Arab petrodollars had a lot to do with the 1973 African diplomatic break with Israel[28] and the 1975 anti-Zionism vote, this is only a partial explanation. One must look for the answer to the new political climate sweeping subsaharan Africa, and the objective record of 15 years of Israeli developmental effort in the continent.

AFRO-ISRAELI TECHNICAL COOPERATION IN PERSPECTIVE

"Contrary to earlier expectations, the 'spillover' or 'demonstration' effects of development in limited sectors and areas have at best been marginal. As a result, the masses of the population have benefited little from, and contributed little to development."[29] This somber conclusion of the International Labour Organization, though no revelation for some time to development administrators in Africa, is a stunning repudiation of the earlier euphoric expectations from the "multiplier" or "spillover" factor in modernization theory,[30] and is in itself one of the more dire warning signals that the transformation of the continent might be a much more complex process than assumed as recently as the 1960's. The I.L.O. conclusion also sums up in a nutshell some of the reasons why Israeli developmental aid—though still widely sought after and appreciated—is no longer that unique (magical?) commodity it was thought to be in the early years of Afro-Israeli cooperation. For though Israeli technical assistance has been solicited, and extended, in a wide variety of fields ranging from the erection of national lotteries (Dahomey, Togo, Cameroun, etc.), reorganization of Foreign Ministry procedures (Dahomey), mapping, surveying and analysing national resources (Upper Volta, Mali, Uganda, etc.), setting up joint construction, shipping and investment companies (Ghana, Nigeria, C.A.R., Ivory Coast, Kenya, Sierra Leone, etc.), military training (Zaire, Liberia, Kenya, etc.)[31] the original and most seducing attraction of the Israeli developmental model to Africa was the former's meteoric socioeco-

nomic development in the 1950's and its important socialist innovations in the areas of communal farming and agrarian modernization,
youth mobilization (for nation-building and agrarian pioneering) and
syndicalism.[32] Indeed, the majority of Israeli experts dispatched to
Africa, or African trainees that arrived in Israel, were in connection with
efforts to implant in Africa versions of Israeli structures or practices in
these three areas. Fully 66.3% of all the Third World trainees in Israel
between 1958 and 1972 (16,352) came to obtain experience in these
three fields, the respective breakdown being 1,078, 6,363 and 3,403.[33]
Yet it was precisely in these areas—where core social change is most
difficult since basic outlooks and cultural frameworks are involved—that the dissimilarities between Israel and Africa seriously
hampered developmental efforts even as the impact of the programs
in the countryside was limited since the then-expected "spillover" did
not in general materialize as the I.L.O. study currently attests.

A detailed discussion of the patterns of successes and setbacks
of Israel's technical cooperation program in its efforts to transplant to
Africa modem developmental and social structures and concepts is
largely outside the scope of this article.[34] It is important to note,
however, that apart from the previously mentioned limitations of the
Afro-Israeli programs, only in a few instances were the host governments either fiscally able to provide the modest infrastructure needed
for the success of the programs, willing to allow the programs to
proceed unencumbered by political or patronage considerations, or
truly committed to the long-run systemic change. Dramatic examples
are provided by the experience of the Israeli Nachal (Fighting Pioneer
Youth) transplants erected in seventeen African states (invariably called
Service Civique or *Jeunes Pionniers* in Francophone Africa, "Builders Brigade"
in Ghana "National Service" in Tanzania, etc.)[35] In several instances
these units were transformed into wasteful patronage machines or
support mechanisms of the regime[36] (e.g. Ghana—under Nkrumah—and Ivory Coast); in other instances (Dahomey, C.A.R.) the host
country's inability to provide the basic fiscal outlay stipulated resulted
in conditions so primitive that youth that had volunteered for the
formations (seeking upward social-mobility via agrarian training) deserted to their villages in droves.[37] Moreover, in many instances (e.g.
Dahomey, Chad) inter-ethnic friction among those recruited into the
youth formations was so intense (leading to major fights and deser-
tions) that recruitment in successive years was restricted to members

of the same ethnic groups, negating the prime rationale of the programs—molding a "national" group of modern youth out of disparate ethnic elements.

Elsewhere (as in Tanzania and Uganda) individual cabinet ministers tried to politicize the youth formations and use them for their own political advancement. And in general many of those completing their basic training (theoretically becoming modern farmers or "animateurs") either promptly deserted for urban areas (especially in Ivory Coast) attempting to use their agrarian diplomas as an entry ticket to the more prestigious civil service[38] or (especially in Upper Volta, C.A.R., Sierra Leone and Dahomey) failed to "animate" traditional life upon their return to their villages and instead rejected their modern training for the sake of social peace in their home villages.

Needless to say Israeli programs aimed at major socioeconomic modernization were not everywhere scaled down or hampered by the harsh and uncompromising realities of African traditional life[39] or political considerations, nor have African governments expressed anything but profuse and sincere appreciation for the Israeli effort. As the Kenyan *Sunday Nation* wrote on the eve of Kenya's reluctant break with Israel : "[the programs] have been more successful than those of most of the major and richer nations...the Israelis have put a great deal in this continent."[40] And at least two "radical" West African states that vociferously broke relations with Israel in 1973 unofficially requested the retention in a private capacity of the entire teams of Israel's technical assistance programs in the two countries. (The probes were rejected). Many other African states likewise requested the retention of economic and cooperation links with Israel despite the diplomatic rupture of 1973. Nevertheless, it is still true that in many instances the original idealism and wildly over-ambitious expectations of the massive transformation of the African socioeconomic reality *a la* Israel with Israeli assistance and quasi-Israeli structures were replaced by much more modest expectations and sealed-down programs. Though these second-generation realistic projects were to prove to be much more successful than their original progenitors, the sealed-down expectations signified the relative, diminution in the value ascribed by Africa to Israeli technical cooperation.

This diminution coincided in the mid and late 1960's with an increase in foreign assistance from a wide variety of donors including a less parsimonious and/or selective program of aid from the Eastern bloc. Israel's technical assistance had in the past been very much valued in Africa because of Jerusalem's ability to very rapidly respond to requests for the dispatch of experts or of scholarships. But the proliferation of sources of aid, including large grants of capital and/or entire industrial complexes (as opposed to training and expertise offered by Israel) further undermined, in African eyes the relative importance of the Israeli technical cooperation program.

This fact was hardly visible in the statistics of Afro-Israeli exchanges for Africa's needs were, and still are, immense, but it was visible in the slow cooling of diplomatic relations. Jerusalem—virtually a fixed stopover on the Africa-Paris-London-Bruxelles travel itinerary of African presidents or ministerial delegations—began to decline in importance as a major marketplace for Africans with shopping lists. And this slow erosion of the relative importance of Israeli influence in the continent also suffered from the progressive radicalization of African elites and the rise to power of more militant groups including the Libyan military clique.

The Radicalization of African Politics

Wallerstein has already bluntly contrasted the dichotomy in Africa between radical rhetoric and the (until recent) conservative *status quo* domestic realities in many states,[41] what I regard the Janus-like rhetoric-reality syndrome that so dominates all things Africana. Other scholars have similarly pointed out the cleavage between ideological and foreign policy militancy of some African states and the neo-colonialist economic subjugation they have tolerated in domestic matters.[42] Whatever the objective worth or the systemic value of radical cantations of ideological purity and lofty declarations of humanistic socio-economic reforms, all unaccompanied by any tangible change or attempts at the implementation of declared goals, the enunciation of such objectives cannot be simply relegated to the realm of empty rhetoric aimed at selected domestic or foreign audiences. While radical rhetoric is indeed often used by conservative elites as a meaningless social palliative, it is as often a statement of ideals or aspirations of (to a greater or lesser extent) reform-minded leaders; declarations that clearly cannot be actualized due to a myriad of domestic and foreign social, economic and developmental obstacles and the grim reality of a world divided into rich and poor nations. The massive transformation and modernization of African society and economy—implicit in most of the radical ideologies—would require not only "structural" policies such as economic nationalism, indigenization of the local service, industrial, bureaucratic and educational sectors and the development of cultural "authenticity" (of a much more honest and sophisticated variety than that espoused under different names in Zaire, Togo, Chad or Dahomey), but also the total transformation of the local splinterized political culture and traditional ethos.[43] Structural changes are easy; they only require governmental decrees. (Nationalization of economic sectors; expulsion of non-nationals; fixing greeting terms—citoyen, camarade; indigenization of service sectors, etc.). But insofar as true systemic change is concerned, that is attitudes, values, lifestyles, beliefs—there are no shortcuts.[44] Indeed, one could possibly even argue that with only a few exceptions the true and full actualization of many of the programs of social change espoused in Africa will never be attained, certainly for most of the continent not within our lifetime. The social and cultural transformation of society is a lengthy and complex process, full of discontinuities, pitfalls and reverses, as the history of Europe so well illustrates. This does not mean, of course, that the status quo is inevitable, but that the systemic goals that many leaders so glibly set for themselves are much more complex than may be expected.

The developmental frustrations of Africa's first decade of independence, coupled with the acute political instability of many states, have dashed aside most of the starry-eyed early expectations of rapid moderation and development. This frustration has been general and quite wide-spread, and not restricted to the previously discussed African disillusionments with the slow and small systemic effects of Israel's technical assistance programs. Unrealistically high expectations of rapid socio-economic transformation and industrialization have clashed with the reality of the complexity of underdevelopment, mismanagement of resources, the Sahelian drought and world-wide inflation, to spark off bitter frustration. And the spectacle of stagnation, or at best only minimal progress towards a better future has led many disgruntled elites to search for better developmental models or ideologies, usually latching onto a variety or local interpretation of Marxism.

The number of Socialist, People's or Popular Republics in Black Africa espousing some form of Marxism has slowly inched upwards until at last count at least seven countries could be said to officially belong in this new and rather nebulous category, with other hybrids possibly also deserving to be noted.[45] And just as it should be immediately qualified that most of these are not by any stretch of the imagination even approximations of East Europe's People's Republics, so it should be noted that many conservative, pro-West African leaders are feeling the same frustrations and (minus the radical rhetoric or pro-East bias) are slowly formulating policies quite similar to those espoused in the first group. Whatever the differences in the various countries' domestic orientations or the disjunctions between stated goals and actual policies, one common denominator has been the radicalization of their foreign postures, the one area where radical credentials can be easily unfurled and displayed without undue destabilizing repercussions.

The slow radicalization of the continent, receiving. a boost from the militancy of O.P.E.C., has further worked to widen the perceived gap between Israel and the Third World. Outwardly paradoxically, but in reality quite understandably, the Israeli foreign posture has slowly become more conservative, more pro-West, as the Third World has moved to the Left. For the "Left" of the Third World has been Russia, China, Cuba, countries that, apart from brief moments in their histories, have been classically opposed to the democratic and pragmatic Socialism of Israel. And as Israel's position in the Third World began to deteriorate, as her bastions of support began to erode, the shift to the center or right has been more pronounced.

Moreover, like many democratic and developed societies the range of Israel's national interests precluded from the outset the kind of single-minded and dogmatic commitment to African goals that Africa demanded from her. Timid Israeli efforts in the early 1960's at a closer integration with the Third World were rebuffed by the latter's Arab and Moslem component. Israel's foreign policy leadership and Israel's indigenous political culture precluded emotional harangues and empty U.N. rhetoric as "means" of legitimating Israel's anti-colonialist credentials; and the hard fact that in the ultimate sense Israel's physical security depended upon the amity of the United States also precluded justified or unjustified public criticism of the U.S., a popular target of the Third World. Geographically part of, and in sympathy with many of the goals of the Third World, and deeply influenced by the democratic ideological currents that gave birth to the Second World,

Israel has always been an integral component of the Western liberal tradition. Her inability and unwillingness to disengage herself full-heartedly from either one of these camps, or to attach herself unreservedly to the Third World, inevitably was to erode Israel's credibility among African states demanding an either/or public posture on issues affecting Africa.

Thus, for example, even when Afro-Israeli relations were at their best and many Israeli public figures were talking of Israel's "integration" with the Third World[46], certain foreign postures were difficult for Israel to adopt. In the pre-1967 era the extremely close Franco-Israeli entente[47] simply precluded the condemnation of France (at the U.N. and elsewhere) over either her atomic tests or colonial war in Algeria, and prevented an Israeli independent policy in Africa, as in the case of the prevarication over the recognition of Guinea's independence. South Africa's racist policies—anathema to most Israeli leaders—were condemned by Israel on numerous occasions. But Israel usually felt it highly imprudent to support the harsher U.N. resolutions, out of a desire not to provoke Pretoria's retaliation against the important resident Jewish community, and out of awareness that the grounds advanced for the expulsion of South Africa from the U.N. could well be used against her as well at a later juncture. China, increasingly viewed by the Third World as unjustifiably excluded from the U.N., had been recognized by Israel as early as January 1950. Notwithstanding this early gesture of friendship and an early dispatch of a goodwill mission to Peking, China adopted a very hostile attitude towards Israel as manifested in the Bandung Conference (1955) and on later occasions. While Israel's relations with the Soviet Union except briefly at the beginning—have also been very poor, China's ideological and military support for the most radical of the Arab terrorist groups (as opposed to states) has inevitably inclined Israel to array herself in the anti-Chinese camp in the U.N. in opposition to much of the Third World.[49] And with the onset of the 1970's Israel's deteriorating diplomatic position has made her dependent upon the goodwill of the U.S. to a degree not existing since the early 1950's, leaving her hardly any leeway in foreign policy-making. Thus the ultimate paradox that with impeccable Socialist credentials, one of the world's earliest anticolonialist liberation movements (Zionism, against the British mandate), consistent sympathy for, and assistance to, the Third World, and a record of uplifting herself from the "have-nots" to the "haves" group of nations via means still attractive and of interest to the Third World, the external exigencies of Israel's position in the Middle East coupled with the radicalization of the Third World have resulted in the portrayal of Israel as a state in the same camp as South Africa and pre-coup Portugal. Thus the stage was set for the entry of the final factor—Libya and Arab petrodollars—that were to help nail the coffin of the Afro-Israeli entente.

Libya and the Petrodollar Influence

What is sometimes loosely called the Petrodollar Era commenced with the September 1969 coup d'etat in Libya and the sudden catapultion into world prominence of a young, zealously pan-Arab junta under the mercurial leadership of Muammar Qaddafi. It took the world several years to realize the significance of the coup in Benghazi; to Israel, however, the significance was crystal-clear and the repercussion immediate. For the first time a truly committed Arab leader had emerged fully able and willing to pledge all his country's oil resources in the ongoing diplomatic and military struggle with Israel. (Though in reality Qaddafi was to prove to he as shrewdly parsimonious with Libya's wealth as all previous Arab leaders). Moreover, Qaddafi's radical anti-Western posture and crusading zealousness provided the prodding necessary to give O.P.E.C. its long-missing teeth vis-a-vis the West, while the Arab world paradoxically was to attain a measure of unity it had not seen previously despite Qaddafi's idiosyncratic antics that isolated Libya from much of the world.

A great deal has been written about Qaddafi, the veritable bedouin product of the Space Age[50], whose fanatical hatred of Israel was to do more to weaken Israel than Arab military power in the preceding twenty-five years. Much of Qaddafi's current attitudes are the product of his early formative years; his poverty as a child inclined him towards asceticism in adulthood; his intellectual isolation as a youth in the remote Fezzan sealed him from foreign influences while providing a fertile background for his imbibing the most rabidly anti-Israel invective of the young Nasser in Egypt. Once in power Qaddafi has been a continuous thorn in the side of first Nasser (who was to him in many respects a surrogate father) and then Sadat, over their "opportunism" in even considering a political (as opposed to military) solution to the Middle East dispute. And after Nasser's death the young Lieutenant-turned-Colonel felt that the Nasserite mantle of leadership of the Arab world had fallen to him.

To Qaddafi the most pressing need in the Arab world is to thoroughly purify Islam of its Western-imbibed decadent mannerisms and a return to the fundamental precepts of Islam,[51] the defence of the Faith and faithful all over the world,[52] the creation of a state based upon Islamic humanism,[53] and the total dismantlement of Israel. The mere existence of Israel, let alone the four humiliating military defeats it dealt to Moslem forces, is to Qaddafi the symbol of the current decadence and decay of dar-el-Islam. This centrality to his thought of the need to physically liquidate Israel is the reason why Israeli sources place some credibility to rumours that Qaddafi has tried to purchase atomic weapons.[54] Thus overnight on September 1, 1969 Libya moved to the forefront of the "confrontation" states with Israel.

Qaddafi's clashes with other Arab leaders notwithstanding, it was under his guidance and support that the Arab propaganda war in the Third World gathered powerful momentum. As has been noted, hitherto Arab propaganda in Black Africa was quite weak and routine; Arab technical assistance—and economic aid—minimal except with respect to the provision of Islamic or Arabic teachers (and even in the area a number of African states applied for and received Israeli teachers), and the African response reflected by unwillingness to support strong condemnatory motions against Israel. Eventually this African foreign policy was modified to oral declarations of solidarity with the Arab powers with quick reassurances to Jerusalem that these had no real significance. Since Jerusalem had become accustomed to this "solution" to what to many African leaders was an embarrassing situation of chasing between "brother and friend" (as Zaire's Mobutu was to phrase it at a later juncture[55]), a delicate stalemate developed between the two Middle East protagonists in Africa.[56]

Libya's role in expelling Israeli influence in Africa has essentially been that of a banker. With the Libyan economy and society dependent itself on between 150,000 and 300,000 foreign (mostly Egyptian) teachers, engineers, doctors and administrators, the country has hardly the skilled manpower to replace even a small part of the Israeli effort in Africa. Rather, low-interest loans and grants, timely offers of subsidies and suggestions for the creation of Afro-Libyan Development Banks, and especially promises of future largesse have been dangled before African leaders willing to adopt more uncompromising attitudes towards, Israel. The above notwithstanding, it should be stressed that explaining Israel's reverses on the continent purely as a function of Arab "bribes" somewhat over-simplifies the issue, gives too much credit to Libya and does an injustice to African leaders. At the time the Libyan effort was beginning to be felt African militancy vis-a-vis the Middle East was also on the rise; a major factor that eased; the Arab effort against Israel was the failure of the well-meant but very naive "Wise Men" Peace Mission.[57] According to one source "the balance seems to have tilted against Israel at the time of the failure of the 1971-72 O.A.U. Peace Mission, in which several leaders not ill-disposed to Israel (Senghor, Gowon, Mobutu) were persuaded that the Arabs were being more reasonable about peace initiatives."[58] Whether or not there is indeed a causal relationship between the progressive deterioration of the Israeli position in Africa and the failure of this peace mission (and many observers assume that there is one), or whether there is but a chronological coincidence, certainly the first visible sign of Israel's eclipse occurred in Uganda.

Libya's anti-Israel drive in many respects began quite by chance as a result of the personality idiosyncracies of Idi Amin who came to power in Uganda in the January 1971 coup. Though originally an Israeli protege, Amin's impetuous and incredible demands from the Israeli government once he rose to power (including, equipment and planes to wrestle a seaport from Tanzania)[59] and his brutalization of domestic real and suspected enemies, resulted in a rapid deterioration of relations between the two. Amin's surprise visit to Tripoli in February 1972 resulted in an important pledge of Libyan funds to the quasi-bankrupt plundered Ugandan treasury (only small portions of this pledge ever reached Kampala) following which Amin announced his diplomatic break with Israel.[60] Before doing so, however, Amin was persuaded to fly to Ndjamena where he convinced the equally fiscally hard pressed President Tombalbaye of the merits of reaching an understanding with Tripoli. Such an understanding was indeed hammered out with Tripoli stopping overt support of the northern Toubou rebels and Siddick's FROLINAT, in exchange for Chad's break with Israel and Tombalbaye's turning a blind eye to Libyan advances in Tibesti to the Mussolini-Laval line. Of the funds pledged to Chad only a small portion had arrived in Ndjamena by the end of 1975.

Several other African states loosened their ties with Israel as the news of Libya's alleged largesse spread. Each particular country did so, however, for different combinations of reasons and only seven states broke with Israel prior to the Yom Kippur war.[61] That so many states did not do so is probably more significant than that seven were swayed to rupture with Jerusalem. Mali provides a good illustration though this country did break with Israel on January 5, 1973. A highly Moslem and extremely poor and country bordering, and historically influenced by, the Maghreb; both under civilian (Modibo Keita) and military rule (since 1968) one of the militant states on the continent; never an important recipient of Israeli technical, assistance, Mali nevertheless did not break with Israel until 1973. Indeed, in the fall of 1972 the entire "Israeli presence" in Mali was two diplomats (and their families), one W.H.O. fisheries expert in Mopti and one navigator (with dual citizenship) with Air Mali.[62] Surely what is most surprising here is the longevity of Mali-Israel relations, cool as they may have been for a number of years.

By 1972 Israel's diplomatic position was fast eroding in Africa. As Colin Legum noted "there is less willingness among the most ardent pro-Israelis to stand against the pressures of the Arab lobby."[63] "Israeli leaders, aware that they had oversold the public to the concept of lasting Afro-Israeli friendship, tried to soften the impending blow (or where they whistling in the dark?) by declaring that though a further deterioration could be expected this would be insignificant ("...not tragic, and one cannot speak of our collapse in Africa."[64] Few could predict the massive break with Israel that was just around the corner. That is hardly surprising, actually, for the 1973 Afro-Israel break—despite rationalizations by statesmen and scholars alike—will remain one of the more bizarre enigmas of diplomatic history. Indeed, possibly because of its unusual nature (of massive ruptures in relations by non-combatants) scholars have assumed that there must have been a *quid pro quo* Afro-Arab understanding.[65]

However that may be, when the Yom Kippur war broke out seventeen states broke with Israel between October 4 and 30, the holdouts—amongst which were the strong Israeli allies of Kenya, Liberia and the Ivory Coast—succumbing during the first two weeks of November. The Israeli presence in the continent was reduced to four small embassies in the conservative Southern Africa, giving credence to Qaddafi's boast that he had "reduced Israel to the level of Taiwan."[66] Most African states paradoxically still maintained that the break in diplomatic relations signified no basic change in their favorable view of Israel, and requested the continuation of Israel's programs of technical cooperation and economic relations.[67] A few bombastically tried to ingratiate themselves as much as they could with the Arab camp by getting as much mileage as they could from the break. Burundi's Micombero, for example, offered the U.A.R. the support of all his armed forces "in order to fight the common enemy."[68] Chad's Tombalbaye, formerly on record an avid admirer of Israel, and one of the few African leaders most certainly "bought off" by Libya[69], stated that " Chad must consider itself at war...a daily airlift will carry meat to the fighting men on the various fronts."[70]

Jerusalem did not react with equanimity or "understanding" to the African assurances that the break in diplomatic relations need not signify a major Afro-Israeli disengagement. Though quite sympathetic to the plight of the few African states that resisted breaking with Israel until practically the entire continent had done so, to Israelis the African rupture was not only totally uncalled for, unparalleled in diplomatic history, but also done in a manner calculated to offend most, in the midst of the Middle East war. Hence the lack of interest on the part of the Israeli Foreign Ministry to exploit the signs of African disenchantment with former pledges of assistance of the Arab world.[71] Such disenchantment—including public criticism of the break itself—had surfaced in several countries practically hand in hand with the Afro-Israeli rupture itself; in others within months of the Middle-East war, and has been accompanied by talk of a rapprochement.[72] To Israelis, however, it seemed futile to appear interested in rebuilding what most felt could never be replaced. Africa's "betrayal" had underscored the worthlessness of reliance on the fickle Third World.

Thus neither Joseph Nyerere (the President's brother) and his suggestion to sell the Arabs the Nile waters for oil, nor Gabon President Bongo's denunciation of his treaty with Libya [73] nor East African regrets over the break with Israel, have been pursued by the Israeli Foreign Ministry, nor taken at face value as harbingers of better days to come. As the respectable *Ha'aretz* editorialized, and in this no doubt reflecting the common Israeli position, "[Africa's] haste to disown us does not add to our respect for the African countries. We shall not forget who abandoned us in this, our hour of dire need...it is unlikely, that the restoration of our position in Africa will be high on Israel's list of priorities for the near future."[74] Or, as more recently enunciated by

Israeli officials, "We would open only one Embassy for three, four or five countries. We wouldn't resume aid projects in 24 hours, but we would resume them..."[75]

The religious daily *Hatzofe* also reflected this "isolationist" attitude towards Africa in its editorial in which it stated *inter alia* "One of Israel's diplomatic errors was its great effort to establish close ties with the African states without first establishing whether these regimes were stable and mature enough to make the effort worthwhile. Careful consideration would have shown that the enormous sums spent in developing Africa would have been put to infinitely better use in absorbing immigrants and in reducing the widening social gap in Israel.[76] And as the influential *Jerusalem Post* so accurately concluded, when Afro-Israeli relations are again restored—and as they inevitably will be—"those links will never be the same again. The taste of betrayal at a time of crisis will remain."[77]

Why the Anti-Zionist Resolution?

If the factors that led to the deterioration of Afro-Israeli relations are kept in mind Africa's general support of the anti-Zionism clause in the United Nations is easy to explain as at least in part a continuation of this process. To a considerable degree the 1973 Afro-Israeli falling apart led inexorably to the 1975 anti-Zionism resolution. If one accepts pious African contentions that the 1973 break was over Israel's "aggression" against Egypt and Syria, or over Israel's refusal to unilaterally withdraw from the Occupied Territories, then nothing had changed by 1975 and the anti-Zionism vote may be seen as further African "pressure" on Israel. If the 1973 break is seen as Africa's response to Arab demands for solidarity, and Arab promises of fiscal largesse, again the 1975 vote is but a continuation of this process. Moreover, there is a certain degree of truth in the Israeli contention[78] that having opted for—or having been pushed into—the harshest form of diplomatic disapprobation in 1973 (break in relations), few African leaders can easily balk even harsher Arab demands today. Any such attempt to draw the line would expose states so inclined to charges of "treason" or of "deserting" the so-called Afro-Arab solidarity bloc. In short, the time to draw the line to unreasonable Arab demands was 1973, not 1975. Many African states, especially the small ones, have been effectively boxed into diplomatic positions lacking any manoeuvrability that they might not have supported in 1973. According to this interpretation, somewhat deterministic, maybe, but certainly containing more than a germ of truth, Africa's unbalanced stampede to the Arab cause in 1973 has straitjacketed many leaders to support resolutions such as the exclusion of Israel from regional groups at UNESCO[79] and anti-Zionism that they could not have been in agreement in 1973 and very reluctantly supported in 1975.

Contentions that the anti-Zionism resolution was part of a well-prepared three-stage plan to destroy Israel[80] can be reconciled with eyewitness reports on the resolution's somewhat opportunistic origins. While the tactical progress of the resolution (from that summer's introduction of similar drafts at three international gatherings[81] need not concern us here,[82] and neither a definition or justification of Zionism is necessary for a European audience, it is important to note that as with all U.N. issues the voting behavior of Africa on the anti-Zionism resolution was affected by a variety of considerations extraneous to the merits of the case itself. Many states were not happy with the sudden Arab exploitation of an originally African issue (the U.N. Third Committee's Decade for Action against Apartheid) by the introduction of seven amendments to the resolutions then debated, naming Zionism as an example of racial discrimination the Decade was to combat. Ultimately, some African states persisted in their opposition to the resolutions as amended; others compromised for the wider "good" of passing out anti-apartheid resolutions, while a third group of countries went along fullheartedly with the de facto anti-semitic resolution.

Moreover, a number of African (and especially Latin American) states that were originally opposed to the by-then consolidated single anti-Zionism resolution, voted in its favor out of anger at either U.S. pressure[83] or U.S. Ambassador Moynihan's October 3rd San Francisco speech in which he stated that Idi Amin ("this racist murderer") was by "no accident" also President of the O.A.U.[84]

Other states simply did not know much about Zionism except that it was an ideology opposed by the Arab powers and/or regarded as acceptable by Western Europe and hence by definition inimical to the Third World. These and other extraneous considerations affected the way the votes were cast. A Sierra Leone-Zambian effort to postpone a vote was defeated by 56 to 48 votes and shortly later the Third Committee passed the draft by 70 votes to 29 with 27 abstentions.

After a strenuous U.S. lobbying effort the General Assembly convened to discuss the three resolutions of the Third Committee, one of which was the anti-Zionism draft. An effort by the Sierra Leone Ambassador to request a postponement of the vote was averted when the Belgian delegate was recognized instead with a similar motion. The vote on deferral was lost by 67 votes to 55 with 15 abstentions, following which the debates commenced. (African states voting for deferral were: Botswana, Ethiopia, Ghana, Ivory Coast, Kenya, Liberia, Malawi, Sierra Leone, Swaziland, Togo, Upper Volta, Zaire and Zambia, with Gabon, Lesotho and Cameroun abstaining[85]. Extraneous considerations again played a role in influencing votes. African and non-African delegations complained of the haste in ramming the anti-Zionism resolution through the General Assembly and of the confusion as to what was being condemned in light of the absence of a definition of "Zionism". Liberia's David Wilson, in opposing the resolution, deplored this lack of definition stressing that "it was an historic fact that anti-semitism gave birth to the Zionist movement" and noted that "some delegations were bitterly disappointed that in all those brilliant and eloquent statements not one word had been said about the Programme for the Decade designed to help our brothers and sisters, some of whom were languishing in the prisons in Namibia, Zimbabwe and South Africa.[86] Similar views were expressed by Kenya's Charles Maina ("rushing this definition through..," "obvious oversimplified definition of Zionism..," etc.)[87] and a few other delegates.

Speaking in favor of the resolution were a number of delegates including Dahomey's Tiamiou Adjibade (who had gained notoriety for defending Amin after Moynihan's San Francisco speech) who in a very lofty speech declared his preference "to see the U.N. dead," rather than "bogged down in compromise," and Mauritius' Radha Krishna Ramphul who quite candidly admitted that Moynihan's eloquent categorization of the U.N.'s activity as "obscene" was swaying votes in favor of the resolution, as was also the strong pressure exerted by the U.S. delegation.[88] There were not a great deal of speeches, however; indeed, extremely few, and quite brief ones, considering the nature of resolution being debated. This was because much of the debate had already taken place at the Third Committee previously, the battle lines were well-defined, and quite a few delegations were somewhat ill-at-ease with what was happening and wanted to be done with the entire matter once and for all.[89]

In the final vote all thirteen countries that had supported the Belgian postponement motion either opposed the resolution (being the only African states to do so: Ivory Coast, Liberia, Malawi, Swaziland and the Central African Republic, the latter originally recording "absent") or abstained; this latter group of states was joined by Mauritius (that had voted against postponement), Gabon and Lesotho (that had also abstained on the deferral motion).[90] In absolute numbers the non-Arab League (including Somalia and Mauritania) African states split with 20 supporting the anti-Zionism resolution, 5 opposing it and 12 abstaining. While many of Israel's former strongest allies either opposed the resolution or abstained, some of them (Dahomey, Madagascar) did not, though for widely divergent reasons. Both Israeli and Western delegates, however, were somewhat more surprised by the greater erosion of support for the West in the Latin American bloc where three states (Guyana, Mexico and Brazil) voted in favor of the resolution, six against and fully nine abstained.

Though the anti-Zionism vote was followed by the strong U.S. and other Western protests mentioned at the beginning of this article, talk of a U.S. link-up of economic aid to U.N. postures of the Third World,[91] and campaigns to discredit states that supported what Moynihan categorized as "a lie, a political lie of a variety well known to the twentieth century and scarcely exceeded in all that annals of untruth and outrage,"[92] the fact still remains that for a variety of reasons the United Nations had gone on record in sanctifying what in the West is clearly perceived as a blatantly unfair and clearly antisemitic resolution, and what Israel considers the most despicable action perpetrated by the Soviet-Third World bloc. The significant support the resolution obtained from Black Africa can only result in the retrenchment of anti-African feelings currently becoming ingrained in the Israeli body-politic, marking the definitive end of an era.

FOOTNOTES

1. See for example Ashley Montagu, "The U.N. Resolution on Zionism," *Bulletin of the American Professors for Peace in the Middle East*, Dec. 1975, p. 5.

2. See the ads that appeared in "The Week in Review" section of the *New York Times*, Dec. 21, 1975, which urged tourists to boycott travel to states

that had voted for the resolution and "visit your friends" listing those, including Belgium, that had opposed the resolution.

3. *New York Times*, Dec. 30, 1975. Rabasa's slip of the tongue in a Mexican press conference where he used the word "Pardon" in explaining that Israeli-Mexican "misunderstandings" had been "forgotten, pardoned and buried" seems to have been the cause of his downfall. See also *New York Times*, Dec. 17, 19, 1975 and Jan. 1, 1976.

4. President Luis Echeverria stated on December 12 that despite his country's vote Mexico "in no way identified Zionism with racism." Nevertheless Mexico's voting record has since been checked though a few abstentions were recorded. See *New York Times*, Dec. 13, 1975 and the "Travel Section" of the latter's Dec. 14, 1975 issue.

5. For the anti-Israel resolution there see the Appendix in George M. Kahin, *The Asian-African Conference*, Ithaca, Cornell University Press, 1956.

6. Most of the regimes that broke with Israel stressed they would prefer that the Israeli technical cooperation teams remain in the country and continue their work.

7. One senior Israeli official, known for his long and devoted service in modernizing the agricultural infrastructure in a West African state, burst out with "I don't want to hear or talk of Africa, period," when interviewed in New York in November 1973 regarding the future of Afro-Israeli relations.

8. Already a reference to the anti-Zionism resolution was inserted in Unesco documents sparking a walkout by twelve nations. *New York Times*, Dec. 18, 19, 1975.

9. For a bibliographic review of the literature up to 1967 see Samuel Decalo, "Israel and Africa," *Journal of Modern African Studies*, vol. 5, no. 3, 1967.

10. For a monumental study of Israel's Foreign Ministry and foreign policy see the twin volumes by Michael Brecher, *The Foreign Policy System of Israel*, and *Decisions in Israel's Foreign Policy*, both published in New Haven by Yale University Press (1972 and 1975 respectively.) See also Samuel Roberts, *Survival or Hegemony: The Foundations of Israeli Foreign Policy*, Baltimore, Johns Hopkins University Press, 1973; Ernest Stock, *Israel on the Road to Sinai*, New York, Columbia University Press, 1963; B. Reich, "Israel's Policy in Africa," *Middle East Journal*, Winter 1964; J. Almo, "Pourquoi Israel va en Afrique," and D. Catarivas, "Sept ans, de relations entre Israel et les Etats francophones d'Afrique" both in *Le Mois en Afrique*, Aug. 1967; A.J. Klinghoffer, "Israel in Africa," *Africa Report*, April 1972 and A. Jacob, "Israel's Foreign Aid Program to Africa," Ph.D. thesis, University of California/Los Angeles, 1969.

11. France, Italy, Great Britain, the Soviet Union, U.S., Canada and Argentina.

12. Samuel Decalo, "Israeli Foreign Policy and the Third World," *Orbis*, Fall 1967.

13. "A Surplus of Brains," *Newsweek*, Aug. 20, 1962.

14. Israel. *Divrei HaKnesset*, Oct. 24-26, 1960, p. 20.

15. Issue for Oct. 16, 1960.

16. For a discussion of this drive see *Israel Economist*, December 1961; Israel Yaffe, The U.N. Votes Against Negotiations," *New Outlook* (Tel Aviv), May 1962. See also the actual resolutions G.A.O.R., 17th and 18th Session Special Political Committee, Draft Resolution A/SPC/L.89+Addl (Dec. 9, 11, 1/2) and Draft Resolution A/SPC/L.100+Add.l (Nov. 18, 20, 1963.)

17. First to the Executive Board of the World Health Organization (1962), then to the board of UNICEF. For more details see *Israel Weekly News Bulletin*, April 1-7, 1964, April 22-28, 1964 and May 23-29, 1962. See also *Jerusalem Post*, January 4, 1962 and Samuel Decalo, *Israel and Africa: The Politics of Cooperation*, Ph.D. thesis, University of Pennsylvania, Philadelphia, 1970.

18. Samuel Decalo, *Messianic Influences in Israeli Foreign Policy*, University of Rhode Island, Occasional Papers in Political Science, 2, 1967; Samuel Decalo, "Messianic Influences and Pragmatic Limitations in Israeli Foreign Policy," in M. Mushkat (ed.), *World Society: Changing Structures and Laws*, The Hague, Mouton, 1974.

19. See for example Julius Braunthal and J. B. Kripalani, *The Significance of Israeli Socialism*, London, Lincolns-Prager, 1958; F. Grevisse, "Reflexions á propos des solutions israeliennes en marge de l'evolution du Congo," *Revue coloniale Belge*, August 1960; Joseph Klatzmann, *Les enseignements de l'experience Israelienne*, Paris, Editions Tiers Monde, 1963; Elie Maissi, "Israel et son exemple," *Cahiers Africains* (Bruxelles), 2, 1961; Jules Moch, "Israel, Yougoslave, Chine. Trois methodes," *La Revue Socialiste* (Paris), 163, May 1963; A. Stime, "Ghanaians Salute Israel," Accra, Guinea Press, 1958; M. Franck, *Cooperative Land Settlements in Israel and their Relevance to African Countries*, Basel, Kylos Verlag, 1968.

20. Compare the figures in Réné Hofherr, "Le probleme de l'encadrement dans les jeunes Etats de langue française," *Tiers Monde*, vol. XIII, 12, Oct. 1962 p. 538 and the figures in Israel. Ministry of Foreign Affairs. Department for International Cooperation. *Accumulative Tables on Trainees and Experts 1958, 1963*, Jerusalem, 1964.

21. Figures from appendices of Shimeon Amir, *Israel's Development Cooperation with Africa, Asia and Latin America*, New York, Praeger, 1974.

22. Personal interview in 1972 in a francophone capital.

23. See *Ethiopian Herald* (Addis Ababa), July 19, 1969.

24. *Izvestiia*, December 12, 1960. For other diatribes against Israel see V. Nikolayev, "Israel's Perilous Course," *International Affairs* (Moscow), 10, 1961 ; G.S. Nikitina, "Ekspansiya Israelya v. Afrike i neokolonialism," *Narodny Azii i Afriki*, 3, 1963; V. Grigoryev, "Israel: A servant of Neo-colonialism in

Africa," in *International Affairs* (Moscow), 1, 1961; S. Astakhov, "Israeli Expansion in the Third World," in *International Affairs* (Moscow), July 1969.

25. For two views of the Egyptian effort see Tareq Ismael, *The U.A.R. in Africa*, Evanston, Northwestern University Press, 1971 and J. Churba, "Israel-U.A.R. Rivalry over Aid and Trade in Subsaharan Africa, 1957-63," Ph. D. Thesis, Columbia University, 1965.

26. As in the case of the Third Afro-Asian Solidarity Conference (Moshi, 1963) when the Chairman (Tanzania's Oscar Kambona) renounced the anti-Israel resolution just passed as "irrelevant to Tanzania." *Ethiopian Herald* (Addis Ababa), February 7, 12, 1963.

27. See for example, "Les Arabes, Israel et nous Maliens," in *Paris-Dakar*, July 4, 1960; also, Peter Enahoro, "Does the Arab-speaking African feel African?" *Daily Times* (Lagos), February 2, 1962; *Le Courrier d'Afrique* (Leopoldville), April 12, 1960; *Ethiopian Herald* (Addis Ababa), February 12, 1962.

28. Only four states maintain relations with Israel: Malawi, Lesotho, Swaziland and Mauritius.

29. International Labour Organization. *Human Dignity, Economic Growth and Social Justice in Changing Africa.* An ILO Agenda for Africa, Geneva, 1973, p. 31.

30. In its simplest terms it assumes peasants observing the success of experimental or model projects would seek to emulate the procedures in order to maximize their own gains. Thus a limited developmental effort (model farms or regional projects) would lead to widescale "spontaneous" spillover of the technology-transfer.

31. For a discussion (though quite dated) of the Israeli technical cooperation projects see Leopold Laufer, *Israel and the Developing Countries*, New York, Twentieth Century Fund, 1967; Mordechai Kreinen, *Israel and Africa : A Study in Technical Cooperation*, New York, Praeger, 1964 and A. Jacob, "Israel's Military Aid to Africa 1960-1966," *Journal of Modern African Studies*, August 1971.

32. The then Ghanaian Trades Union Congress Secretary General John Tettegah is quoted as saying at the end of a brief study tour of Israel "Israel has given me more in eight days than I could have obtained in two years in a British University," *Jerusalem Post*, July 23, 1957.

33. Computed from figures in Amir.

34. But see Samuel Decalo, "Afro-Israeli Technical Cooperation: Successes and setbacks," in Michael Curtis (ed.), *Israel and the Third World*, New York, Transaction Press, 1976. Documentation of some of the facts that follow, well-known to experts who served in the field, is sparse in light of the sensitivity of the subject, especially to Afro-Israel relations. See, however, Z. Y. Hershlag (ed.), *Israel-Africa Cooperation*, Tel Aviv University, 1973, and especially the *Progress Report 1970*, limited circulation version.

35. Those interested might care to look into the following literature: C. Rossillon, "Civic Service and Community Work in Mali," *International Labour Review*, Jan. 1966; Israel, Departement de la cooperation internationale, *Plan fondamental pour la creation d'un mouvement de jeunesse pionnere en République du Tchad*, Jerusalem, 1964; D. Boni, "Le Service civique ivoirien et l'assistance technique israelienne," *Le Mois en Afrique*, August 1967; Ross Baker, "The Civic Service of the Ivory Coast," *International Development Review*, Dec. 1967; J. Mowly, "The Young Pioneers Movement in the Central African Republic," *International Labour Review*, Jan. 1966; G.W. Griffin, "The Kenya National Youth Service" *Bulletin of the Inter-African Labour Institute*, Feb. 1965; Peter Hodge, "The Ghana Workers Brigade: Project for Unemployed Youth," *British Journal of Sociology*, June 1964; C. Rossillion, "Economic and Social Work for Young People during Defence Service," *International Labour Review*, Jan. 1966; Dahomey. Ministère de la defense nationale. *Le Service Civique*, Cotonou, 1971.

36. For a few examples see Hershlag; also, *West Africa*, September 14, 1968, p. 1082.

37. Field work in Dahomey in 1971 indicated attrition rates of recruits were as high as 70% of original intake.

38. From interviews with Israeli personnel in Ivory Coast and Upper Volta (1971, 1972) and interviews in Jerusalem 1972.

39. For some reports of the spectacular successes see especially Israel and Africa. "Cooperation Brings Grass-Roots Revolution," *Africa Report*, April 1972 and the three articles in *Kidma* (Tel Aviv) by Y. Abt and E. Maoz, "Integrated Rural Development: Case Study of the Kafuba-Kafula Project in Zambia," (Vol. 1, 4, 1974) and by Gideon Naor, "Israel's Cooperation Projects Observed," in two parts (vol. 1, 2, 3, 1974); A. Jacob, "Foreign Aid in Agriculture: Introducing Israel's Land Settlement Scheme to Tanzania," *African Affairs*, April 1972.

40. Cited in *Jerusalem Post*, October 29, 1973.

41. Immanuel Wallerstein, "Left and Right in Africa," *Journal of Modern African Studies*, vol. IX, 1, 1971.

42. See in particular some of the literature on Congo/Brazzaville: Arthur H. House, "Brazzaville: Revolution or Rhetoric?," *Africa Report*, April 1971; Samuel Decalo, "Revolutionary Rhetoric and Army Cliques in Congo/B." in S. Decalo, *Coups and Army Rule in Africa. Essays on Military Style*, New Haven, Yale University Press, 1976.

43. The experience of Japan cogently underscores that while the traditional infrastructure need not be dismantled, socioeconomic development does seem to require social mobilization, national unity and modern outlooks.

44. See Samuel Decalo in M. Curtis (ed.), *Israel and the Third World*.

45. The seven countries are Guinea, Guinea-Bissau, Mozambique,

Somalia,Congo/Brazzaville, Dahomey (Benin), soon (?) to be joined by Angola. Possible additional hybrids that can be added now, or in the future, include Mali, Malagasy Republic and Ethiopia.

46 Samuel DECALO, Orbis, Fall 1967.

47 See S. K. Crosbie, *A Tacit Alliance: France and Israel from Suez to the Six Day War*, Princeton, Princeton University Press, 1974; Paul Balta and Claudine Rulleau, *La politique arabe de la France de de Gaulle á Pompidou*, Paris, Sinbad, 1974.

48. For some literature on Israel-Russia relations, recently becoming plentiful see especially A. Dagan, *Moscow and Jerusalem: Twenty Years of Relations between Israel and the Soviet Union*, New York, Abelard-Schuman, 1970; M. Confino and S. Shamir, *The USSR and the Middle East*, New York, Halsted Press, 1973; Charles McLane, *Soviet-Third World Relations*, New York, Columbia University Press, 1973; Y. Rash, "Moscou et Jerusalem," *Reuve franRevue Française d'etudes Politiques mediterranéennes*, Sept.-Oct. 1975.

49. For literature on Israel-China see in particular, "Peking and Jerusalem," *Jerusalem Post*, Feb. 22, 1972; M. Nahumi, "China and Israel," *New Outlook* (Tel Aviv), July-August 1966; Joseph Dunner, "Israel and China," *Southeast Asian Perspectives*, December 1972 and Moshe Ma'oz, "Soviet and Chinese Relations with the Palestinian Guerrilla Organizations," *Jerusalem Papers on Peace Problems*, no. 4, 1974.

50. Samuel Decalo, "Libya's Qaddafi: Bedouin Product of the Space Age," *Present Tense*, vol. 1, no. 2, Winter 1974. See also in particular Edward R.F. Sheehan, "Colonel Qaddafi, Libya's Mystical Revolutionary," in *New York Times Magazine*, Feb. 6, 1972; A. McDermott, "Qaddafi and Libya," *The World Today*, Sept. 1973; Pierre Rondot, "La philosophie politique du Colonel Kadhafi," *Le Mois en Afrique*, Sept. 1972; Ruth First, Libya, Penguin Books, 1974.

51. Among Western "influences" banned were nightclubs, casinos, bars, prostitutes and hairdressing salons. As one Libyan put it, "He [Qaddafi] is turning all of Libya into a mosque." See Sheehan.

52. Including support for the Moslem rebellion in the Philippines, the Toubou rebellion in Chad, the Eritrean Liberation Front and even the I.R.A. in Ireland.

53. The first steps in that direction included the cultural revolution, nationalization of most sectors of the economy, etc.

54. This belief was to cause the February 1973 shooting down of the Air Libya plane that overflow Israeli territory.

55. Cited in *Jerusalem Post*, October 5, 1973.

56. For the period 1965-69 see Colin Legum, "Israel's Year in Africa," in *Africa Contemporary Record 1969-70*; Samuel Decalo, "Africa and the Mid-East War," *Africa Report*, Oct. 1967; H. Strauch, "Le vote des pays africains á

l'Assemblée générale de l'O.N.U.," *Géneve-Afrique*, vol. VI, no. 2, 1967; "Israel, the Arabs and Africa," *West Africa*, June 10, 1967; July 8, 1967.

57. R. Kochan, "An African Peace Mission to the Middle East," *African Affairs*, April 1973; S. Gitelson, "The O.A.U. Mission and the Middle East Conflict," *International Organization*, vol. XXVII, 3, 1973; Jon Woronoff, "The O.A.U. enters the Middle East," *New Outlook* (Tel Aviv), Feb. 1972; Yassin El Ayouty, "O.A.U. Mediation in the Arab-Israeli Conflict," *Géneve-Afrique*, vol. XIV, 1, 1975 and C. Casteran, "Les sages de l'O.U.A. au Caire et á Jerusalem" *Le Mois en Afrique*, Dec. 1971.

58. *West Africa*, Oct. 15, 1973, p. 1443.

59. Israel. Ministry for Foreign Affairs. "Israel and Uganda," Jerusalem, 1972; Colin Legum, "Israel's Year in Africa," in *Africa Contemporary Record 1972-3*.

60. J. Gueriviere, "Ouganda. Traversée du desert pour Israel," *Le mois en Afrique*, April 1972; R. Mergui, "Ouganda-Israel," *Jeune Afrique*, April 15, 1972; *Africa Research Bulletin*, vol. IX, 3, April 1972, p. 2423; *Afrique Nouvelle* (Dakar), April 20, 1972 and *Uganda Argus* (Kampala), March 27 and 31, 1972.

61. In chronological order from Uganda (March 20, 1972), Chad, Congo/B, Niger, Mali, Burundi to Togo on September 21, 1973. For the full lists and dates see *Revolution africaine*, Nov. 9-15, 1973, reprinted in *Afrique contemporaine* (Paris), Nov.-Dec. 1973.

62. Fieldwork in Mali, August 1972. Interviews at the Israel Embassy, Bamako.

63. "Israel's Year in Africa," in *Africa Contemporary Record 1972-73*, p. A123. See also "African Relations" in the chapter on Libya in Colin Legum (ed.), *Africa Contemporary Record 1973-74*, p. B63-64.

64. Foreign Minister Eban qoted in the *Washington Post*, January 7, 1973.

65. Ernest J. Wilson, *The Energy Crisis and African Underdevelopment*, in *Africa Today*, Oct.-Dec. 1975, p. 30.

66. *Le Monde*, October 23, 1973.

67. For some typical reactions see "Middle East War: West African Reactions," *West Africa*, Oct. 22, 1973; "Africa and the Middle Eastern War," *West Africa*, Oct. 15, 1973; *Africa Research Bulletin*, Oct. 1973, p. 3022-3027; "The Middle East and Africa," *Africa Confidential*, Oct. 19, 1973; "Zaire breaks with Israel," *West Africa*, Oct. 15, 1973; "L'Afrique et la crise Israelo-arabe," *Afrique nouvelle*, Oct. 7-13, 1971; D. L. Greener, "Israeli-African Relations. The End of an Era," Africa, vol. XXIX, 1974, and *West Africa*, Nov. 19, 1973.

68. Radio Bujumbura, October 8, 1973.

69. "Chad, Peking and Israel," *West Africa*, Dec. 18, 1972; "Chad-Libya,"

Africa Report, Jan.-Feb. 1973; "Chad Relations with the Arabs," *West Africa*, March 12, 1973; "Libya Money Arrives," *West Africa*, June 11, 1973. Also, the sections on Chad and Libya in *Africa Contemporary Record*, volumes for 1971-73.

70. Radio Ndjamena, October 12, 1973.

71. "Arab Oil Politics Attacked," *West Africa*, Nov. 26, 1973; "Africans et Arabes face á la crise du petrole," *Afrique contemporaine*, Jan.-Feb. 1974; "Ghana Warning to Oil States," *West Africa*, July 1, 1974; Z. Cervenka, "Afro-Arab Relations. Exploitation or Cooperation?" *Africa*, 34, 1974; *The Ghanaian Times*, May 8, 1974; *East African Standard*, June 19, 1974; Colin Legum, "Africa, Arabs and Oil," *Africa Contemporary Record*, 1974-75.

72. See for example *East African Standard* (Nairobi) June 19, 20, 1974 and *Ethiopian Herald* (Addis Ababa), August 14, 1974.

73. "The state of our relations with Arab countries is nothing but negative, except with Algiers. They are people who are hardly serious and who do not bother to abide by the agreements they have signed," *West Africa*, July 29, 1974.

74. *Haretz*, Nov. 2, 1973.

75. *New York Times*, Feb. 17, 1974.

76. Cited in *Jerusalem Post*, Nov. 5, 1973.

77. *Jerusalem Post*, Oct. 26, 1973.

78. From interviews at the Israel Mission to the United Nations.

79. Or the more recent actions there. See *New York Times*, Dec. 19, 20, 1975; January 6, 1976.

80. Prepared by intellectuals associated with Beirut's Institute for Palestinian Studies. See the very perceptive "Infight at the U. N. Corral," in *The Sunday Times*, Nov. 30, 1975.

81. International Women's Year Conference (Mexico City, July), Organization of African Unity (Kampala, August), Conference of Non-Aligned Nations (Lima, August.)

82. See the previously cited article from *The Sunday Times*, Nov. 30, 1975 and Tom Buckley, "Brawler at the U.N.," *New York Times Magazine*, Dec. 7, 1975.

83. *The Sunday Times*, Nov. 30, 1975.

84. *Ibid.*

85. See *U.N. Chronicle*, Dec. 1975, p. 38.

86. *Ibid*, p. 40, 41.

87. *Ibid*, p. 41.

88. *Ibid*, p. 39.

89. Interviews at the U.N.

90. For the votes see *U. N. Chronicle*, Dec. 1975, p. 38-39 as well as the *New York Times*, Nov. 11, 1975.

91. *New York Times*, Jan. 9, 1976; *Washington Post*, Jan. 10, 1976.

92. *U. N. Chronicle*, December 1975, p. 43. The campaign has taken various forms but usually includes dissemination of facts about nations that voted for the resolution and their score on civil or political rights or freedom. See for example Freedom and U.N. General Assembly Resolution 3379 (30), in *Bulletin of the American Professors for Peace in the Middle East* (New York), Dec. 1975, p. 4.

10 THE RISE, DECLINE AND REBIRTH OF THE AFRO-ISRAELI ENTENTE*

In 1972/73 twenty-eight African states severed relations with Israel in what remains to this day one of the most unusual episodes in the history of diplomatic relations. Only three—Lesotho and Swaziland, firmly in the South African orbit, and maverick Malawi—resisted the frenzied snowballing condemnation of Israel that followed its victory in the 1973 Yom Kippur War and its occupation of a tiny sliver of continental Africa. Israel—after a decade and a half of diplomatic superpower status in Africa, second only to France in its representation on the continent—was at one stroke transformed into a virtual pariah. Although Afro-Israeli economic relations did not grind to a halt and considerable informal contact and co-operation continued unabated (many African leaders having been very reluctant to break off diplomatic relations), only in recent years, paradoxically, has there been a modest interest among some African states in repairing the damage of 1973. Between 1984 and 1986 five African countries resumed formal diplomatic relations with Israel—Liberia, Zaire, Cote d'Ivoire (Ivory Coast), Cameroon and Togo—with Kenya joining the group on December 23, 1988; at least half a dozen more (including Sierra Leone and the Central African Republic) are known to be waiting for an "auspicious moment" to follow suit without incurring the wrath of the Arab world. Does this presage the beginning of a second Afro-Israeli entente?

The Origins

Born as it was in the midst of a dual struggle for self-determination—a struggle against British mandate rule, and a struggle against Arab military invasions attending that mandate's termination—security considerations have always played a paramount role in the formulation of Israeli foreign policy. And since the successful War of Inde-

*Published in *Journal of Contemporary African Studies*, vol. 8/9 no. 1/2, 1989/1990, pp. 3-25.

pendence in 1948 clearly only assured the new state a breathing space until the ominously oft-promised Arab "second round", the quest for international legitimation, diplomatic recognition and military allies was likewise of overriding concern to early Israeli foreign policy-makers.

Israel's initial steps in the international arena sought to chart a neutral course in the cold war between the two global power blocs whose joint diplomatic support in 1948 had made independence possible. At the time, such a policy also meshed well with prevailing domestic ideological sentiment and, moreover, seemed eminently suitable for a new state primarily concerned with national reconstruction and the ingathering of the exiles. The Soviet shift of support in favour of the Arab powers rapidly foreclosed the non-aligned option, and Israel increasingly found itself riveted to every action and policy-nuance emanating from Washington—seemingly its sole international ally. Yet Israel's acute diplomatic and economic weakness made overly close association with that state a major liability, especially with the United States involved at that very time in forging a variety of Western alliances in the region. Rebuffed by the East and kept at arm's length by the West,[1] increasingly incensed by the double standards prevailing at the United Nations,[2] and even regarded as an alien polity in its own continent,[3] Israel by 1955 found itself in a major diplomatic cul de sac—just at a time when its security situation was also progressively deteriorating.[4]

The failure of Israel's early policy of reliance on the West for its security must be seen in the context of the trauma brought about by the anti-Israeli resolutions passed at the Afro-Asian Bandung Conference of 1955. Indeed, prior to the 1973 Afro-Israeli break, Bandung was Israel's greatest diplomatic setback. As one high-ranking official of the Israeli Foreign Ministry put it: "That two and one-half billion people could be united in such a way against 1,8 million people in Israel was in itself soul-shattering to all of us in the Foreign Ministry."[5] The trauma of Bandung, coupled with Israel's international isolation and increased military vulnerability, played a major role in the November 1955 leadership shuffle that brought David Ben-Gurion back to power and, in June 1956, Golda Meir to the Foreign Ministry. It also triggered a powerful diplomatic drive on the Third World (with Asia as the major focus at the outset) that, despite a number of half-hearted and fiscally hamstrung initiatives in the past, had been suffering from benign neglect. Underlying this shift in attitude towards the Third World—one that soon was to involve a monumental shift in attention and resources—was Israel's realization of one simple, fundamental fact: retaining the amity and support of the West, and especially the United States, must remain the cornerstone of Israeli policy; but it was by then also clear that, paradoxically, only an independently strong Israel, an Israel posing no liabilities to the West in its relations with other states, could aspire to have its security interests given serious consideration in Washington. Moreover, if Israel were also diplomatically secure, this might finally convince the Arab world of the futility of further bouts of hostilities in order to reverse their loss of the "first round" and lead to a negotiated settlement in the Middle East, Israel's ultimate goal. Thus the road to greater influence in the centres of Western power, and indeed to peace in the Middle East, was clearly perceived to run through the Third World, a Third World that had to be actively courted and won over, not just casually acknowledged and intermittently explored for potential.

Defending Israel's new diplomatic drive in the Third World, Prime Minister Ben-Gurion prophesied in a *Knesset* session that "our ties with the new nations will do more to strengthen our position in the world than anything else".[6] The influential daily *Haaretz* elaborated on this theme by stressing that "African countries are not rich but...their votes in international institutions are equal in value to those of more powerful nations".[7] One key Foreign Ministry official emphasized the centrality of the newly-emerging African states to Israel's immediate as well as long-term vital, national interests by forcefully stressing that "Africa is a battleground between Israel and the Arabs. It is a fight of life or death for us..."[8] Thus, from being only of tangential interest prior to 1956,[9] the Third World, and Afro-Asia in particular, moved to centre-stage in Israeli diplomacy.

These pragmatic considerations impelling Israel towards closer relations with the Third World meshed perfectly with an array of ideological drives in Israeli society at the time, which further "sanctified" the new diplomatic option. During the first years of Israel's independence there were considerable "messianic strivings" in the Israeli body politic. A number of important secular leaders from all walks of life, including Pinhas Lavon and David Ben-Gurion, were indeed grappling at this very time with the highly philosophical issue of whether Israel had a preordained "mission" or "role" to play in global affairs.

The political rebirth of Israel—an event foretold in the Scriptures, and zealously awaited by Jews over the centuries—had been a momentous event for both the secular and the religious. With the miraculous fulfilment of the 2000-year-old prophesy, debate in those heady early days of the state of Israel focused on the question of what Israel's ordained "mission" was to be in the modern world. Was the new polity to be merely "a state like all others in the community of nations?"—independence being an end in itself. Or was in its rebirth Israel somehow taking the first step towards fulfilling yet another prophesy in the Scriptures—that of providing "a Light to all Nations", a shining example to the gentiles? By the 1960's much of this sort of debate ended, the euphoria of the attainment of a 2000-year-old dream swamped by the normal tribulations and preoccupations of statehood. But during the 1950's these questions were vibrant topics for debate in many circles and in many public forums.[10] Delegations from Asia, Africa and Latin America suddenly started flocking to the hitherto isolated state of Israel to learn of its unique socioeconomic innovations (*kibbutz, moshav, nachal, gadna,* desert reclamation, rural resettlement, syndicalism, and so forth). The wide acclaim these innovations attracted overseas[11] lent credence to the view that Israel had indeed a quasi-divine mission to serve as a bridge between the "haves" and the "have-nots" of the world, assisting new nations in their quest for national reconstruction and socioeconomic development.

Only by taking cognizance of the role of the powerful "messianic" vector of the 1950's, as briefly sketched above, can we appreciate both the crusading zeal with which Israel pursued the "African option", and the inter-party consensus in the normally polarized *Knesset* whenever issues relating to costly programmes of co-operation with the Third World came up for debate. The fact that idealism meshed perfectly with pragmatism in Israel's foreign policy towards Africa was succinctly recognized by the *Manchester Guardian* when it observed that:

> Israel's policy towards Black Africa should perhaps be seen in wider terms, and should be recognized to be not just part of its defence line against the Arab world, but also of a genuine desire to be of help. Africans respond because they recognize this.[12]

An Asian state, Burma, proved to be Israel's door to Africa. Warm relations and extensive technical co-operation in the mid-1950's between U Nu's Burma and Israel[13] vindicated the arguments of Israel's

"Asia lobby" that the continent of Africa was not axiomatically lost to Israel. And it was in Rangoon (during the first session of the Asian Socialist International Conference) that the first recorded contacts took place between Israeli officials and African trade unionists. Several of the latter, notably from the former Gold Coast, were soon to visit Israel, and on their return home spread the gospel of the importance to Africa of the Israeli development model. When Ghana attained independence, an Israeli Embassy was already in situ—one of only seven in the world—testimony to the importance attached in Jerusalem to its newly-found allies and/or its mission in Africa. By 1960 that embassy was the most influential in Accra; and its ambassador was the envy of the diplomatic corps, being the sole foreign envoy to have immediate access to President Kwame Nkrumah.[14]

Expansion and Collapse

As decolonization proceeded in Africa, so did Israel's aggressive diplomatic expansion. No longer restricted by fiscal considerations, and solidly anchored in a bedrock of pragmatic and ideological legitimacy, Afro-Israeli relations became a *sine qua non* fixture of Israeli foreign policy. From having only six embassies in 1956, Israel by 1964 boasted 75—the world's fourth largest diplomatic network after the United States, France and Great Britain, and second only to France in Africa.

If Burma was Israel's door to Africa, Ghana was the key to that door.[15] Contacts between Israeli and Ghanaian unionists at International Labour Organization (ILO), International Confederation of Free Trade Unions (ICFTU) and various socialist conferences resulted in several early visits of Ghanaians to Israel. Following the 1957 visit of John Tettegah (Secretary-General of the Ghanaian Trade Union Congress) and his highly-publicized exclamation that "Israel has given me more in eight days than I could obtain from two years in a British university",[16] there started an extensive exchange of personnel between the two countries. Scores of ventures were embarked upon, including joint companies, a civic service movement (the Builders' Brigade), experimental farms, an aviation school (which threatened vested British military interests), and a joint merchant marine. The cream of the engineers, doctors and managers of companies/organizations such as Solel Boneh (construction), Tahal (construction/agricultural engineering), Zim (shipping), and Hadassah (medical services) began the pilgrimage to Accra as Israelis suddenly became "possibly the most welcome strangers in Africa".[17]

The case with which Israel's first foothold in Africa had been secured,[18] the speed with which diplomatic relations with the continent's new states expanded, and the bountiful benefits of Israel's newly-found global legitimacy, added further momentum to Israel's African policy. Coming after a decade in the diplomatic wilderness, it certainly appeared as if Israeli diplomacy had finally reached the Promised Land—and this despite concerted Arab efforts to block Israel's leapfrogging over the Arab global trade and diplomatic boycott[19] and vicious Soviet attempts to portray Israel as no more than "fulfilling the role of a Trojan horse for NATO [the North Atlantic Treaty Organization] in Africa".[20]

In 1958, Golda Meir made the first of her five visits to Africa; and in 1962, to underscore Africa's intrinsic value to Israel, seriously-ailing President Itzhak Ben-Zvi was prevailed upon to undertake a series of colourful state visits to five African countries. By 1966 Israel was represented in every single independent sub-Saharan African state except Mauritania and Somalia. (Later, Djibouti also refused to enter into diplomatic relations.) And, despite strident Arab objections, the majority of Africa's leaders had visited Jerusalem at least once. In 1960/61, for example, seven such state visits took place, shattering the provinciality of a capital that had witnessed but one such occasion in its twelve years of independence.

By 1965, over 6,600 African cadres from 37 countries had completed training in Israel in a whole array of skills, and some 2,000 Israeli experts had visited Africa on a variety of missions. These figures were to virtually double by the time of the 1973 Afro-Israeli rupture in diplomatic relations. (In comparison some 5,000 Asians came to Israel during the first period, with 850 Israeli experts travelling to various countries in Asia. Corresponding figures for South America were more modest.) And it should be noted that despite the formal break in relations in 1973, the number of cadres trained in Israel had grown by 1988 to 90,000—over one-half arriving from Africa. Indeed, an additional 1,400 to 1,500 trainees, of whom 35 percent are from Africa, continue to arrive in Israel annually. And as if these figures were not impressive enough, one Ethiopian journalist has calculated that on a per capita basis (one that would more accurately reflect the relative magnitude of Israel's aid, given its small population and developing economy) the 1962 Israeli effort would have been the equivalent of the United States granting Africa one million training bursaries for that year and dispatching 360,000 technical experts to the continent![21]

Details of this remarkable story of technical co-operation need not detain us here, they having been voluminously written up in the 1960s.[22] It is enough to note that by the early 1970s an economically and militarily much stronger Israel had been greatly buttressed by what *Newsweek* referred to as "one of the strangest informal alliances in the world".[23] At the UN, Israeli candidates began to be elected for the first time, with strong African backing, to a variety of posts and committees as representatives of Afro-Asia; and in the General Assembly the first resolutions were submitted calling upon the Arab states to enter into peace negotiations with Israel.[24]

Why then the devastating diplomatic rout in 1973 when 28 African states broke off relations with Israel in a debacle that has no equal in the annals of diplomatic history? How are we to account for the desertion from the Israeli camp of even staunch allies, especially since Egypt was the clear aggressor in the 1973 Yom Kippur War? Still more perplexingly, why has the Afro-Israeli rift not been healed in the decade and a half since then, in spite of the two main combatants in 1973 having long since signed a formal peace treaty?

The answer to these questions is somewhat complex, for a host of factors played a role in eroding the close Afro-Israeli entente of the 1960s. While *Haaretz* was quite correct in drawing attention to the fact that the "brutal pressures of the Arab states in the economic and military spheres"[25] drove many African countries from the Israeli camp, this was but the tip of the iceberg: an array of other important considerations lay concealed. Among these we might note, first, the emergence of Libya's Muammar Gaddafi as Israel's most implacable foe,[26] and the only one willing to pledge his country's resources towards the goal of isolating Israel at every level. While the number of African states actually seduced into breaking with Israel by Gadaffi's "inducements" was small (essentially only Uganda, Chad and Niger),[27] the prospect of securing similar future benefits from Libya undoubtedly played a secondary role in many more. Second, and also of importance, is that Africa's progressive economic pauperization made many states more susceptible to such financial blandishments than to the benefits of continued technical co-operation with Israel. Third, there is of course Africa's ultra-sensitivity to the intrusion of foreign military actors, pushing them automatically to side with a sister African country (Egypt) when "invaded" from beyond the continent's bounds.[28] Fourth, Africa's progressive radicalization (one-fifth of all African countries are currently Marxist) was, moreover, by the 1970s rendering the continent evermore susceptible to anti-Israeli ideological drives. Israel's resistance to calls for the imposition of sanctions and/or the expulsion of South Africa from all international organizations[29] increasingly came to be viewed as proof of Israel's ambivalence in a matter of cardinal importance to the satisfaction of Black African aspirations. And finally, the qualitative and quantitative decline in African eyes of the usefulness of Israel's development model and technical assistance, the relevance of which increasingly came to be questioned in the light of the apparent non-transferability of Israeli models to African situations. This fact, in and of itself, goes a long way towards explaining the magnitude and rapidity of the Israeli diplomatic rout in 1973, and the lengthy freeze in Afro-Israeli relations since then. Let us now examine some of these factors in more detail.

The 1973 Debacle

Indications that Israel's relations with many African states were not truly secure, and that it remained vulnerable to the corrosive influences of a politicized Islam, were not long in the offing. Despite the actual number of African states to maintain diplomatic relations with Israel, a sizeable group could not be counted as firm allies. Two, Somalia and Mauritania, had from the outset refused to establish relations; they were to be joined later by Djibouti and the Comoros. Guinea broke with Israel in the aftermath of the 1967 Six Day War[30] and, despite rosy expectations at first, relations with Tanzania were always very difficult and soon to be severed.[31] A number of other states, such as Ghana and Mali—having joined the militant Casablanca group, which included the Arab Maghreb states, in the years preceding the creation of the Organization of African Unity (OAU)—found themselves under pressure to fall in with the variety of anti-Israeli stances that such membership entailed. Still others, such as the Congo, Dahomey (now Benin), and Malagasy (now Madagascar), drifted from the Israeli orbit with the ousting either of their founding fathers or of some *ancien regime* predisposed in Israel's favour: their radicalization and new international allies now moved them squarely into a confrontational stance vis-a-vis Israel. In other instances, such as in Nigeria and Senegal, the persistent pressure of powerful *mullahs* and other Muslim religious leaders—progressively mobilized in the vendetta against Israel—finally bore fruit as national political leaders withdrew their support from Jerusalem.

It should be noted here that, although there were exceptions in those countries where Israel's effort (public and private) had been greatest, the diplomatic rupture in relations came latest and most reluctantly; and that in most of the countries concerned the Israeli effort had been, objectively viewed, quite modest. The overall statistics on Israel's development role in Africa had all along camouflaged the fact that Israeli aid had been spread quite unevenly. A small minority of key states, economically or politically-speaking, such as Kenya, Cote d'Ivoire, Ghana, Liberia, Nigeria, and to a lesser extent Uganda and Zaire, had over the years received inordinate amounts of aid and attention from Israel; most of the others had benefited only marginally from their relations with Israel. (That they also tended to receive only minimal attention from other donors was irrelevant.) At the same time the drying up of much of Africa's sources of credit owing to global recession and international disenchantment with the continent's prospects, increased the relative value to many African states of fiscal (that is, unencumbered monetary) aid. This was a commodity Israel had rarely provided, but one which Libya and other petro-dollar states could offer in superabundance.

The tenuousness of Israel's position in much of Africa was actually visible prior to the Libyan Revolution of 1969, though it took Gaddafi's arrival on the broader African scene to accelerate the process. Even before fighting broke out in the Middle East in 1973, six states severed relations with Israel—Uganda, Chad, Niger, Burundi, the Congo, and Mali. Libya's hand was clearly visible in the action of the first three, with Idi Amin acting as Gaddafi's surrogate bully to persuade Burundi. (The Maghreb-pulled Mali had always offered but an insecure toe-hold for Israel; and the Congolese break had primarily ideological roots.) Though Israeli officials at the time tended to minimize the rollback of Israel's presence in Africa,[32] it was clear that a new and more dynamic Arab-Israeli tug-of-war had developed in sub-Saharan Africa. The failure of the well-intentioned but naive six-man

"African Sages" peace mission to the Middle East in 1971/72, which
concluded that Israel was the most obdurate of the protagonists, had
tilted against Israel the sentiments of a number of influential non-
aligned African statesmen. And the 1973 Yom Kippur War tipped the
scale completely.[33] As President Mobutu Sese Seko of Zaire most aptly
put it, when faced with a conflict between a brother (Egypt, an African
state) and a friend (Israel), Africa had no choice but to side with the
former.[34]

But the debacle in Africa, leading to the freeze in Afro-Israeli
relations that remains to this very day, had other reasons beyond those
already mentioned. Although one influential Source in the 1970s
noted that "the basic line underlying Israel's policies today is complete
integration with Afro-Asia"[35]—a position to which most Israeli statesmen intermittently paid lip-service—at no time was this even remotely
true. Sincere sympathy for Africa did exist in many Israeli quarters. But
Israel's fundamental national interests were only very indirectly linked
with those of the African continent—so that, although at times great
pains were taken not to offend African sensitivities (as with the
reluctant tilt against South Africa),[36] in any clash between vital Israeli
national interests (close relations with the West, considerations of
military security, protection of World Jewry, and so forth) and mere
secondary interests (the amity of Afro-Asia), the latter inevitably had
to yield. It is indeed difficult to escape the conclusion that never, at
any point, was there truly a commonality of interests between Africa
and Israel beyond the mutual quest for economic development. For
Israel's most basic security interests precluded non-alignment: its
diplomatic allies and military suppliers were exclusively in the West;
and the communist nations were implacable enemies. Israelis, moreover, were loathe to pay lip-service to goals and policies they did not
believe in, such as non-alignment, merely to curry favour with the
Third World. Consistently, then, Israel and Africa had for long been on
different sides of the ideological fence.

Even in economic matters there was little true commonality of
interest between the two erstwhile partners. For quite some time,
rhetoric apart, Israel had no longer been part of the "developing world",
except possibly geographically. The country's stunningly rapid socioeconomic advances and modernization had as early as the 1950s
placed Israel squarely in the ranks of the world's highly developed
states. By the 1980s, Israeli economic indicators had surpassed those

of all but a handful of West European states, pointing to Israel as being among the most developed countries in the world. Ideological philosophizing and diplomatic platitudes notwithstanding, Israel's economic interests were those of an increasingly sophisticated industrial power, and thus fundamentally in opposition to those of Third World primary commodity producers. And of the Third World group, Africa was of only tangential economic importance to Israel. Trade with the continent had never been very extensive. Israeli officials had always made a great deal of the so-called "leaps and bounds" in Afro-Israeli trade, but apart from a limited number of commodities (for example, diamonds and timber, and these from only a few countries—Gabon, the Central African Republic, and Sierra Leone) imports from Africa had always been depressed, and this despite the fact that Israel artificially restricted its importation of tropical products from Latin America in order to favour those from Africa.[37]

Finally, Israel's attraction to Africa had largely worn off. Quantitatively Israel's development role in Africa had been largely taken over by much richer latecomer donors who by the mid-1960s had got their act together, while qualitatively the most innovative of the Israeli socioeconomic experiments were increasingly being seen as not replicable in an African environment, and hence irrelevant. In 1973 the International Labour Organization concluded that "contrary to earlier expectations, the "spillover" or "demonstration" effects of development in limited sectors and areas have at best been marginal. As a result, the masses of the population have benefited little from, and contributed little to, development"[38]—a stunning repudiation of earlier euphoric expectations that, through the multiplier effect, rapid socioeconomic modernization was feasible in developing societies. Much of Israel's efforts in the Third World had rested on this, now disproves, assumption that widespread socio-economic change could be effected through spontaneous self-motivated societal emulation of key model projects, a sequence to be spearheaded and assisted by Israeli-trained "animators". Moreover, Africa had been attracted to some of Israel's socioeconomic and developmental innovations—communal farming, nation-building structures, agricultural- pioneering youth cadres, land reclamation, agrarian training projects, and so on—which turned out to be particularly resistant to implantation in the radically different cultural context of Africa, or were fundamentally transformed when so transplanted.

Structures aimed at eroding primordial loyalties and binding people from various groups to the concept of a new nation, for example, were found to be unworkable in Africa. Indeed, whenever communal settlements, youth structures, paramilitary hierarchies or even agrarian courses were set up with multi-ethnic intakes, points of internal friction often arose that led to inordinately high rates of attrition or desertion. In Dahomey, Nachal-style programmes suffered from attrition rates as high as 70 percent, and compulsion, even force, had to be employed to keep the rest in line—completely contrary to the voluntarism of the Israeli prototype. Communal farming, whether of the kibbutz or moshav type, often proved unworkable as well. Even the prestige of former President Julius Nyerere's brother—who was personally involved in efforts to create kibbutzim in Tanzania—was to no avail. Modern agricultural technology practised on model farms, and leading to vastly-increased productivity, was simply not emulated by farmers in neighbouring traditional villages where this new creation of agrarian surpluses by new technology threatened fundamental and prized values—social status and harmony—and long-term inter-village social relations. Even mounting straightforward agrarian training courses did not necessarily increase the country's cadre of modern agriculturalists. At the conclusion of one such Israeli training programme in Cote d'Ivoire in the mid-1960s, fully 80 percent of the graduates of the eighteen-month course promptly vanished overnight into the country's urban centres to seek clerical work on the strength of their newly-gained agrarian certificates.

In a somewhat different vein, joint companies set up by Israel and host governments were plundered by local political appointees who proved to possess immunity no matter what their misdeeds. In several countries (Togo, Cameroon, Sierra Leone) Israeli-administered national lotteries were ordered by the host government to pay out on patently forged or fraudulent winning tickets presented by "untouchable" political or military personnel—thus siphoning off funds from their intended social betterment targets. Elsewhere, youth and/or youth paramilitary hierarchies were transformed into either machines of patronage (as in Ghana and Cote d'Ivoire) or politicized props for whatever leader happened to be in office (as in Malawi and Uganda). All such developments inevitably undermined much of the credibility of the Israeli aid effort in Africa, as well as threw deeper doubt on its fundamental value to the continent.[39] It is against this setting that the

Libyan petro-dollar drive and the Arab diplomatic campaign for continental solidarity found fertile ground in the aftermath of the 1973
Yom Kippur War.

Towards Normalization

Because Israel's involvement with Africa was not motivated solely by
considerations of self-interest or the quest for UN votes, and because
a great deal more than money and manpower had been invested in
the continent, the diplomatic break when it came was a very traumatic
event for most Israelis. As one official noted: "Nearly every Israeli has
had some intimate contact with Africa and our effort in that continent,
either personally or through a member of his family or a close friend."
Consequently their expulsion from Africa was felt by most Israelis as
a slur on the nation, as well as a personal affront.[40] Bitterness at the
African "betrayal", for so it was referred to in public, was compounded
by the fact that the African states had previously consistently, and
emotionally, affirmed their friendship for Israel—and much higher
standards of behaviour are expected from friends! The stunning collapse of the entire Afro-Israeli diplomatic edifice certainly suggested
that Israel's African policy had been built on shifting sands—indeed a
monumental waste of effort. As the influential *Haaretz* editorialized,
closely mirroring widespread popular sentiment: "...[Africa's] haste to
disown us does not add to our respect for the African countries. We
shall not forget who abandoned us in this, our hour of dire need...[and]
it is unlikely that the restoration of our position in Africa will be high
on Israel's list of priorities for the near future".[41] As the *Jerusalem Post*
also predicted "when Afro-Israeli relations are again restored—and they
inevitably will be—those links will never be the same again. The taste
of betrayal at a time of crisis will remain.[42]

   This sense of betrayal was made yet more bitter by the fact that
with the diplomatic break of 1973 and the eclipse of Israeli influence
in Africa, the continent suddenly lay wide open to its mobilization
behind even more radical anti-Israeli stances. Increasingly crisscrossed
by emissaries from some of Israel's harshest foes, Libya, Iraq and
Kuwait, seduced by promises of developmental largess, and swayed by
the vitriolic rhetoric of the new Palestine Liberation Organization (PLO)
offices which supplanted Israeli embassies throughout the continent,

many African states swung through a full 180 degrees to support a plethora of anti-Israeli positions at the United Nations. The most notorious examples of these were, of course, the 1975 Anti-Zionism Resolution which secured astonishing support from Africa,[43] and the subsequent efforts to oust Israel from the UN and its specialized agencies, efforts that ultimately were to result in the resignation of the United States from the UN Economic, Social and Cultural Organization (UNESCO) on the grounds of its excessive politicization. The venom with which this new anti-Israeli sentiment was expressed in public debates (often by former "staunch allies") and the petty spitefulness of some of the actions taken by African states (such as allocating vacated Israeli embassy premises and staff housing to newly-accredited PLO representatives) further entrenched consensus in Israel that the entire Israeli effort in Africa had been an exercise in futility. Not only had it failed to gain Israel any true allies, but it had signally failed to spread in African circles even an awareness of the intrinsically democratic and peaceful values for which Israel stood.

With Black Africa written off as a bad debt, Israeli foreign policy found itself, of course, freed of a number of hitherto constraining obligations. Israel's strong links with the United States, for example, had been somewhat obscured in the 1960's by the rhetoric of solidarity with the Third World. Now the natural sympathies for the US could again be given free rein. Military options vis-a-vis Israel's Arab neighbours that might have been shelved as potentially disruptive of Israel's standing in the Third World were now pursued without concern for such considerations: the long-range bombing of Iraq's nuclear reactor, and the assault on the PLO offices in Tunisia, to mention only two.[44] And relations with South Africa, previously strained through the need to cater to African sensitivities, received a major boost after 1973.[45]

In the mid-1980's, nevertheless, the Afro-Israeli freeze began to thaw, even though formal relations were not re-established. Many African civic leaders, parliamentarians. and newspapers had condemned at the time the 1973 break in relations—especially the abrupt form it had taken. These initial misgivings received powerful impetus with the realization that the economic blandishments employed to win African states to the Arab cause were extremely miserly, tardy in arriving, or largely fictitious.[46] Thus second thoughts on the wisdom of breaking with Israel surfaced in numerous African capitals, in some instances within months of the diplomatic rupture. Moreover, in many countries, especially in those that had clambered aboard the 1973 bandwagon most reluctantly, a "business as usual" policy had meant that the bulk of Israeli effort remained unaffected by the absence of formal diplomatic relations. Political contacts were now handled through an Israeli Interests Office in some friendly European embassy (for example, Denmark or the Netherlands), or even direct, though without official status—at times within a stone's throw of the newly-established PLO offices, as in Nairobi. The break in diplomatic relations thus did not really mean the complete ousting of Israeli enterprise, effort and personnel from the continent. Indeed, paradoxically, in some countries (notably in Kenya and Cote d'Ivoire) there was a *far greater* Israeli presence after 1973 than before, owing to a local economic boom! Despite the absence of formal political relations decade and a half, for example, Solel Boneh—the giant Israeli construction company to be found in several African countries—continued to transform the physical landscape of Abidjan and Nairobi, possibly doing more for Israel's standing and reputation in Cote d'Ivoire and Kenya than normal diplomatic exchanges could have effected.[47]

In the matter of formal Afro-Israeli contacts, however, despite anti-Arab grumblings in many African quarters, the die was cast. Having moved into the Arab camp in the most unequivocal manner possible, African states found themselves with little room to manoeuvre—even were they so inclined—when faced by exhortations to continued "continental solidarity", especially since the official *casus belli* had not changed. Thus, despite a shift in Africa's mood in favour of Israel, and despite the fact that in many states the break had implied no decline in economic relations, no regularization in the diplomatic field could have been expected until the Israel-Egypt Peace Treaty at last provided an acceptable rationale for a few mavericks to bolt.

With the signature by Israel of the peace treaty with Egypt (the sole "African" belligerent in the Middle East wars) the grounds were laid for Afro-Israeli rapprochement. Yet the ensuing diplomatic normalization was an extremely modest one, and proved to be a very slow-moving process. From Israel's standpoint some African countries (including a few with whom diplomatic relations had previously existed—or example, Mali) can still be seen as irretrievably hostile, fully in the orbit of militant Islam. Most African states are not in fact hostile, but rather exhibit inertia in the absence of any compelling reasons to shift diplomatic allegiance yet again; some, obviously, are only waiting for an "auspicious moment" which will allow them to return to the Israeli fold without undue Arab ostracism.[48] Yet powerful diplomatic drives on Africa have not, as in previous decades, emanated from Jerusalem in order to sway waverers to Israel's orbit. The 1987 and 1988 African visits of Shimon Peres and Itzhak Shamir were motivated more by a desire to plaster over cracks in the minimalist Israeli diplomatic network in Africa than aggressively expand it. Clearly the basic paradigms of Israel's Third World policy have changed radically since 1973.

The Israel of the 1980s is substantially different from the Israel of the 1960s. The country is no longer merely a modest Middle East regional power, but increasingly a global actor of significant economic, political, military and—as is now clear—nuclear clout. Though facing the same intractable difficulties in the Middle East as in previous decades, Israel's international foundations are solidly established. Its importance to the United States as a sincere and reliable ally is beyond question, as was revealed by its unfortunate middleman role in the Irangate Affair. And Israel's sources of advanced military technology are progressively internal, making it an important supplier of sophisticated war material, as well as increasingly self-sufficient and hence not easily pressured by others. The recent thaw in Soviet-Israeli relations has as much to do with these Israeli strengths as it has with Mikhail Gorbachev's reforms in the Soviet Union. To such an Israel the diplomatic importance of African allies has very seriously declined, especially since the continent's acute fickleness has been demonstrated.

There is also an intense awareness in Israeli circles that their highly emotional attachment of the past to Afro-Israeli amity had been fundamentally unhealthy in that it nurtured exaggerated expectations on either side. As one source put it: "Expectations on both sides have been tempered by the period of strained relations...both sides have come to understand that good intentions alone cannot be concrete expressions without regard to the constraints of real political life."[49] And this is quite apart from the fact that the 1950's debate on Israel's possible messianic role in the twentieth century was by the 1980s half-forgotten history to most blase Israelis and hard-nosed political leaders. Moreover, in the context of the shift to the right in the centre of gravity of Israeli politics, the previous period's over-concentration on social and political relations wit Africa to the exclusion, in many instances, of economic considerations, was likewise rejected by the new generation of Israeli policy-makers as not conducive to normal and stable relations. Avi Primor, former Assistant Director-General of the Israeli Foreign Ministry and Director of its Asia and Oceanic Division, expressed these changed perceptions in Jerusalem when he noted that in the 1960's "economic ties were neglected in comparison to social and political aims. This we have acknowledged as having been a mistake and thus we are currently emphasizing economic ties."[50] In Israel itself the state was progressively decreasing its role in the parastatal sector, privatization proceeding under right-wing or national unity governments. Clearly, in any instance of Afro-Israeli rapprochement, it would be the Israeli private sector that would now be expected to take the lead; and this almost by definition implies that future Afro-Israeli relations would have to be based purely on pragmatic considerations, on mutual interest—again a major departure from the unbridled state-to-state aid of earlier decades.

In such a dramatically changed context, "normalization of relations" assumes a different meaning. While Israel still values diplomatic allies and is fundamentally committed to offer technical assistance to Africa, the scale of its effort is much more modest and its scope more realistic. Gone are the golden days of frantic diplomatic lobbying, Afro-Israeli politicking for a greater slice of the cake, grandiose dreams of a powerful Afro-Israeli juggernaut entente, and noble but Quixotic assaults on the social ills of the day. Israeli embassies in Africa are incredibly lean these days, as if to underscore the principle that the new Israeli toe-holds on the continent are grudgingly there in the first place and should be prized by the host government. Israeli staff in the embassies in Lilongwe and Abidjan in 1988, for example, comprised exactly two career diplomats (aided by 2 to 4 support personnel in each capital), down dramatically from the numbers that staffed, for instance, the bustling key Israeli outpost in Abidjan in the 1960's! Moreover, Israeli officials warn that even should a massive diplomatic rapprochement develop in the future, few African countries would house full-fledged resident Israeli embassies.

This much scaled-down Israeli presence in the continent, and the fact that no longer do offers of training scholarships or other forms of state aid come readily, have inevitably led to aggrieved complaint from those (such as Zaire) that had expected far greater benefits, as in "olden days",[51] from the resumption of relations with Israel. It also throws light on the reasons why African states that might politically be inclined to re-establish diplomatic relations with Israel, see no particular economic "inducements" or urgency for doing so. For if their national economies offer little of interest to Israeli entrepreneurs, relations are likely to be little more than diplomatic formalities: admittedly akin to those they maintain with much of the world, but hardly worth antagonizing the Arab world over.

The fact that in the new Israeli diplomacy, private enterprise now has pride of place has at times caused great embarrassment to Israel. Shady international consortia have always been attracted to a number of mineral-rich countries in Africa (for example, the diamond-rich Central African Republic), and an Israeli "connection" has increasingly been visible in various fiascos on the continent. Claims that Israel is after all "a nation like all other nations", and that its government cannot be held accountable for the fast dealings of some of its nationals, hardly cut much ice with offended host governments. The Kalmanowitch Affair, for example, ruffled many African feathers and shook a number of political thrones. Repercussions created major embarrassment for several of the South African "homelands" in which Shabtai Kalmanowitch was involved, and indeed played a role in the attempted 1987 coup against Lucas Mangope in Bophuthatswana. (Kalmanowitch had been known there as "Mangope's Rasputin", and full details of his economic dealings have never been revealed.) Other Israeli peccadilloes have periodically surfaced in Transkei and Ciskei; but this could have been expected: the homelands have always been irrelevant internationally, and little more than South African-sanctioned patronage outlets and cesspools of corruption aimed at consolidating a measure of collaborationist African elite support for the beleaguered regime in Pretoria. More disappointing to Israel was the fact that because of Kalmanowitch's major economic role in diamonds in Sierra Leone, where he had close personal relations with President Joseph Momoh, the anticipated re-establishment there of relations with Israel was postponed.[52] And though Sierra Leone was hardly a key state, this setback was enough to arrest the momentum of the Israeli "return to Africa" until the December 1988 decision by Kenya to formalize its long-standing and extremely close relations with Israel.

It is a strange fact of international life that apart from the construction/hydraulic engineering activities in Africa of several of Israel's larger companies, recently scaled down as a result of the economic downturn, and the multifaceted investments of scores of private entrepreneurs, much of the new Israeli effort in Africa in recent years has been in the security field, where both private and state expertise has been solicited by African states constantly threatened by praetorian assault from within. Israeli technical and manpower infusions have strongly bolstered the presidential guards in Liberia, Zaire, Cameroon, and Togo, among others. Some informants even suggest that in two of these four countries diplomatic relations may have been resumed solely in order to secure this benefit from Israel! In Liberia, Israeli-trained troops (commanded by Israeli instructors) foiled the dangerous, allegedly Central Intelligence Agency (CIA)-sponsored coup of 1985 against President Samuel Doe.

And even in Marxist Ethiopia, Israel played a crucial military role in the late 1970s, selling the embattled regime war material (Soviet booty captured from the Arabs in previous wars), training its elite combat troops, and even assisting in the unloading and readying of war materiel flown in to Addis Ababa airport from the Soviet Union and Libya!

Conclusion

The nature of Afro-Israeli relations in 1989 is therefore quite different from what it was in the early 1970s. Much more "normal" and healthy in many respects, it better reflects different national interests and balanced pragmatic expectations on both sides. The much reduced official Israeli presence on the continent merely reflects the continued reality of the polarization of Afro-Asia over the Middle East dilemma. Yet despite Africa's split on this issue, a residue of amity for Israel remains in many states. As Primor has noted: "If we consider the voting patterns in international organizations ... we can derive satisfaction that African voting patterns over the last few years have improved significantly in Israel's favour".[53] In the real world of the 1980s this may possibly be all that can be expected; and from Africa, for the much stronger Israel of today, this may be all that is desired.

FOOTNOTES

1. See Eytan, W., *The First Ten Years*, Simon and Schuster, New York, 1958; Dagan, A., *Moscow and Jerusalem: Thirty Years of relations between Israel and the Soviet Union*, Abelard-Schuman. New York, 1970 and Safran, N., *The United States and Israel*, Harvard University Press, Cambridge (Massachusetts), 1963.

2. For Israeli perceptions of the United Nations, See Carnegie Endowment for International Peace. *Israel and the United Nations*, Manhattan Publishing Co., New York, 1956, pp. 289 and 293.

3. A leading Burmese newspaper highlighted this when it noted: "...though white men, Israelis consider themselves Asians." See *Jerusalem Post* (Jerusalem), March 25, 1956. In 1962, Prime Minister David Ben-Gurion complained that Israel's struggle for self-determination and independence against Britain was the only liberation movement in Asia not recognized as a genuinely anti-colonialist struggle; see *Israel Weekly News Bulletin* (Jerusalem), May 16-22, 1962.

4. For an early definitive study of Israel's foreign policy, see Michael Brecher's two volume study *The Foreign-Policy System of Israel*, Yale University Press, New Haven (Connecticut), 1972 and 1975. See also Roberts, S., *Survival or Hegemony: The Foundations of Israeli Foreign Policy*, Johns Hopkins University Press, Baltimore (Maryland), 1973.

5. Cited in Decalo, S., "Israeli's Foreign Policy and the Third World", in *Orbis* (Vol. 11 No. 3, Fall 1967), p. 729.

6. Divrei Haknesset, October 24-26, 1960, p. 12. See also the report in Israel Economist (Jerusalem), July 1961, p. 115; and Lengyel, E., "Israel's Campaign in Africa", in The Reporter (Jerusalem), February 4, 1960, pp. 11-13.

7. *Haaretz* (Tel-Aviv), August 19 1962.

8. Interview conducted by the author in Jerusalem on July 19 1964.

9. Though most of Africa became independent after 1957, Israel's fixation on Washington and European capitals, coupled with an extremely parsimonious policy regarding the accreditation of full-scale embassies, resulted in Israel having only seven embassies throughout the entire world in 1957. The one in Argentina was, moreover, the sole Embassy in the Third World.

10. For a fuller exploration of this theme, see Decalo, S., *Messianic Influences in Israeli Foreign Policy* (Occasional Papers in Political Science No. 2, University of Rhode Island, Kingston, 1967); and Decalo, S., "Messianic Influences and Pragmatic Limitations on Israeli Foreign Policy", in Mushkat, M. (ed.), *World Society: Changing Structures and Laws*, Mouton, The Hague, 1973, pp. 373-382.

11. A great deal of literature was published in the 1960's on the relevance of Israeli socialism to the Third World. See, inter alia, Braunthal, J. and J.B. Kripalani, *The Significance of Israeli Socialism*, Lincolns-Prager, London, 1958; Klatzmann, J., *Les enseignements de l'experience israelienne*, Editions Tiers-Monde, Paris, 1963; Maissi, E., "Israel et son exemple", in *Cahiers Africaines* (vol. 2, 1961); Franck, M., *Cooperative Land Settlements in Israel and their Relevance to AfricanCountries*, Kylos Velag, Basel, 1968; and Moch, J., "Israel, Yougoslavie, Chine: Trois Methodes", in La Revue Socialiste (No. 163, May 1963).

12. Cited in *Jerusalem Post* (Jerusalem), August 17, 1962.

13. Including assistance in the creation and management of Burma's Five Star Line (shipping), military training, assistance with the establishment of communal settlements, and so forth. See also Medzini, M., "Reflections on Israel's Asian Policy", in *Midstream* (Vol. 18, No. 6, June-July 1972), pp. 22-35.

14. Oakes, J.B., *The Edge of Freedom*, Harper and Row, New York, 1961, p. 45.

15. For an annotated bibliography of the early literature, see Decalo, S., "Israel and Africa", in *Journal of Modern African Studies* (vol. 5, No. 3, November 1967), pp. 385-399.

16. Cited in *Jerusalem Post* (Jerusalem), July 23, 1957.

17. *New York Times* (New York), October 16, 1960.

18. Liberia and Ethiopia, the only two historically independent African states, had been virtually ignored by Israel until after 1957.

19. See Ismael, T., The *UAR in Africa*, Northwestern University Press, Evanston (Illinois), 1971.

20. *Izvestiia* (Moscow), December 12, 1960. See also the diatribes against the growing Israeli effort in Africa in the issues of Moscow's *International Affairs* (Vol. 7, No. 1, January 1961; Vol. 7, No. 10, October 1961; and Vol. 15, No. 7, July 1969); and Nikitina, G.S., "Ekspansiya Israelya v. Afrike i neokolonialism", in *Narodny Azii i Afriki* (No. 3, 1963).

21. *Ethiopian Herald* (Addis Ababa), July 19, 1969.

22. See, inter alia, Churba, J., UAR-Israel Rivalry over Aid and Trade in Sub-Saharan Africa (PhD. Thesis, Columbia University, New York, 1965); Amir, S., *Israel's Developmental Cooperation with Africa, Asia, and Latin America*, Praeger, New York, 1974; Decalo, S., Israel and Africa: The Politics of Cooperation—A Study of Foreign Policy and Technical Assistance (PhD. Thesis, University of Pennsylvania, Philadelphia, 1970); Curtis, M. (ed.), *Israel and the Third World*, Transaction Press, New Brunswick (New Jersey), 1976; Rodin, T.S., Political Aspects of Israeli Foreign Aid in Africa (PhD. Thesis, University of Nebraska, Lincoln, 1969); Jacob, A., Israel's Foreign Aid Program in Africa (PhD. Thesis, University of California, Los Angeles, 1969);

Jacob, A., "Israel's Military Aid to Africa, 1960-66", in *Journal of Modern African Studies* (Vol. 9, No. 2, August 1971), pp. 165-187; Reich, B., "Israel's Policy in Africa", in *Middle East Journal* (Vol. 18, No. 1, Winter 1964), pp. 14-26; Almog,J., "Pourquoi Israel va en Afrique", in *Revue Française d'Etudes Politiques Africaines* (No. 20, August 1967), pp. 17-21; Catarivas, D., "Sept ans de relations entre Israel et les Etats francophones d'Afrique", in *Revue Française d'Etudes Politiques Africaines* (No. 20, August 1967), pp. 31-42; Klinghoffer, A.J., "Israel in Africa: The Strategy of aid", in, *Africa Report* (Vol. 17, No. 4, April 1972), pp. 12-14; Laufer, L., Israel and the Developing Countries, Twentieth Century Fund, New York, 1967; and Kreinin, M., *Israel and Africa: A Study in Technical Cooperation*, Praeger, New York, 1964.

23. See "A Surplus of Brains", in *Newsweek* (New York), August 20, 1962.

24. See, inter alia, Decalo, S., "Africa and the Mid-Eastern War", in *Africa Report* (Vol. 12, No. 7, October 1967), pp. 57-61.

25. *Haaretz* (Tel-Aviv), November 2, 1973. Gitelson, in her own research, distinguishes between the bullying tactics at the UN of the Libyans, the soft-sell approach of the Egyptians and the statesmanship of the Tunisians as they worked to swing the African states against Israel see Gitelson, S.A., "Israel's African Setback in Perspective", in Curtis, M. (ed.), *Israel in the Third World*, Transaction Press, New Brunswick (New Jersey), 1976, pp. 182- 199. ,

26. See Decalo, S., "Libya's Qaddafi: Bedouin Product of the Space Age", in *Present Tense* (Vol 1, No. 2, Winter 1974), pp. 50-54; and Rondot, P., "La philosophie politique du Colonel Kadhafi", in *Revue Française d'Etudes Politiques Africaines* (No. 81, September 1972), pp, 106-117

27. Gueriviere, J., "Ouganda: Traversée du desert pour Israel", in *Revue Française d'Etudes Politiques Africaines* (No. 76, April 1972), pp. 15-17; and Legum, C., "Israel's Year in Africa: Study of Secret Diplomacy", in *Africa Contemporary Record, 1972-73*, Africana Publishing Co., New York, 1973, pp. A123-A136.

28. A photograph which appeared in much of the Israeli press showing Israeli troops driving into Egypt under a banner proclaiming "We Have Returned to Africa" was reprinted in several African newspapers and did Israel incalculable harm.

29. A voluminous literature has blossomed around this theme: see the distinctly different assessments of Israeli-South African relations contained in, inter alia, Hunter, J., *Israeli Foreign Policy: South Africa and Central America*, South End Press, Boston, 1987; Gastratian, S.M., *Izrail i UAR: tseli i formu sotrudnichestva*, Nauka, Moscow, 1987; Adams, J., *The Unnatural Alliance*, Quartet Books, London 1984; Bergman, E., *South Africa and Israel: Different Countries with Common Problems*, South African Institute of International Affairs, Johannesburg, 1988; Benabdallah, A., *L'Alliance raciste israelo-africaine*, Editions Canada-Monde Arabe, Montreal, 1979; Osia, K., *Israel, South Africa and Black.Africa: a Study of the Primacy of the Politics of Expediency*, University Press of America, Washington, DC, 1981; Bunzi, J., *Die Vereinigter Staaten, Israel und Sudafrika,*

Austrian Institute of International Affairs, Vienna, 1981; *South Africa and Israel*, Madison Area Committee on South Africa, Madison, Wisconsin, 1971; and Stevens, R.P. and A. Elmessiri, *Israel and South Africa*, New World Press, New York, 1976. See also the two-part article by Kreindler,J.D., "Israel et l'Afrique du Sud", in the August-September and October-November 1982 issues of *Revue Française d'Etudes Politiques Africaines*.

30. Guinea was probably "lost" to Israel in any case, consequent on Israel's unwillingness to antagonize France (then, its prime ally) by recognizing the country that had just been expelled by Charles de Gaulle from the French Community. For the broader issues, see Crosbie, S.K., *A Tacit Alliance: France and Israel from Suez to the Six Day War*, Princeton University Press, Princeton (New Jersey), 1974; and Balta, P. and C. Rulleau, *La Politique Arabe de la France de de Gaulle a Pompidou*, Sindbad, Paris, 1974.

31. See the report on his tenure as Israel's first Ambassador to Dar es Salaam by Rafael Rupin: *Schlichut LeTanganyika* [Assignment to Tanganyika], Ministry of Defence, Tel-Aviv, 1986.

32. When the author was conducting research in Mali, in the summer of 1972, Israeli Embassy officials in Bamako rationalized the deteriorating relations and imminent diplomatic break primarily by referring to the minimal aid effort Israel was capable of mounting in a country historically pulled towards the Maghreb, and the latter's militantly anti-Israeli religious message. At the time, the entire Israeli presence in Mali consisted of two diplomats and their families, a fisheries expert sponsored by the World Health Organization and based in distant Mopti, and a navigator working for Air Mali in his, private capacity. Nevertheless, considerable goodwill for Israel existed, as was clearly manifest by the numerous and spontaneous expressions of condolence the Embassy received following the 1972 Munich Olympics massacre from casual passers-by and from Mali cadres trained in Israel.

33. Kochan, R., "An African Peace Mission in the Middle East: The One-Man Initiative of President Senghor", in *African Affairs* (Vol. 72, No. 287, April 1973), pp. 186-196; and Gitelson, S.A., "The OAU Mission and the Middle East Conflict", in *International Organization* (Vol. 27, No. 3, 1973), pp. 413-419.

34. Cited in *Jerusalem Post* (Jerusalem), October 5, 1973. See also Rash, Y., "Les Annees Israeliennes en Afrique: Un bilan", in *Revue Française d'Etudes Politiques Africaines* (No. 171/172, February-March 1981), pp. 18-26.

35. See report in *Israel Economist* (Jerusalem), September 1970, p. 35.

36. Though often indicating repugnance for the practices of racist South Africa, Israel has always opposed the imposition of mandatory sanctions. This has been largely consequent to very pragmatic considerations relating to, *inter alia*, an awareness that a precedent of mandatory sanctions could later be employed against Israel as well (as had indeed been demanded several times in the past by the Arab states); a retention of access

to South Africa's mineral resources; and the protection of the status of that country's important Jewish community.

37. Israel has been a prime importer of a number of commodities from African states such as Gabon (at one time Israel was the latter's second-best customer for tropical hardwoods), and the Central African Republic and Sierra Leone (diamonds); conversely, Africa has periodically been a prime importer of a number of Israeli commodities. However, overall Afro-Israeli trade has always been negligible, accounting for only between 2 and 4 percent of Israel's global trade.

38. International Labour Organization. *Human Dignity Economic Growth and Social justice in Changing Africa:* An ILO Agenda for Africa. ILO, Geneva, 1973, p. 31.

39. For further analysis in this vein, see Decalo, S., "Afro-Israeli Technical Cooperation: Patterns of Setbacks and Successes", in Curtis, M. (ed.), *Israel and the Third World*, Transaction Press, New Brunswick (New Jersey), 1976 pp. 81-99. For some detailed case studies, especially of implementation problems and fiascoes, see Hershlag, Z. Y. (ed.), *Israel-Africa Cooperation*, Tel-Aviv University, Tel-Aviv, 1973.

40. Interview conducted by the author in Jerusalem on July 17, 1979.

41. *Haaretz* (Tel-Aviv), November 2, 1973 (emphasis added).

42. *Jerusalem Post* (Jerusalem), October 26, 1973.

43. For details of the UN debate and its background, see Decalo, S., "Africa and the UN Anti-Zionism Resolution: Roots and Causes", in *Cultures et Developpement* (Vol. 8, No. 1, 1976), pp. 89- 117.

44. Interview conducted by the author in Tel-Aviv in February 1987.

45. Apart from the multitude of trade interests the two countries have in common. Israel served in the 1980's as one of South Africa's prime sanctions-busters. Moreover, South Africa has served as a magnet for Israel's surplus intelligentsia and unemployed. All this has brought impassioned outcries from liberal critics in Israel, and dismay in American circles. Particularly galling has been the cooperation between the two countries in military and nuclear matters, consummated by the explosion in the South Atlantic of an Israeli nuclear device, and the revelation that South Africa's nuclear industry had been assisted by Israel's. Furthermore, when the *Knesset* met to finally scrap Israel's controversial Lavi aircraft project, South African Armscor officials were waiting outside the Israel Arms Industries buildings with incredibly lucrative contracts to sign on up to 60 top Israeli engineers.

46. Gabon, Equatorial Guinea, the Central African Republic, Sierra Leone, Senegal and Nigeria—though in the latter two instances the likelihood in the near future is slim.

47. In Cote d'Ivoire, Solel Boneh was the officially-favoured prime contractor for a host of government projects (including, most recently, the mammoth futuristic Abidjan Cathedral, and the upgrading of Yamoussoukro Airport to international standards).

48. As Aynor summed it up: "The African states have learned their lesson...got nothing out of the break... [and were] taken for granted by the Arabs." See Aynor, H. S., "Africa-Israel: Trade and Commercial Relations", in *Israel Economist* (Jerusalem), Special Issue, February 1988, p. A52.

49. Mollov, B., "Expectations for the Future", in *Israel Economist* (Jerusalem), Special Issue, February 1988, p. A7.

50. *Ibid*, p. A8.

51. See, for example, the ire of Zaire as reported in "Zaire/Israel: Reality Sets In", in *Africa Confidential* (vol. 29, No. 16, August 12, 1988), p. 8.

52. See "Sierra Leone: Middle East War", in *Africa Confidential* (vol. 29, No. 16, August 12, 1988), p. 8.

53. Mollov, B., "Expectations for the Future", in *Israel Economist* (Jerusalem), Special Issue, February 1988, p. A8.

11 A NATION LIKE ALL NATIONS: THE NORMALIZATION. ISRAEL AND AFRICA IN THE NINETIES—AN EPILOGUE*

The trauma on the Israeli body-politic of Africa's 1972/73 "betrayal"—the near-total rupture of diplomatic relations between Africa and Israel—took a decade to heal, and it was Africa that suffered from the break in relations. For the vacuum created by Israel's departure from Africa was not filled well by the Arab world, if only because money was all most could (if they wished to) offer. Africa's massive tilt towards the Arab camp did result in the establishment (often visibly reluctantly) in many of them of new Arab Embassies and PLO Offices), while Libyan petrodollars (especially) brought about an infusion of capital to some fifteen states for cultural projects (e.g. the construction of mosques, koranic schools, medresas, etc.) But fewer were the African states to receive (parsimoniously doled-out) development funds from their new benefactors (mostly for joint companies, banks, etc.), which, in any case, were as often as not largely defunct by the mid-1980's.

A number of African states (e.g. Ghana, the Central African Republic) retained informal relations with Israel (via special Interests Offices Israel attached to friendly Embassies in Africa), and bilateral economic relations actually mushroomed with several (e.g. Cote d'Ivoire, Nigeria, Kenya, Gabon) well beyond levels prevailing in 1973. Solel Boneh, Israel's large construction builder, for example, landed huge contracts in Nigeria, Kenya and Cote d'Ivoire for a decade after the break, and in the latter country, until the economic malaise of the mid-1980's there were two large Israeli schools serving the educational needs of children of Israelis working in the country.[1] But these countries, were, first of all, the exceptions, and secondly, residual Afro-Israeli relations had, by the turn of the decade become purely commercial in nature. In 1980, for example, Israeli exports to Africa

*First time published.

had more than tripled to $110 million, and this was to progressively increase in subsequent years.

Israel's technical assistance program did not completely whither after 1972/73, but it did dramatically contract. While most African states requested that Israel continue her aid programs despite the diplomatic rupture in relations, the idea was untenable in practice and repugnant to Jerusalem. Thus in 1978 there were only 23 Israeli experts working in all of Africa, down from the hundreds that had formerly been dispatched annually. And if before 1972 one could hardly move around in Israel without noticing African faces everywhere, by 1980 these were very rare indeed.

This ossification in Israel's technical assistance effort was also, as noted elsewhere[2], due to the fact that Israel's socio-economic innovations did not strike root well in Africa, and because the financial pauperization of most African economies left few funds available for development projects, let alone those, such as Israel's, targeting rural populations. But the core reason was Jerusalem's total disinclination to play a double-faced game and lay out aid for countries diplomatically hostile to her.

In turn, many African states that in 1972/73 were trapped, cajoled, or persuaded to break relations with Israel, found it impossible in subsequent years to resist Arab pressures for other harsh denunciations at the U.N., especially as now freed from African constraints Israeli ties with South Africa rapidly escalated. Africa's heavy (though hardly unanimous) support for the November 1975 anti-Zionism vote in particular riled many in Israel, including key officials. One of them remarked, over a decade after the event with disgust in his voice "it is unbelievable with what venom and gratuitous spite some of those we thought were friends rose to denounce us at international forums."[3]

As the drive for peace in the Middle East acquired momentum after the 1979 peace treaty between Israel and Egypt (as the only African country in the conflict, allegedly the *cassus belli* for the Afro-Israeli rupture in relations), the diplomatic balance tilted slightly towards Israel.[4] Many Africans, formerly trained in Israel, had reached senior positions, and were pushing for a new entente; others had opposed the break all along; and yet others were by now thoroughly disenchanted with the parsimonious aid the Arab world had granted, by the loss of Israeli know-how and cooperative ventures, and increasingly by Qaddhafi's expansionist and de-stabilizing efforts in Black Africa.[5]

Throughout the 1970's, however, Israel did nothing to try to repair the damage in Africa, and, somewhat more surprisingly, there was little effort in Jerusalem to exploit the tensions and contradictions in the new Afro-Arab entente that had emerged. Africa ceased to exist as even a secondary, or minor, focus of interest for the Foreign Ministry. For many policy-makers the continent had fallen over the edge of the world, and they did not wish to be reminded of their earlier quixotic dreams of an Afro-Israeli juggernaut.

Moreover, Israel was rapidly evolving into a mature and *global* power, economically, politically, militarily, and even diplomatically. On every per capita indicator Israel was in the 1980's integrally part of the First World, and on some indicators—e.g. doctors per capita, newspaper readership, literacy and education—Israel was a front-runner. Even on per capita income, despite massive Israeli moanings (a function more of heavy taxation for defence purposes), the country actually was *ahead* of many West European states! The country had thus completely distanced itself from most of the Third World, whose fickleness and double-facedness a new generation was conditioned to be extremely suspicious of. Within such a changed context, to paraphrase the parlance used in an earlier article, the road to Washington, Paris and London, no longer went through Rangoon or Accra: indeed, a direct superhighway by now linked Jerusalem with Washington. And as the 1990's dawned a score of pauperized African states suddenly discovered that *their* road to salvation via the West went through Israel![6]

If the 1970's was the "lost decade" in Afro-Israeli relations, the 1980's, first under Foreign Minister Itzhak Shamir (and later Ariel Sharon), and with Dr. David Kimche (one of Israel's Third World experts) as Director General, saw the first major new effort at mending fences with Africa. But this new thrust was one of extreme pragmatism, divorced of even a whiff of earlier "messianic" strivings. The "era of tachlis"[7] is how one author referred to the 1980's: they can equally well be called the decade when Israel finally became "a nation like all nations" motivated primarily by core national interests. And within such a context, Africa could not but play a minor role.

The normalization of diplomatic relations in the 1980's was an excruciatingly slow process, and for several reasons, inertia on the part of Africa certainly being one. On the Israeli side despite a few task forces spanning several ministries set up to facilitate the drive (and especially one between the foreign and the defence ministries, that now replaced the ministry of agriculture that had been the dominant one in the 1960's), the drive was selective, targeting the economically stronger countries, and those that had never voiced rabid anti-Israel rhetoric. Additional factors that slowed the normalization was the fact that with only a few exceptions (and even then belatedly, reluctantly, and minimally) Israel refused to offer serious economic inducements to those African states (e.g. Zaire) who wanted to barter their allegiances. Moreover, Israel was now willing to settle for informal *modus vivendi* relations (that would facilitate trade) that she had largely rejected in the 1970's. Since this allowed African states to continue to straddle the fence, gaining the best of both worlds, many did so. And, finally, by now Israel's massive cooperation with South Africa (where an incredible 200,000 Israelis now resided) had become a major stumbling bloc for many an African state, and especially those (e.g. Nigeria) that envisaged themselves as African pace-setters.

Still, in the early and mid-1980's numerous secret and not so secret contacts were forged by the Israeli Foreign Ministry as it mounted its "comeback," and various military protocols were signed with states such as Zaire, Gabon and the Central African Republic. With others (e.g. Cote d'Ivoire, Togo, Kenya) such formal treaties were simply unnecessary, as their leaders had maintained warm relations with Israel throughout the difficult 1970's. Limited non-military technical assistance was also progressively granted, but this time usually in the form of courses for African trainees in Israel, fully subsidized by external donors such as Sweden, the Netherlands and the USA.[8]

Ultimately it was military cooperation that opened the door to Africa for Israel in the 1980's. With most states under acute internal stress, external subversion, and intermittently reeling under internal coup bids,[9] African leaders sought out from Israel assistance in its acknowledged *forte*, security—to set up praetorian guards against internal enemies, elite units against external ones, and secure Intelligence data (often of CIA origin) on Libyan designs in Africa. Indeed, though some leaders still sought out Israeli aid in agriculture (the prime field of cooperation in the 1960's), by the 1980's virtually all sought out military aid.[10] Not paradoxically, in their quest for such benefits former hard-line anti-Israel foes—e.g. Chad's Habre, Ethiopia's Haile Mariam, and Liberia's Doe—made complete diplomatic somersaults to secure Israeli aid. But for long—despite constant rumours about one or another African state—Zaire and Liberia were the only to officially renew relations with Israel.[11]

While the earlier era's "messianic" thrust in Africa was not particularly opposed in Israel (and if criticisms did arise, these were mainly about unfunded local agendas that had to be sacrificed), the new "military" links with the continent triggered considerable opposition in liberal and intellectual circles.[12] Until then Israelis had prided themselves of their moral righteousness. Suddenly their allies were Africa's pariahs, and the worst dictators of the continent: South Africa's Vorster (who visited Israel, and with whom nuclear cooperation was agreed to boot), Zaire's Mobutu, Liberia's Doe, Haile Mariam's Ethiopia!

It was only in the mid-1980's that the first real break came. On February 12, 1986 President Houphouet-Boigny—with whom "non-relations" had been warmer than formal relations with many a state—announced Cote d'Ivoire would re-establish diplomatic relations, and an Embassy in Jerusalem. President Biya of Cameroun—whose Presidential Guard had been completely revamped by Israel earlier, and with whom close relations had mushroomed—soon followed suit. Indeed in August Prime Minister Peres paid a State Visit to Yaounde, becoming the first Israeli Premier to be hosted in any African capital in twenty years. Togo joined suit the next year, in June 1987, within days of which the new Prime Minister, Shamir, paid a State Visit to Lome. Nigeria, however, continued to straddle the fence, despite considerable domestic pressure for a diplomatic normalization, and the fact that by now over 1,400 Israelis were working in the country, carrying out major work that "would not disgrace a semi-power." (At the time throughout the continent various Israeli companies were carrying out projects valued at over $500 million.[13]

A reassessment in the Foreign Ministry at the time resulted in a partial policy shift with levels of Israeli technical assistance going up. Once again agrarian training and trade union leadership courses (now heavily for Southern Africa) began to be mounted, though military aid retained pride of place. The five vintage Israeli centers involved with Africa were again the Mt. Carmel Center in Haifa, that organized seminars for African women in an array of development tasks; the Settlement Study Center in Rehovot, that offered training in regional planning and agrarian research; the Agricultural Center, providing experts and technical assistance for optimal usage of resources; the Foreign Training Department, teaching the "multiplier effect" to rural animators; and the Afro-Asian Institute of the Histadrut, teaching an array of trade union activities. The latter, in particular, was active in serving the "new" South Africa, part of a conscious effort to mend faces with the ANC and Mandela, both of whom had been relatively ignored during the days of apartheid, in favor of Chief Gatsha Buthelezi.[14]

The trickle of the mid-1980's continued, as African states slowly came back to the Israeli fold, but it was really in the post-liberalization era of the 1990's that it assumed the proportions of a flood. A massive re-establishment of diplomatic relations with Israel took place in 1991/92, and not just on the part of Africa. This was one benefit of the collapse of global Marxism, that saw the removal from office of Africa's so-called People's Republics, and other radical regimes, that had been among Israel's most implacable foes.[15] In rapid succession in mid-1992, for example, eight African states, including Zambia, Congo, Gambia, Seychelles, and Nigeria (in May 1992)[16] normalized their status with Jerusalem, as one of Israel's darkest episodes finally came to an end. Indeed, when in January 1993 two of Eritrea's key leaders were flown to Israel for treatment for cerebral malaria, no one even gave a moment's thought to the fact that only a few years earlier the Eritrean Liberation Front (fighting for independence from Ethiopia) had been wholly under the sway of rabid pan-Arabists!

Today, in 1997, the circle is thus complete. Israel is back in full strength in Africa. But despite her presence, the effort expanded today is only commensurate to Israel's global interests and Africa's importance. The basic guidelines of the new Israeli foreign policy, visible as early as 1981, are still in place. State-to-State to aid is still extended, but frugally and cooperatively; Israeli Embassies in Africa are lean and understaffed—intentionally so. Private enterprise and trade have pride of place, as the normalization proceeds. A more normal and healthier relationship has been laid in place, based on a mutuality of interests, and it is more likely to be sustained than the old emotional one of the sixties and early 1970's.

FOOTNOTES

1. Including Israelis helping build the massive Basilica in President Houphouet-Boigny's home-town.

2. See chapters 5 and 9 in this volume.

3. Interview in Jerusalem, December 12, 1988.

4. For a summary of some African reactions to the peace accords see Susan Aurelia Gitelson, "African Press Reactions to the Camp David Summit and to the Israel-Egypt Treaty," *Geneve-Afrique*, vol. 17 no. 1, 1979, pp. 183-195.

5. "Afro-Arab and Muslim Relations," in Colin Legum (ed.), *Africa Contemporary Record 1985-86.* New York: Africana Publishing Co., 1986, pp. A162-A175.

6. Certainly a significant number of states that sought rapprochement with Israel, starting with Zaire and Liberia, but including Togo and Chad, did so out of a feeling that this would endear them, or "clean" their hitherto tarnished credentials with Washington!

7. Lawrence P. Frank, "Israel and Africa: the Era of Tachlis," *Journal of Modern African Studies.*

8. *Jerusalem Post,* April 20, 1984.

9. Samuel Decalo. *Coups and Army Rule in Africa.* New Haven, Ct.: Yale University Press, 1990.

10. *Ma'ariv* (Tel Aviv), January 18, 1983.

11. When Mobutu was criticized for breaking ranks with African solidarity with the Arab world by re-establishing relations with Israel in May 1982, he sharply denounced Arabs as "slave-taking caravanners with riding-crops and turbans." *Africa Research Bulletin,* Political Series, June 15, 1982, p. 6472. See also J. Coleman Kitchen Jr., "Zaire and Israel," *CSIS Africa Notes,* March 21, 1983, and Noah Dropkin, "Israel's Diplomatic Offensive in Africa: The Case of Zaire," *Transafrica Forum,* Spring 1992.

12. See especially Naomi Chazan (later to become a Knesset member) strong critique in her "The Fallacies of Pragmatism," *African Affairs,* vol. 82, no. 327, pp. 169-199.

13. Cited in "Afro-Arab and Muslim Relations," *Africa Contemporary Record 1985-86.* New York: Africana Publishing Co., 1987, p. A171.

14 "[Israel] must mend its fences with the ANC," stated the influential *Jerusalem Post,* on November 17, 1991, shortly before the first Israeli meeting with Nelson Mandela, the future President of Africa's most powerful country, in December 1992.

15. Samuel Decalo, "The Process, Prospects, and Constraints of Democratization in Africa," *African Affairs,* January 1992, pp. 16-31.

16. See "Israel: A Second coming in Africa," *Africa Confidential,* Oct. 21, 1994.

12 | ISRAEL AND AFRICA: A SELECTED BIBLIOGRAPHY*

Israel shares the distinction, together with only a handful of other nations, of being a "newsworthy" country. Even before the recent war, hardly a week passed without at least a reference to Israel in either the daily or periodical press. Various American, British, and European weeklies consistently carry articles on Israel. On a per capita basis, probably no other country receives as much world press attention as Israel. Yet, despite this profuseness of printed material, very few articles and fewer books present competent analyses of the Israeli polity and foreign policy. And if one narrows one's attention to Israel's involvement with Africa, the paucity of first-rate work is even more evident. Because of these limitations, this article will attempt to reconcile the diametrical opposites—being both all-encompassing, yet still selective enough for the discriminating scholar.

Israeli Foreign Policy

Israel's foreign policy may be divided into two basic periods (1950-55 and 1957 ff.), with a few intervening years (1949-50, 1955-6) constituting transitional stages. The first period was marked by a general Israeli fixation on the actions and reactions of the major world powers and the United Nations. Israel's diplomatic efforts centred overwhelmingly upon the major European capitals, Washington, and New York, in an attempt to garner the international support deemed vital for Israel's security. The trauma of the Bandung Conference (1955) and the events leading to the Sinai Campaign (1956) irrevocably shattered this fixation. The general re-evaluation of operational goals and values that followed brought about an attendant shift in foreign policy. Though hesitant and not clearly perceptible at the outset, the shift signified a conscious attempt on the part of Israel at greater identification and

*Published in the *Journal of Modern African Studies*, vol. 5, no. 3 (1967), pp. 385-99.

international alignment with the emerging forces of the Third World. There have been some indications in the past few months, and especially since the recent Middle East war, that Israel's foreign policy is entering into another assertive and more mature phase. It is, however, much too early to make any hard and fast conclusions on this point.

No discussion of Israel's foreign policy—in either period—can be adequate without at least perfunctory homage to some of the unique peculiarities of the Israeli polity which affect so much her international stance. One good article exists-written by a senior Israeli official[1] Shabtai Rosenne, "Basic Elements in Israel's Foreign Policy", in *India Quarterly* (New Delhi), October 1961, pp. 328-58. The messianic ideological configurations that frequently colour policy-enunciation especially during the Ben Gurion era are treated in greater depth in the author's "Messianic Influences in Israeli Foreign Policy", in *Occasional Papers in Political Science*, No. 2 (Kingston, R.I., University of Rhode Island, 1967.) Other references to this interesting cluster of influences, which help to illuminate an important aspect of Israel's involvement with Africa, are to be found in David Ben Gurion's "The Vision of Isaiah for Our Time", in *New York Times Magazine*, 20 May 1963, and to some extent in Pinhas Lavon, "A Chosen Society and a Normal People", in *New Outlook* (Tel Aviv), February 1962, pp. 3-9. Two basic works in Hebrew survey Israel's foreign policy during the first years of statehood: A. A. Ben-Asher, *Yachasei Hutz 1918-1953* [Foreign Relations 1918-1953], (Tel Aviv, Ayanot Press, 1954), and David Ben Gurion, *Mediniut Hutz* [Foreign Policy] (Tel Aviv, Ayanot Press, 1954-55.) One could also note Ben Gurion's discourse (printed in pamphlet form), *Israel Among the Nations* (Jerusalem, Government Printer, 1952), which surveys Israel's envisaged role in the community of nations. Walter Eytan (former Israeli delegate to the armistice conferences and former director-general of the Israeli Foreign Ministry) surveys the same era—though extended to 1956—in *The First Ten Years* (New York, Simon and Schuster, 1958.) This book, written essentially for American laymen, can be frustrating to scholars because of what it doesn't reveal, while tantalising them with the thought that, if anyone could have written the definitive study of Israel's foreign policy, it would have been this author.

A much more recent work, of academic calibre, which surveys, *inter alia*, the entire 1948-63 period, is Nadav Safran's *The United States and Israel* (Cambridge, Harvard University Press, 1963.) This, too, is a slightly aggravating study, which stems in part from certain methodological deficiencies; moreover, the value of the entire study is appreciably reduced by the omission of all footnotes—and this in a book published by a university press! Notwithstanding the above flaws, the work is possibly the best introductory study of Israel's polity and foreign policy.

Growing Israeli discontent with foreign policy reverses in the international arena contributed directly to the re-evaluation of policy goals that occurred in the transition period, 1955-6. This re-evaluation led in turn to the aggressive diplomatic drives in Africa and Asia. The Israeli discontent and general feeling of isolation is forcefully documented, *inter* alia, in Carnegie Endowment for International Peace, *Israel and the United Nations* (New York, Manhattan Press, 1956.) David Ben Gurion's *Israel's Security and her International Position Before and After the Sinai Campaign* (Jerusalem, Government Printer, 1960?) is central for any analysis of the Sinai campaign, and contains in its latter part frequent references to the new direction of Israel's diplomacy.

By 1958 the general outlines of Israel's "new" Afro-Asian policy could be discerned. In that year Paul Giniewski wrote his rather pessimistic *Israel devant l'Afrique et l'Asie* (Paris, Librairie Durlacher, 1958.) *Politique Etrangere* (Paris) paid particularly close attention to Israeli foreign policy during this period with three articles: Paul Giniewski, "Tendances de la politique asiatique et africaine d'Israel", in XXII, 4, 1957, pp. 463-78; Paul Giniewski, "Strategie et politique d'Israel en 1959", in XXIV, 3, 1959, pp. 315-28; and Jacob Tsur, "Les fondements de la politique etrangere d'Israel", in XXII, I, 1957, pp. 27-38. Indeed, the output of articles on Israel's foreign policy jumped significantly during 1958-60 with the mounting Israeli drives in Afro-Asia. *The Economist* (London) published a number of brief articles on these developments; see especially the issues of 26 July 1958, 16 August 1958, 16 May 1959, 17 September 1960, 19 March 1960, and 10 June 1961. *West Africa* (London) published on 13 June 1959 an article by Eliashiv Ben-Horin (then director of the Africa-Asia desk of the Israel Foreign Ministry), "Israel in Africa".[2]

Among other articles appearing in the British press one should include "Israel Looks Toward Africa and Asia", in *The World Today* (London), January 1958, pp. 37-47; Walter Schwartz, "Israel goes Afro-Asian", in *The Spectator* (London), 16 January 1959, p. 65; M. Z. Frank, "Israel: Afro-Asian Bridge", in *New Leader* (London), 7 March 1960, p. 13;

Leo Kohn's substantive "Israel's Foreign Relations", in *International Affairs* (London), XXXVI, 3, July 1960, pp. 330-41; Norman Bentwich, "Israel's Afro-Asian Dilemma", in The *New Statesman* (London), 11 August 1961, pp. 178-9; Norman Bentwich, "Some Aspects of the Israeli Penetration in Africa", in *Scribe* (London), IV, June 1963, pp. 63-5; the rather significant article by Amos Ben-Vered, "Israel's African Dilemma", in *The Jewish Observer and Middle East Review* (London), XII, 40, 4 October 1963, pp. 6-7; Natanel Lorch, "Israel and Africa", in *The World Today*, August 1963, pp. 358-68; N. Shepherd, "Israel and Africa", in *The New Statesman*, 28 August 1964, pp. 274 ff.; and an article by the ex-ambassador to Ghana and Nigeria, Hanan Yavor, "Israel in Africa', in *The Statist* (London), 12 June 1964, pp. 47-8.

Among some of the more pertinent articles appearing on the Continent, one may especially note "Israel en Africa", in *Mededeeling van het Afrika Instituut* (Rotterdam), 13 January 1959, pp. 323-34; "L'Etat d'Israel en 1961", in *Chronique de politique etrangere* (Bruxelles), March 1962, pp. 153-65; C. Bloch, "Die Aussenpolitischen Probleme des Staates Israel", in *Europe-Archiv* (Frankfurt-am-Main), 25 June 1964, pp. 449-56, and "Les Problemes fondamentaux de l'etat d'Israel", in *Politique etrangere* (Paris), XXVIII, 6, 1963, pp. 493-513.

On the other side of the Atlantic, Israel's African policy has been analysed by Arnold Rivkin, "Israel and the Afro-Asian World", in *Foreign Affairs* (New York), XXXVII, 3, 1959, pp. 486-95; Dwight Simpson "Israeli Policy for Survival", in *Current History* (Philadelphia), XXXVI, February 1959, pp. 70-7; Y. Leo Kohn, "Israel and the New Nation-States of Asia and Africa", in *The Annals of the American Academy of Social and Political Science* (Philadelphia), CCCXXIV, July 1959, pp. 96-102; Emil Lengyel, "Israel's Campaign in Africa", in *The Reporter* (New York), 4 February 1960, pp. 23-4; Michael Brecher, "Israel and Afro-Asia", in *International Journal* (Toronto), XVI, Spring 1961, pp. 107-37; Aaron Segal "Israel in Africa", in *Africa Report* (Washington), April 1963, pp. 19-21; Bernard Reich, "Israel Policy in Africa", *Middle East Journal* (Washington, D.C.), XVIII, I, Winter 1964, pp. 13-26; S. Decalo, "Israel and the Third World: a 1967 assessment", in *Orbis* (Philadelphia), Fall 1967, forthcoming; and the unpublished doctoral dissertation, S. Decalo, "Israel and Africa: the politics of co-operation—a study of foreign policy and technical assistance" (University of Pennsylvania, 1967.)[3]

As would be expected, there have been frequent references to Israel's African policy in the Israeli domestic press. Most of these are in

Hebrew. Possibly the most significant for English-speaking scholars would be: Ehud Avriel, "Israel's Interest in New Africa", *Jerusalem Post* (daily), 30 September 1960; "Israel, Africa and Asia", in *Israel Economist* (Tel Aviv), special supplement July 1961; "Israel's Relations with Africa and Asia", *Israel Economist*, special supplement July 1962; Natanel Lorch, "Basic Factors in Israel-Africa Relations" (Hebrew with English summary), in *Hamizrach Hehadash* [New East] (Jerusalem), 12, 1962, pp. 1-18; Shalom Cohen, "Israel and Africa in 1970", in *New Outlook* (Tel Aviv), September 1964, pp. 26-30; and David Horowitz (President of the Bank of Israel), "Israel and the Developing Nations", in *Jerusalem Post Weekly*, 3 December 1965.

To round off the picture, one should also note—because of the intimate connection—four articles dealing with Israel's Asian policy: E. Ben Horin, "Kavey yesod le'maamada shel Israel be'asia" [Basic guidelines to Israel's stand in Asia], in *Hamizrach Hehadash*, VII, 4, 1957, pp. 245-52; Josef Canaan et al., "Israel in Asia", in *Far Eastern Economic Review* (Hong Kong), 14 July 1960, pp. 61 ff.; and Eliahu Elath's two articles, "Israel's Relations with the Emerging States in Africa and Asia, in *Jewish Social Studies* (New York), April 1962, pp. 69-78, and "Israel's Relations with the Emerging States in Asia", in *Royal Central Asia Journal* (London), L, 1, January 1963, pp. 21-9.

Israeli diplomatic efforts in Africa in the decade since 1956-7 have brought about an immense improvement in the international position of Israel. Growing amity for Israel on the part of Africa has expressed itself on numerous occasions and in a variety of ways. Afro-Israeli co-operation in the United Nations, for example, has appreciably dulled Arab anti-Israel propaganda in that organisation. Beginning in 1961, a number of resolutions sponsored by countries from the Third World (with significant African participation) have called for direct negotiations in the Middle East. And, moreover, by 1966 Israel found herself elected to a number of executive positions in U.N. agencies as the official representative of the whole of Afro-Asia. Such co-operation has not been, needless to say, one-sided. Israel has had to modify certain of her stands and postures in the U.N., in order to accommodate African interests. Two authors who discuss some of these changes are Yitzhak Artzi in his 'Changes in Israeli Foreign Policy', in *New Outlook*, September 1963, pp. 14-19, and Victor Cygielman, "Can Israel go Neutralist?", in *New Outlook*, October 1964, pp. 18-25.

By 1965 Israel had established diplomatic relations, and maintained technical co-operation ties, with all but two (Somalia and Mauritania) of the sub-Saharan nations. Indeed, in that year Israel's diplomatic network was larger than that of any country in the world except France, United States, and Great Britain. These advances have not occurred without strong resistance from a variety of sources. Vehement Arab opposition to this encroachment in their "backyard" has been enhanced by similar Soviet, East European, and Chinese protests published by *Pravda, Trud,* and *Peking Review.* Documentation of Soviet views on Israel, and Israeli activities in Africa, is available in *Mizan* (London), Supplement A. In many instances the "cold war" in Africa is a term more appropriate to denote the Arab-Israeli competition for influence on that continent.

No specific study has examined all aspects of this struggle, though references to it are numerous. Possibly the deepest analysis is that of Joseph Churba's doctoral dissertation, "U.A.R.-Israel Rivalry over Aid and Trade in Sub-Saharan Africa" (Columbia University, 1965.) Other significant contributions are L. A. Fabunimi, "Egypt and Africa", in *West Africa,* 21 December 1957, p. 1209, and 28 December 1957, p. 1231; the two Israel Ministry for Foreign Affairs monographs, *Expansion nasserienne en Afrique* (Jerusalem, 1958), and *Nasserite Objectives and Methods in Africa* (Jerusalem, 1960); "Israel, Egypte en de minde rout wikkel de gebieden in Afrika", in *Mededeeling van het Afrika Instituut,* 12 January 1958, p. 65; "Vaulting the Arab Boycott", *The Economist,* 27 August 1960; J. B. Adotevi, "Les Relations africano-arabes", in *Communaute France-Eurafrique* (Paris), March 1962, pp. 30-1; and A. N. Polack "Afrikaniyut ve'arviyut" ['Africanism and Arabism'], in *Molad* (Tel Aviv), 175-6, January 1963, pp. 20-6.

The Arab position can possibly be best perceived from two articles (among others) in *Nahdatu Ifriquiah* (Cairo): Abdul Monim El-Khedry, "The Israel Infiltration in Africa," in no. 50, January 1962, pp. 16-20, and Wera Amhito, "Can Israel be Africa's Friend?" in no. 54, May 1962, pp. 14-18.

For some of the African reactions to this struggle for influence one could refer to "Les Etats arabes, Israel, et nous Maliens", in *Paris-Dakar* (Dakar, daily), 4 July 1960, and Peter Enahoro's extremely perceptive "Does the Arab-speaking African feel African?", in *Daily Times* (Lagos), 2 February 1962. Other more general sources of information include "Egypt's Policy in Africa", in *Hamizrach Hehadash,* 1-2, 1962, pp. 19-27; "An African Policy for Egypt", in *Egyptian Economic and Political*

Review (Cairo), August 1956, pp. 21-4 (containing a most candid proposal for an Egyptian power-gambit in Africa); and Jacques Baulin, *The
Arab Role in Africa* (Harmondsworth, 1962.)

As has been previously noted, there have been some tentative
indications in the last few months, and especially since the recent
Middle East war, that Israel's foreign policy is shifting into yet another
phase—a more mature, assertive, and self-confident one.

The recent war has captured the imagination of numerous
political commentators who have turned out a spate of articles on the
conflict and its aftermath. Much of this material is of relatively ephemeral value, especially insofar as Africa is concerned. The bulk of the more
significant research is only obviously yet to come. Possibly the best
coverage of the origins and significances of the conflict is contained in
Walter Laqueur, "Israel, the Arabs and World Opinion", in *Commentary*(New York), August 1967, pp. 49-59; Richard Hudson, "The U.N. and
the Middle East", in *War/Peace Report* (New York), June-July 1967, pp. 3-6;
and in the *New Statesman* (London), 9 June 1967.

The author attempts a tentative evaluation in his "The Third
Middle East War: African reactions", in *Africa Report*, October 1967. The
best sources for such evaluations at this time are the various African
newspapers; especially the issues of *Afrique Nouvelle* (Dakar) for 15-21
and 22-28 June 1967, and *West Africa* (London) for 10 and 24 June, and
8 July 1967. Other significant material may be gleaned from the
excellent *Africa Research Bulletin* (Exeter), and from the chronologies in
AfricaReport and *Africa Digest* (London.)

Trade

Afro-Israeli commerce has never figured prominently in Israeli trade
statistics, fluctuating between three and six per cent of total Israeli
imports and exports. Of necessity, the bulk of Israel's import require-
ments—be they heavy machinery, foodstuffs, or armaments—have
had to be purchased from European and North American suppliers.
And conversely, the bulk of Israeli exports—mostly quality-ori-
ented—have also been aimed at the mass markets of these continents.
Nevertheless, in her quest for new markets and new friends, the
potentialities of Africa have not gone unrecognised in Israel. Moreover,
African imports of a number of Israeli commodities (e.g. furniture,

cement, distilled soya oil), even if small in absolute figures, have amounted to over 50 per cent of total Israeli exports of these items. There are a number of other commodities (e.g. asbestos pipes, pharmaceuticals, carpets) of which Africa purchases over 25 per cent of the Israeli exports, with significant purchases of others below this figure (vehicles and spare parts, cotton thread, paints, chemicals, and so on.) In like manner, Africa is Israel's prime supplier for a number of tropical products, though again absolute trade figures are relatively small. For example, Israel's imports of woods for her booming furniture industry have made her Gabon's third best global customer for this commodity (1961), and the Central African Republic's prime purchaser of diamonds (1962-7.)

Statistical data on Afro-Israeli trade are readily available and easily accessible to foreign scholars, even if little interpretative and analytical work has been done in this field. The prime sources, excellently organised under specific commodity and country headings, are the monthly and annual cumulative issues of *Israel's Foreign Trade*, published in Jerusalem by the Central Bureau of Statistics of the Israel Government. Further data may be obtained from the annual *Shnaton Hamemshala* [Government Yearbook], published in Jerusalem by the Information Division of the Prime Minister's Office.

A number of other publications frequently carry significant information about Afro-Israeli trade, even if sometimes one has to search hard for it. The excellent Parisian weekly, *Marches tropicaux et mediterranneens*, often contains notes of this nature. So do the *Israel Economist* (Tel Aviv, monthly), and the *Israel Export and Trade Journal* (Tel Aviv, monthly.) Three of the most important articles here have been "Israel's Links with West Africa", in *Israel Export and Trade Journal*, special supplement to the June 1961 issue; "Israel and East Africa", in *Israel Export and Trade Journal*, February 1962, pp. 19-45; and "Israel's Trade with Africa", in *Israel Economist*, July 1963, pp. 135-6. Two other articles should also be noted in this section: "Israel-Ghana Trade Agreement", in *West Africa*, 23 August 1958, discusses Israel's first trade agreement with an African state: and David Yaghil, "Rapports economiques entre Israel et le continent Africain", in *Etudes Mediterraneennes* (Paris), 10, Autumn 1961, pp. 79-85, analyses the entire topic of Afro-Israeli commerce. See also "Africa and Israel", special supplement to *Israel Economist*, June-July 1966, pp. 135-54, and the entire July 1967 issue of *Israel Export and Trade Journal*, entitled "Trade Relations with East African Countries".

Technical Co-operation

Published material on Israel's programmes of technical co-operation with Africa is much more voluminous, even if at times it is too general. However, some of the most significant reports and documents—those issued by the Department of International Co-operation in the Israel Ministry for Foreign Affairs—are not always easily obtainable, being subject to some of the most preposterous bureaucratic red tape possible.

The most ambitious study available on the Israeli programmes is Mordechai Kreinin's *Israel and Africa: a study in technical co-operation* (New York, Praeger, 1964.) This rather brief work, sparsely footnoted, is especially good in its chapters on agrarian organisation and economic development programmes. It also contains short chapters on other facets of Afro-Israeli co-operation—youth organisation, health, joint companies, and so on. Two other good introductions to Israel's activities in Africa are Michael Brecher, "Israel and Afro-Asia", Chapter 5 in his recent *The new States of Asia* (New York, Oxford University Press, 1966), and E. Kanovsky, "Israeli Technical Co-operation: a review", in *American Journal of Economics and Sociology* (New York), XXV, April 1966, pp. 215-24.

Yaacov Yanay's "Technical Co-operation between Israel and the Developing World", in *International Development Review* (Washington), VI, 3, September 1964, pp. 10-15, is extremely useful, despite its brevity, for it includes the results of an opinion poll made among ex-trainees in Africa regarding their stay in Israel.[7]

Other, more general articles include: Ursula Wasserman, "Israel in Africa", *New Outlook*, July 1959, pp. 11-16; A. Bone, "Hakalkala Hamedinit shel siyua le'aratzot nechshalot" ["The National Policy of Assistance to Developing Countries"], in *Hamizrach Hehadash*, X, 1-2, 1959, pp. 1-6; Oded Remba, "Israel's Aid Program to Africa and Asia", in *Midstream* (New York), Spring 1961, pp. 3-21; Hugh H. Smythe, "Israel and Africa: some common problems", in *Jewish Social Studies*, April 1962, pp. 97-107; and M. Neirynck, "Israels unieke mogelijkheden bij de hulp aan nieuwe landen", in *Gids op maatschappelijk gebied* (Bruxelles), March 1962, pp. 223-39. Of a briefer nature, but still meriting attention, are: Shamir Yoram "Africa Turns to Israel", in *New Leader* (London), pp. 10-11; "Israel Helps the Developing Countries", in *Review of International Co-operation* (London), May 1962, pp. 132-5; Ron Tamari, "Israel and Africa", in *Jewish Frontier* (New York), April 1961 supplement, pp. 10-12; Fabiene Lacombe, "La Cooperation entre Israel et l'Afrique", in Communaute France-Eurafrique, April 1962, pp. 16-18; A. Rauchfuss, "Die Entwicklungilfe Israels in Afrika", in *Neues Afrika* (Munich), September 1962, pp. 357-8; E. Avriel's "Africa and Israel: a working partnership", reprinted in English by the Israel Embassy to the United States, from the Hebrew original in *Ha'aretz* (Tel Aviv, daily), 13 March 1963; Moshe Bar-Natan, "Israel in Africa", in *Jewish Frontier* (New York), July-August 1966, pp. 4-6; Moshe Leshem, "The Roots of Friendship", in *Israel Economist* (Tel Aviv), June 1966, pp. 20-7; G. Gersh, "Israel's Aid to Africa", in *Commonweal* (New York), 25 November 1966, pp. 226-8; M. Nahumi, "Ten Years of Relations with Ghana", in *New Outlook*, February 1966, pp. 21-9, and Leopold Laufer, "Israel's Technical Assistance Experts", in *International Development Review* (Washington, D.C.), March 1967, pp. 9-14.

A voluminous amount of official literature is published in Jerusalem every year. Most of it is issued by the Department of International Co-operation in the Ministry for Foreign Affairs, and may be difficult to obtain abroad, as noted earlier. It would be futile to attempt to list all of this material here. Instead, only a few of the more important monographs will be noted, essentially to indicate to the reader the nature and variety of the material available.

Among the more significant reports/documents are: *Trainees in Israel in the Year 1961* (1962); *Programme of Co-operation with Countries of East Africa* (1962); *Israel's Programme for Training Opportunities* (1962); *Programme for Itinerant Courses in Africa* (1962); *Cumulative Tables on Trainees and Experts, 1958-1963* (1964); *Programme of Co-operation with Kenya, Malagasy Republic, Tanganyika, and Uganda* (1963.)

One further publication of general interest may be cited. This is the irregular (though presumably quarterly) *Shalom*: Alumni Bulletin of Israel Trained Students, issued by the Department of International Cooperation since 1963. The publication serves as a link between ex-trainees and Israel; it includes a potpourri of news about returning students, and reports on activities of Ex-Israel Trainees Clubs in Africa.

The establishment of national, agrarian-centred, youth organisations aimed at the promotion of civic consciousness has been one of the major emphasises of Israel's programmes of technical co-operation. These organisations, patterned with some modifications along the lines of the Israeli *Gadna* and *Nachal* structures, have been established in approximately two dozen African states. Possibly the most comprehensive coverage of the Israeli structures is to be found in C.

Rossillion, "Economic and Social Work for Young People during Defence Service: the Israeli formula", in *International Labour Review* (Geneva), January 1966, pp. 66-79; Avraham Aderet, *The Pioneer Youth Movements* [Hebrew] (Jerusalem, Szold Foundation, 1963), Gidon Levitas, *Nahal: Israel's Pioneer Fighting Youth* (Jerusalem, Youth and Hechalutz Department of the World Zionist Organisation, 1967), and Irving Heymont, "The Israeli Nahal Program", in *Middle East Journal*, Summer 1967, pp. 314-24.

What was to become a Ghanaian hybrid of the Israeli Nachal is briefly noted by Colin Legum, "Ghana Starts Builders Brigade", in *Jerusalem Post*, 22 December 1957; Peter Hodge analyses the Ghanaian organisation in much greater depth in his "The Ghana Workers Brigade: project for unemployed youth", in *British Journal of Sociology* (London), vol. 2, June 1964, pp. 113-28. One should also mention the photocopied document, Dean Cochran, "Report to the Minister for the Builders' Brigade" (Accra, 8 February, 1960.) Official reports recommending the types of structures to be established (all issued by the International Co-operation Department) include: *Report on Youth Organisation in Mauritius* (1962); *Youth Leadership Course-Uganda* (1962); *A Pioneer Youth Training Centre for Tanganyika* (1962); and *Project for the Establishment of an Ethiopian National Youth Organisation* (1963.)

The particular structures actually established in Africa, and the problems of youth that evoked the need for such solutions, have been rather extensively documented in the International Labour Review. The following articles are all from that most valuable periodical: "Special Manpower Mobilization Schemes and Youth Programmes for Development Purposes", January 1966, pp. 1-4; E. Costa, "Practical Organization of Manpower Mobilization Schemes in Developing Countries", March 1966, pp. 248-80; C. Rossillion, "Youth Services for Economic and Social Development: a general review", April 1967, pp. 315-26; "Unemployed Youth: an African symposium", March 1963, pp. 183-205; G. Ardant, "A Plan for Full Employment in the Developing Countries", July 1963, pp. 15-51; "Youth Employment and Vocational Training Schemes in the Developing Countries", September 1962, pp. 209-34; A. Dawson, "Economic Development, Employment and Public Works in African Countries", January 1965, pp. 14-46; G. W. Griffin, "The Development of Youth Centres in Kenya", July 1963; pp. 52-65; C. Rossillion, "Civic Service and Community Works in Mali", January 1966, pp. 50-65; E. Costa, "Back to the Land: the campaign against unemployment in Dahomey", January 1966, pp. 29-49; and J. Mouly,

"The Young Pioneers Movement in the Central African Republic",
January 1966, pp. 19-28.

Trade union co-operation and the mass training of African
union leaders is yet another project stressed in Israel. As is known, the
Histadrut model is widely admired in the developing countries, and
has served—again with some modifications—as a prototype for the
reorganisation of certain trade union federations in these countries.
There has been no detailed research on Afro-Israeli co-operation in this
field: the best sources are the two Ph.D. dissertations already cited
(Churba and Decalo) and the brief chapter in Kreinin's book.

Afro-Israeli co-operation in this sphere was first cemented via
the contacts of John Tettegah of the Ghana T.U.C. and the Histadrut.
Ghanaian cadres were promptly dispatched to study the Israeli model
while a Histadrut branch was established in Accra to aid Tettegah in
the reorganisation of the G.T.U.C. For the latter process (the end-product of which did not necessarily please the Israelis) see especially T. O.
Elias, *The British Commonwealth: the development of their laws and constitutions, vol.
x: Ghana and Sierra Leone* (London, Stevens, 1962.) See also *West Africa*,
1 February and 29 August 1958, 17 and 27 January and 7 November
1959, and 8 October 1960. Of particular interest also is Ghana Trade
Union Congress, *New Charter for Ghana's Labour* (Accra, Guinea Press, 1958.)

Brief notes on the Afro-Asian Institute for Labour Studies and
Cooperation in Tel Aviv, which turns out some 30-50 trained leaders
every 3-4 months, are to be found in Arnold Zack, *Labor Training in
Developing Countries* (New York, Praeger, 1964), pp. 37-8, and in Eliahu
Elath, "Afro-Asian School Teaches Progress under Democracy", in *The
American Federationist* (Washington), June 1961, pp. 10-11. Assistance in
the creation of new agrarian structures and co-operatives has been yet
another field of intense Afro-Israeli effort. By and large the Israeli *kibbutz*
system, though widely admired, has not been deemed appropriate for
Africa. (Nevertheless a few Kibbutzim have been established in e.g.
Ivory Coast, Biafra, Central African Republic, and Tanzania.) Modifications of the Israeli *moshav* prototypes have, on the other hand, been
quite successfully transplanted to Africa.

For an introduction to the Israeli prototypes, and the whole field
of collectives, see H. Desroche, *Au pays du kibbutz: essai sur le secteur cooperatif
israelien* (Basle, Union suisse des cooperatives de consummation, 1960);
Harry Viteles, *A History of the Cooperative Movement in Israel* (London, Val-
lentine, Mitchell, 1966); J. Shatil, *L'Economie Collective du Kibboutz Israelien*

(Paris, Editions de Minuit, 196o); Melford Spiro, *Kibbutz, Venture in Utopia* (New York, Schoken, 1963); Eliyahu Kanovsky, *The Economy of the Israeli Kibbutz* (Cambridge, Mass., Harvard University Middle East monographs, 1967); H. Darim-Drabkin, *Le Kibboutz á l'epreuve de l'efficience economique* (Paris, Bureau d'Etudes Cooperatives et Communautaires, 1962), and the special 1966 issue of the excellent *Revue des Etudes cooperatives* (Paris), no. 145-6; Y. Goussault, "La Participation des collectivites rurales au developpement", in *Tiers Monde* (Paris), January 196i, pp. 27-40; J. Stanovik, "The Role of Collective Farms in the Economy of Countries passing Economic Underdevelopment to Economic Maturity", in *Annals of Collective Economy* (Liege), April 1960, pp. 167-208; and Maurice Milhaud, "Le developpement communautaire instrument de developpement economique et sociale en Afrique", in *Tiers Monde*, January 1962, pp. 313-20.

For specific references to Afro-Israeli co-operation in this sphere, see Mordechai Kreinin's *Israel and Africa*, which is particularly well versed in this field. One could also note the following articles: Mordechai Kreinin, "The Introduction of Israel's Land Settlement Plan to Nigeria", in *Journal of Farm Economics* (Ithaca, N.Y.), August 1963, pp. 535-46; "Farm Settlement Scheme in Nigeria", in *Nigerian Trade Journal* (Lagos), January 1962, pp. 2-6; Government of West Nigeria, *Future Policy of the Ministry of Agriculture and National Resources* (Ibadan, 1959); R. Delprat "Fermes-ecoles an Dahomey", in *Developpement et civilisations* (Paris), June 1960, pp. 59-64; and (among others) the following reports issued by the Israeli Department of International Co-operation: *Report on the Creation of an Organisational Framework for the Villagisation of Tanganyika* (1963), *Report on Consumers' Co-operatives in Uganda* (1964), *Rapport sur l'agriculture au Mali* (1962), *Agricultural Settlement and Development in Kenya* (1962), *Propositions pour le developpement des regions en Cote d'Ivoire* (1961), *Development of Co-operatives in Eastern Nigeria* (1961), and *Rapport de la mission agricole israelienne en Haute Volta* (1963.)

Sources of information on other forms of Afro-Israeli co-operation are sparse and have to be gleaned from the daily press (a selected list of the most useful papers concludes this article.) Several brief articles on a wide variety of fields have, however, been published: "Zim Serves Africa", in *Israel Export and Trade Journal*, July 1963, special Afro-Israeli co-operation issue; "Israel Aids Africa's Health", in *West African Review* (London), June 1962, pp. 65-7; Yoram Dinstein, "Legal Aid to Developing Countries", in *Israel Law Review* (Jerusalem), October 1966, pp. 632-51.

The collected papers and reports delivered during the three

Rehovoth Conferences in Israel have been assembled and published in three volumes. These are: Ruth Gruber (ed.), *Science and the New Nations* (New York, Basic Books, 1961); Ra'anan Weitz (ed.), *Rural Planning in Developing Countries* (Cleveland, Western Reserve University Press, 1966); and David Krivine (ed.), *Fiscal and Monetary Problems in Developing States* (New York, Praeger, 1967.)

The fact that the majority of the African states have been greatly impressed by the plethora of Israeli socioeconomic innovations, and have emulated some of them in their own countries, has prompted some scholarly speculation as to Israel's role as a developmental model for the modernising countries. Representative samples of this sort of literature include, B. Ady-Brille-Bidot, "Y-a-t-il une voie israelienne du socialisme?", in *L'Afrique et l'Asie* (Paris), 58, 1962, pp. 41-7; Julius Braunthal and J. B. Kripalani, *The Significance of Israeli Socialism* (London, Lincolns-Prager, 1958); F. Grevisse, "Reflexions a propos des solutions israeliennes en merge de l'evolution du Congo", in *Revue coloniale belge* (Bruxelles), August 1960, pp. 23-7; Joseph Klatzmann, *Les Enseignements de l'experience israelienne* (Paris, Editions Tiers Monde, 1963); Elie Maissi, "Israel et son exemple", in *Cahiers Africains* (Paris and Bruxelles), 2, 1961; Jules Moche, "Israel, Yugoslavie, Chine: trois methodes, in *La Revue socialiste* (Paris), 163, May 1963, pp. 459-479; and Robert O. Perlman, *Israel's Cooperation as the new Alternative to Communism, Socialism and Capitalism* (Jerusalem, Institute for the Advancement of Philosophy, 1961.)

It would be appropriate to conclude this bibliography with a list of newspapers and other publications that frequently carry information on Israeli activities in Africa. By far the best, though slightly difficult to obtain, is the *Israel Weekly News Bulletin*, published in Jerusalem by the Government of Israel Press Office. The mimeographed *Bulletin* contains full documentation of visits of foreign dignitaries as well as extracts from policy statements and Israeli editorials.

Another good source of information is Israel, *Divrei Haknesset* [Parliamentary Debates], especially for debates on the budget of the Ministry. There are numerous official reports published by the Department of International Co-operation. for Foreign Affairs. Among Israeli periodicals, the most useful are *Hamizrach Hehadash* [New East], *Israel Digest* (Jerusalem), and *New Outlook* (Tel Aviv.) Among the foreign publications, the following publish news on Israeli activities in Africa more frequently than others: *Marches tropicaux et mediterraneennes* (Paris); *Afrique nouvelle* (Dakar); *Abidjan-matin* (Abidjan); *Jewish Observer and Middle East Review*

(London); and *Africa Research Bulletin* (Exeter.) The U.S. Department of State publishes *External Research* (volumes for Middle East, Africa, and International Relations), which is also useful to scholars wishing to learn of current academic research.

FOOTNOTES

1. It would be proper to note from the outset that a large percentage of the interpretative articles on Israeli foreign policy are written by high-ranking government officials.

2. Somewhat similar to the same author's "Israel and Africa", in *Africa South* (Cape Town), December 1957.

3. To avoid repetitious reference to this work, the following break-down of chapters is noted: Chapters 1-5, "Israeli Foreign Policy in Africa"; Chapter 6, "Afro-Israeli Trade"; Chapters 7-10, giving an introduction to, and specific programmes of, Israel's technical co-operation with Africa; Chapter 11, "Israel as a Developmental model for the Third World?".

4. A very large number of "perpetual amity" treaties have been signed by Israel and the African states. See Israel, *Kitvei Amana* [Treaty Series] (Jerusalem.)

5. For an extremely interesting revelation of how Lebanese communities in West Africa are forced to participate in anti-Israel activities, see *Liberian Age* (Monrovia), 19 January 1962, and *West Africa*, 14 October 1961.

6. Particularly useful are that periodical's occasional tables ranking the major Commodity suppliers of African states.

7 The author is acquainted, for example, with an instance when an Israeli scholar was refused permission to glance through some of these (unclassified) reports at the Israel Mission to the United Nations prior to receipt of official permission from Jerusalem. This, while the very same reports were available in two public libraries not more than ten blocks away.

8. For articles on African cadres in Israel, see especially, Adjingborn A. Syme, *Ghanaians Salute Israel* (Accra, Guinea Press, 1958); "West Africans in Israel", *West Africa*, 27 August 1960; Hal Lohrman, "Campus in Jerusalem", in *Midstream* (New York), Spring 1960, pp. 42-60; Harold Flender "Africans in Israel", in *Jewish Frontier* (New York), November 1961, pp. 13-15; and Arm Morrisett, "Africans in Israel: Canaan meets Cush", in *Midstream*, Spring 1962, pp. 53-9.

9. Frequently this form of assistance has gone hand in hand with youth training, i.e. similar to the Nachal formations in Israel.

10. Of a briefer nature but still relevant are: "Western Nigeria's New Agricultural Programme", and "Training Western Nigerians in Modern Farming Techniques", in *African World* (London), August 1958, p. 23 and October 1962, p. 11; Gabriel Akin Deko, "West Nigeria's Pioneer Farmers", in *West Africa*, 24 February 1962, p. 199 and to September 1960, p. 1021; "Western Nigeria's Pioneering Settlers", in *West African Review* (Liverpool), September 1961, pp. 14-16; "Cooperative Farming: West Nigeria's exciting £20 million scheme", in *Africa Trade and Development* (London), September 1961, pp. 12-13; "The Ivory Coast Seeks Cooperative Solutions", in *Review of international Cooperation* (London), June 1962, pp. 157-60; and S. R. Hatch, "The Kibbutz-New Plan for Tanzania", in *Venture* (London), XVII, 10, 1965, pp. 22-4.

13 A SUPPLEMENTAL SELECTED BIBLIOGRAPHY*

If at the time the preceding bibliographic essay was written one could snugly fit within the confines of a dozen pages most of the key literature on Israel's foreign policy vis-a-vis Africa, and annotate it as well, this is no longer the case today. During the 1970's (especially) and the 1980's a voluminous literature mushroomed – both books and articles– on these topics. A significant number of contributions also began to be published, either historiographically critical of Israel's foreign policy, or written in support of the Arab cause. Many monographs also began to appear, analyzing Israel's international relations *vis-a-vis* the major powers, often anchoring data on the Third World within such contexts. Israel's controversial relationship with the apartheid regime in Pretoria has also received extremely heavy critical coverage.

Today any student of Israeliana would encounter in many academic centers several library shelves of books on Israel and her foreign policy. And even a cursory count of what has been published in the periodical press would reveal several hundred articles written in English and French alone. Since much of this outpouring is today accessible either via the electronic media or in a number of bibliographical compendia (with the holdings of the Library of Congress and New York's Public Library in particular useful), it would serve no purpose to replicate these here. Rather, a small selection of those that I have found most valuable, easily accessible, or representative, are listed alphabetically below, with the following few bibliographic comments.

First, notwithstanding the significant academic outpouring the selection represents, there remains a surprising imbalance in terms of the coverage. For example, the early formative years of Israel's foreign policy have only received the attention of Bialer (see the bibliography) in the past two decades. Apart from the fact that his work seems

---

*First time published.

oblivious of antecedent published research, no additional work has been published in this important field. Likewise, and equally surprising, no Israeli or foreign scholarship has explored the foreign policy and/or leadership of Moshe Sharett, though virtually every other Israeli leader's role and contributions have been assessed, at least cursorily.

Second, there has not appeared yet much systematic treatment in monograph form, of Israel's relations and/or cooperation with any specific African state; nor for that matter have there appeared detailed comparative analyses of Israel's technical assistance efforts. True, a few writers (such as, for example, Codo) have written a number of single-country articles, and a few former Israeli envoys have written their memoires (as for example the ambassadors to the Central African Republic, and to Tanganyika, the latter in Hebrew.) And this despite the fact that a solid effort in that direction (see Hershlag) does exist. Seemingly also, very few scholars have conducted fieldwork, at least in the context of research on Afro-Israeli relations. Yet, there is ample data for several PhD dissertations at least, in this area, including on countries that superficially may appear to have not had a very extensive or prolonged Israeli presence. Dahomey, Togo, Uganda, Kenya, and the Central African Republic are several countries that immediately come to mind. That such research gaps exist does not imply that primary data is non-existent or has not been collected already. The surprising thing is that a large amount of archival data does exist in Israel, and also in several African countries.

Notwithstanding this, it is unlikely that much new work along these lines will be published in the future. The high tide of interest in Afro-Israeli relations came in the 1970's. In the 1980's the focus dramatically shifted to become much more the diplomatic battle for U.N. votes, rather than the technical assistance effort, and its failures or successes. Moreover, shifting vagaries of academic research, the effect of the trauma of Africa's diplomatic "betrayal" of 1973, the gradual political and economic marginalization of the continent, and the maturing of Israeli foreign policy, have by the late 1980's made Africa of relatively minor interest to most Israelis. It is striking how very little factual news is published in the Israeli press today on a continent that not so long ago riveted the attention of the entire nation. To a considerable extent, however, this is quite understandable. It was, after all, the intensely close "Afro-Israeli honeymoon" of the 1950's-1970's that was abnormal!

The Bibliography

Abd al-Rahman, Awatif. *Israil wa-Afriqiya, 1948-1985* [Israel and Africa, 1948-1985]. Cairo: Dar al-Fikr al-Arabi, 1985.

Abegunrin, Layiwola. "The Arabs and the Southern African Problems." *International Affairs* vol. 60 no. 1, 1983-1984, pp. 97-105.

Adams, J. *The Unnatural Alliance: Israel and Africa*. London: Quintet Books, 1984.

Adefuye, Ade. "Nigeria and Israel," *International Studies*, vol. 15 no. 4, October-December 1974.

Adisa, Jimni. "Nigeria, Israel and Diplomatic Ties: The Conditional Thesis," *International Problems*, vol. 24 no. 1-4, 1985, pp. 60-89.

Agyeman, Opoku. "Pan-Africanism versus Pan-Arabism: A Dual Asymmetrical Model of Political Relations," *Middle East Review*, vol. 16 no. 4, Summer 1984, pp. 2-16.

Ajami, Fouad and Martin A. Sours. "Israel and Sub-Saharan Africa: A Study of Interaction," *African Studies Review*, vol. 13 no. 3, december 1970.

Akinsanya, Adeoye. "The Afro-Arab Alliance: Dream or Reality." *African Affairs* vol. 75 no. 1976, pp. 511-529.

————— . "On the Lagos decision to Break Relations with Israel," *International Problems*. Spring 1978, pp. 67-79.

Akinyemi, Boladji. "Open Letter to members of the National Assembly on Nigeria-Israel Relations." *Nigerian Forum* no. 2, July-September 1982, pp. 731-739.

Alencastre, Amilcar. *Le sionisme et le tiers monde*. Algiers: S.N.E.D., 1972.

"Alliance between Tel Aviv and Pretoria." *International Affairs* (Moscow) vol. 17, 1977, pp. 53-58.

Aluko, Alajide. "Israel and Nigeria: Continuity and Change in Their Relationship," *African Review*, vol. 4 no. 1, 1974.

Amir, Shimeon. *Israel's Development Cooperation with Africa, Asia, and Latin America.* New York: Praeger, 1974.

Amson, Daniel. *De Gaulle et Israel.* Paris: Presses Universitaires de France, 1991.

Andriamirado, Sennen. "Afrique Noire: Israel Revient." *Jeune Afrique*, May 8, 1985, pp. 24-28.

———. "Cote d'Ivoire/Israel: Le Retour de l'ami Israelienne." *Jeune Afrique*, 8 january 1986, pp. 31-32.

Argov, Shlomo. *An Ambassador Speaks Out.* London: Weidenfeld and Nicholson, 1983.

Aribsala, Femi. "Thought-Piece on the Question of Nigerian-Israeli Rapprochement." *Nigerian Forum.* no. 2,4 and 5, 1982, pp. 525-531.

Asante, S. K. B. "Africa in World Politics: The Case of the Organization of African Unity and the Middle Eastern Conflict." *International Problems* vol. 20 no. 2-4, 1981, pp. 111-128.

Astakhov, S. "Israel's Expansion in the Third World." *International Affairs* (Moscow), vol. 7, 1969, pp. 53-58.

Awala, Agola. "Afro-Arab Solidarity." Nairobi: League of Arab States, 1976.

Ayari, Chedly. *Afro-Arab Cooperation: Facing the Challenges of the 1980's.* Khartoum: Badea, 1985.

———. "The Reality of Afro-Arab Solidarity," *Africa Report*, vol. 20 no. 6, November-December 1975.

Aynor, H. S. "Black Africa's Rediscovery of Israel: Motivations and Expectations." *Jerusalem Journal of International Relations*, vol. 12 no. 1, 1990, pp. 102-111.

———. *Notes from Africa.* New York: Praeger, 1969.

———. "Relations between Israel and States in Asia and Africa: A Guide to Selected Documentation," no. 4, Ghana; no. 7, Cote d'Ivoire. Jerusalem: Hebrew University Harry S. Truman Research Institute, 1988-1992.

Bahbah, Bishara. *Israel and Latin America: The Military Connection.* New York: St. Martin's Press, 1986.

Bard, Mitchell G. "The Evolution of israel's Africa Policy." *Middle East Review,* Winter 1988/89, pp. 21-29.

Beit-Hallahmi, Benjamin. "Israel and South Africa 1977-1982: Business as Usual and More," *New Outlook,* vol. 26 no. 2, March-April 1983.

———. *The Israeli Connection: Who Israel Arms and Why.* London: Pantheon Books, 1987.

Beker, Avi. *The United Nations and Israel: From Recognition to Reprehension.* Lexington, Mass.: Lexington Books, 1988.

Benabdallah, Abdelkader. *L'Alliance raciste israelo-sud-africaine: Israel et les peuples noirs.* Montreal: Editions Canada-Monde-Arabe, 1979.

Beshir, Mohamed Omer. *"Israel and Africa,"* Khartoum: Khartoum University Press, 1974.

Bialer, Uri. Between East and West: *Israel's Foreign Policy Orientation, 1948-1955.* Cambridge: Cambridge University Press, 1990

———. "Our place in the World: Mapai and Israel's Foreign Policy Orientation, 1947-1952." Jerusalem: Jerusalem Papers on Peace Problems, 1981.

Bin Barakah, al-Mahdi. "Israel and Zionist Penetration in Africa." Cairo: Permanent Secretariat of the Afro-Asian Peoples' Solidarity Organization, 1967.

Bourgui, Albert. "Afrique Noire-Israel: Une Relance Problematique." *Revue d'Etudes Palesriniennes,* no. 11, Spring 1984, pp. 47-60.

Brodie, Joan. "Transfer of Problem-Solving Techniques from Israel to Africa." PhD dissertation, University of Denver, 1969.

Carol, Steven S. "Israel's Foreign Policy towards East Africa." PhD dissertation, St. John's University, 1977.

Cefkin, Leo J. "Israel and South Africa: Reconciling Pragmatism and Principle." *Middle East Review.* Winter 1988/89, pp. 29-40.

Cervenka, Zdenek. "Afro-Arab Relations: Rxploitation or Cooperation?" *Africa*, no. 34, June 1974.

Chaabra, Hari Sharan. "The Competition of Israel and the Arab States for friendship with the African States," *India Quarterly*, vol. 31, 1975, pp. 362-370.

Chazan, N. "The Fallacies of Pragmatism: israeli Foreign Policy Toward South Africa," African Affairs, vol. 82 no. 327, April 1983, pp. 169-199.

———. "Israel and Africa in the 1980's: The Dilemma of Complexity and Ambiguity," in O. Aluko (ed.), *Africa and the Great Powers in the 1980's*. Lanham: University Press of America, 1987.

———. "Israel in Africa," *Jerusalem Quarterly*. no. 18, 1981, pp. 29-44.

———. "Israeli Perceptions on Israel-South African Relations," London: *Institute of Jewish Affairs Research Report* 9-10, 1987, pp. 12-19.

———. and Victor L. Levine. "Africa and the Middle East: Patterns of Convergence and Divergence," in John W. Harbeson and Donald Rothchild (eds.) *Africa in World Politics*. Boulder, Co.: Westview, 1991, pp. 202-227.

Chibwe, E. C. *Afro-Arab Relations in the New World Order*.London: Julian Freidman, 1976.

———. *Arab Dollars to Africa. London*: Croom Helm, 1976.Clement, Claude. Israel et la Ve Repubique. Paris: O. Orban, 1978.

Codo, Leon Cesar. "L'Afrique Noire et Israel: inversion d'une dynamique diplomatique," *Politique Africaine*, no. 30, 1980, pp. 50-68.

———. "Les elites Africaines et l'Etat Hebreu: perceptions, images et representations." *Annee Africaine 1987-1988*. Paris: Pedone, 1988, pp. 157-175.

———. "Israel et l'Afrique Noire," *Le Mois en Afrique*, vol. 20, no. 233/4 1985, pp. 3-25; vol. 21 no. 235/6, 1985 pp. 36-51.

———. "Israel's Return to sub-Saharan Africa," *Jerusalem Journal of International Relations*, vol. 11 no. 1, 1989, pp. 58-73.

————. "La normalisation Cote d'Ivoire-Israel: raisons de coeur et raisons d'etat," *Afrique Contemporaine*, no. 153, 1990, pp. 42-60.

"Commentary: Roundtable Discussion on the Establishment of relations with Israel by Nigeria." *Nigerian Forum* vol. 2 no. 7-9, 1982, pp. 645-730.

Curtis, Michael. "Africa, Israel and the Middle East," in M. Curtis (ed.) *The Middle East Reader*. New Brunswick, N. J.: *Transaction Press*, 1986, pp. 415-432.

————. and S. Gitelson (eds.). *Israel and the Third World*. New Brunswick: Transaction Press, 1976.

Dajani, S. "Israel and South Africa: the US connection," *American-Arab Affairs*, no. 24, 1988, pp. 74-98.

Decalo, Samuel. "Africa and the Mid-Eastern war." *Africa Report*, vol. 12 no. 8, 1967, pp. 57-61.

————. "Africa and the U.N. Anti-Zionism Resolution: Roots and Causes." *Cultures et Développement*, vol. 8 no. 1, 1976, pp. 89-117.

————. "Israel and Africa: The Politics of Cooperation: A Study of Foreign Policy and Technical Assistance." PhD dissertation, University of Pennsylvania, 1970.

————. "Israeli Foreign Policy and the Third World." *Orbis*, vol. 11 no. 3, 1967, pp. 724-745.

————. "The Rise, Decline and Rebirth of the Afro-Israeli Entente," *Journal of African Contemporary Studies*, vol. 8/9 no. 1/2, 1989/1990, pp. 3-25.

Decraene, Phillipe. "Is the Romance with Africa over?" *Africa Report*, May-June 1973, pp. 20-24

Decter, Moshe. *To Serve, to Teach, to Leave: The tory of Israel's Development Assistance Program in Black Africa*. New York: American Jewish Congress, 1977.

Diallo, Sirandiou. "Cote d'Ivoire-Israel: Les secrets d'une Recontre." *Jeune Afrique*. 22 january 1986, pp. 28-29.

Dropkin, Noah. "Israel's Diplomatic Offensive in Africa: The Case of Zaire," *Transafrica Forum*, vol. 9 no. 1, 1992, pp. 15-26.

Ebo, E. C. "A Call on Nigeria and the other African states to Renew Normal Diplomatic Relations with Israel," Lagos: 1982.

_____ . "Extracts from a Motion in the National Assembly on the Renewal of Dimplomatic Relations by Nigeria and Other African States." *Nigerian Forum*. no. 2, July-September 1982, pp. 740-745.

Eger, Akiva. *What Asians and Africans Learn in Israel*. Jerusalem: Israeli Academic Committee on the Middle East, 1968.

El-Ayouty, Yassin. "OAU Mediation in the Arab-Israeli Conflict." *Geneva-Africa* vol. 14 no. 1, 1975, pp. 5-29.

_____ . "The OAU and the Arab-Israeli Conflict: A Case of Mediation that Failed," in Yassin El-Ayouty (ed.) *The Organizationof African Unity after Ten Years: Comparative Perspective*. New York: Prager, 1975, pp. 189-212.

El-Khawas, Mohammed A. "African-Arab Solidarity: The Emergence of a New Alliance." *Current Bibliography on African Affairs*, vol. 8 no. 2, 1975, pp. 134-145.

Frank, L. P. "Israel and Africa: The Era of Tachlis," *Journal of Modern African Studies*, vol. 26 no. 1, 1988, pp. 151-155.

Freundlich, Yehoshua (ed.). *Documents on the Foreign Policy of Israel. Jerusalem: The State Archives*, 5 vol.

Gaillard, Phillipe. "Israel en Campagne." *Jeune Afrique*, 26 December 1984-2 January 1985, pp. 50-53.

Geldenhuys, Deon. *Isolated States: A Comparative Analysis*. Cambridge: Cambridge University Press, 1990.

Gil, Avil. "Israel's 'Quiet' Relations with Black Africa," *Jewsih Observer and Middle East Review*. 17 March 1977.

Gitelson, Susan Aurelia. "African Press Reactions to the Camp David Summit and to the Israel-Egypt Treaty," *Geneve-Afrique*, vol. 17 no. 1, 1979, pp. 183-195.

_____ . "Arab Aid to Africa: How Much and at What Price?" *Jersualem Quarterly*, Spring 1981, pp. 120-127.

———— . "Israel's African setback in perspective." Jerusalem: Hebrew University Leonard Davis Institute for International Relations, 1974.

———— . "The OAU Mission and the Middle East Conflict." *International Organization* vol. 27 no. 3, Summer 1974.

———— . "Unfulfilled Expectations: Israeli and Arab Aid as Political Instruments in Black African United nations Voting," *Jewish Social Studies.* vol. 38 no. 2, Spring 1976, pp. 159-175.

———— . "Why Do Small States Break Diplomatic Relations with Outside Powers? Lessons from the African Experience." *International Studies Quarterly* vol. 18 no. 4, December 1974, pp. 451-484.

Goell, Yosef. "Israel/South Africa: A View from Jeruslaem." *Africa Report,* November-December 1980, pp. 18-22.

Golan, Tamar. "Israel and Africa: What Future after Mutual Disengagement?" American-Jewish Committee, Foreign Affairs Department, April 1975.

Golubev, V. "Israeli Penetration of Africa." *International Affairs* (Moscow), no. 12, December 1983, pp. 120-127.

Goren, Amon. "Yisrael ba'amim: Al Yachasey Hahutsz shel Yisrael," [Israel among the nations: On the foreign relations of Israel] Jerusalem: Foreign Ministry, 1983.

Grose, Peter. *A Changing Israel.* New York: Vintage Press, 1985.

Hamid, Muhammad. *The Unholy Alliance: Indo-Israel Collaboration against the Muslim world. Lahore:* Islamic Book Center, 1978.

Hakim, Najim and Richard P. Stevens. "Zaire and Israel; An American Connection," *Journal of Palestine Studies,* vol. 74, Spring 1983, pp. 41-53.1

Harkabi, Yehoshofat. *Arab Strategies and Israel's Response.* New York: The Free Press, 1977.

Hellyer, Peter. *Israel and South Africa: Development of Relations 1967-1974.* london: Palestine Action, 1975.

Hershlag, Z. Y. *Israel-Africa Cooperation*. Tel Aviv: Tel Aviv University Report, 1973.

Hirschmann, Erwin. "Israel Seeks African Friends." *Africa Now*, October 1983, pp. 35-40.

Hunter, Jane. "Israel and the Bantustans." *Journal of Palestine Studies*. 1985.

——— . *Israeli Foreign Policy: South Africa and Central America*. Boston: South End Press, 1987.

——— . *Undercutting Sanctions: Israel, the U.S. and South Africa*, Washington: Washington Middle East Associates, 1987.

Hurley, Andrew J. *Israel and the New World Order*. Santa Barbara: Fithian Press, 1991.

Husain, Azim. "The West, South Africa and Israel: A Strategic Triangle." *Third World Quarterly*. vol. 4 no. 1, January 1982, pp. 44-73.

Inbar, Efraim. "The Energence of Pariah States in World Politics: The Isolation of Israel." *Korean Journal of International Studies*. vol. 15 no. 1, Winter 1983/1984, pp. 55-83.

——— . "Outcast Countries in the World Community," Denver: University of Colorado Monograph Series in World Affairs, vol. 21 no. 2, 1985.

Ismael, Tareq. *The UAR and Africa*. Evanston, In.: Northwestern University Press, 1971.

Israel. Ministry of Foreign Affairs. *Israel's Programme of International Cooperation*. Jerusalem, 1967.

"Israel." *Nigeria Forum*, July-September, 1982, pp. 740-745.

"Israel: A Second Coming in Africa." *Africa Confidential*. 21 October 1994, pp. 6-7.

Israel-South Africa: Cooperation of Imperialistic Outposts. Bonn: Progress Dritte Welt, 1976.

"Israel-South Africa: The Natural Alliance." London: Palestine Solidarity Campaign, 1985.

Jacob, Abel. "Foreign Aid in Agriculture: Introducing Israel's Land Settlement Scheme to Tanzania." *African Affairs* vol. 71 no. 283, April 1972.

———. "Israel's Military Aid to Africa, 1960-1966," *Journal of Modern African Studies,* vol. 9 no. 2, 1971, pp. 165-187.

———. "The Political Outcomes of Foreign Aid: Israel's Foreign Aid Program to Africa." PhD dissertation, university of California, Los Angeles, 1969.

Johnson, Willard R. "Africans and Arabs: Collaboration with Cooperation, Change without Challenge," *International Journal,* vol. 35 no. 4, Autumn 1980, pp. 766-793.

———. "The Role of the Arab Bank for Economic Development in Africa," *Journal of Modern African Studies,* vol. 21 no. 4, December 1983.

Jolloh, Abdul Aziz. "The Policies of the Black African States Toward the Arab World: An Overview." in UNESCO. *Historical and Socio-Cultural Relations Between Black Africa and the Arab World from 1935 to the Present.* Paris: UNESCO, 1984.

Kanarek, Jehudi J. *Israeli Technical Assistance to African Countries.* Geneva: Geneva-Africa Institute, 1968.

Kashin, Y. "Israeli Designs on Africa." *International Affairs* (Moscow), no. 2, February 1972, pp. 62-66.

Kaufman, Edy, Yoram Shapira and Joel Barromi. *Israel-Latin American Relations.* New Brunswick, N.J.: Transaction Press, 1979.

Keimach, Burt. "Israel and Black Africa." *Focus,* May 1987.

Khapoya, Vincent B. "The Rupture in African-Israeli Relations." *TransAfrica Forum* Fall 1986, pp. 77-91.

Kitchen, J. Coleman Jr. "Zaire and Israel." *CSIS Africa Notes* no. 10, March 21, 1983.

Klieman, Aaron S. *Israel and the World after Forty years.* Washington: Pergamon-Brassey's International Defense Publishers, 1990.

———. (ed.). *Israel in American Middle East policy.* New York: Garland Press, 1991.

_____ . *Statecraft in the Dark: Israel's Practice of Quiet Diplomacy.* Boulder: Westview Press, 1988.

Klinghoffer, Arthur Jay. "israel in Africa: The Strategy of Aid," *Africa Report.* vol. 17 no. 2, April 1972, pp. 12-14.

Klitch, Ignacio. "Israel Returns to Africa," *Middle East International*, 4 June 1982.

Kochan, Ran. "An African Peace Mission in the Middle East: The One-Man Initiative of President Senghor," *African Affairs*, vol. 72, no. 287, April 1973, pp. 186-196.

Kokole, Umari. "The Islamic Factor in African-Arab Relations." *Third World Quarterly* vol. 6 no. 3, 1984, pp. 687-702.

Kreindler, J. D. "L'Afrique du Sud et Israel." *Le Mois en Afrique*, no. 201/2, Oct.-Nov. 1982, pp. 16-34.

_____ . "Israel et l'Afrique du Sud." *Le Mois en Afrique*, no. 200, Sept. 1982, pp. 38-55.

Land, Thomas. "Black Africa Poised to Restore Relations with Israel," *New Outlook*, vol. 23 no. 2, March 1980.

Laufer, L. "Israel and the Third World." *Political Scvience Quarterly.* vol. 87 no. 4, December 1972.

Legum, Colin. "Africa, Arabs and Oil," in Legum, C. (ed.), *Africa Contemporary Record 1974-75.* New York: Africana Publishing Co., 1975.

_____ . "Africa, the Arabs and the Middle East," in Legum, C. (ed.), *Africa Contemporary Record 1973-74.* New York: Africana Publishing Co., 1974, pp. A5-16.

_____ . "Afro-Arab and Muslim Relations." in Legum, C. (ed.), *Africa Contemporary Record 1985-86.* New York: Africana Publishing Co., 1986, pp. A162-179.

_____ . "Afro-Arab Relations in 1983," in Legum, C. (ed.), in Legum, C. (ed.), *Africa Contemporary Record 1983-84.* New York: Africana Publishing Co., 1984, pp. A152-166.

———. "Afro-Arab Relations." in Legum, C. (ed.) *Africa Contemporary Record 1984-85*. New York: Africana Publishing Co., 1985, pp. A122-139.

———. "Afro-Arab-Muslim Relations in 1986." in Legum, C. (ed.), *Africa Contemporary Record 1986-1987*. New York: Africana Publishing Co., 1987, pp. A149-169.

——— "Afro-Arab relations after the Summit." in Legum, C. (ed.), *Africa Contemporary Record 1976-77*. New York: Africana Publishing Co, 1977.

———. "The Afro-Arab Summit, 1977." in Legum, C. (ed.), *Africa Contemporary Record 1976-77*. New York: Africana Publishing Co., 1977.

———. "Israel's Year in Africa: A Study of Secret Diplomacy." in Legum, C. (ed.), *Africa Contemporary Record 1972-73*. New York: Africana Publishing Co., 1973.

Levenfeld, D. "Israel and Black Africa." *Midstream*, vol. 30 no. 2, February 1984, pp. 7-11.

Le Vine, Victor. "The Arabs and Africa: A Balance to 1982," *Middle East Review*, Spring/Summer 1982.

———. and Timothy W. Luke. *The Arab-African Connection. Political and Economic Realities*. Boulder, Co.: Westview Press, 1979.

Levtzion, Nechemia. "International Islamic Solidarity and its Limitations." Jerusalem Papers on Peace Problems no. 29, 1979.
Lewis, Bernard. "The Anti-Zionist Resolution," *Foreign Affairs*, vol. 55 no. 1, Oct. 1976, pp. 54-64.

Liba, Moshe. "Perek Hadash Be'yachassei Yisrael-Afrika" ["New Chapter in Afro-Israeli Relations."] *International Problems*, vol. 13 no. 4, September 1974, pp. 20-27.

Lieber, Joel. "The Arabs and Black Africa," *Midstream*, vol. 12 no. 2, 1966.

Lorch, Netanel. "The Knesset and Israel's Foreign Policy," *Jerusalem Journal of International Relations*. vol. 9 no. 2, June 1987, pp. 117-131.

Lottem, Emmanuel. "The Israeli Press – Israel's Relations with Africa," *International Problems* (Tel Aviv), vol. 14 no. 3-4, Fall 1975.

Lustick, Ian S. (ed.). *Arab-Israeli Relations in World Politics*. New York: Garland Pub., 1994.

Lyall, Michael. "Arab Aid to Black Africa: Myth versus Reality," in Dunstan M. Wai (ed.) *Interdependence in a World of Unequals*. Boulder, Co.: Westview Press, 1982.

Madison, Marlyn annette. "A Trilateral Approach to Development Cooperation: Afro-Arab Solidarity." PhD dissertation, University of California, Berkeley, 1985.

Mahmoud-Okereke, N. Enuma el. *Israel and Black Africa: Time to Normalize*. Lagos: Emmcon Books Nigeria, 1986.

Marmont, J. "Israel and the Socio-economic Status of South Africa's Jewish community," *Journal of Modern African Studies*, vol. 27 no. 1, 1989, pp. 143-152.

Mathiot, Elisabeth. *La collaboration entre Israel et l'Afrique du Sud*. Paris: Editions France-Pays arabes, 1977.

Mazrui, Ali. "Black Africa and the Arabs," *Foreign Affairs*, vol. 53 no. 4, 1975.

———. "Black Africa and the Arab-Israel Conflict," *Middle East International*, no. 87, 1978.

———. "The Semantic Impact on Black Africa: Arab and Jewish Cultural Influences," *Issue*, vol. 13, 1984.

———. "Zionism and Apartheid: Cooperative Segregation." *Africa Events* (London), February 1986.

Medzini, Meron. "Israel and Africa: What Went Wrong?" *Midstream*, vol. 18 no. 10, 1972, pp. 25-34.

———. *Israel's Foreign Relations*. Jerusalem: Israeli Foreign Ministry, 5 vol.

Meir, Golda. *A Land of our Own*. New York: G. P. Putnam's Sons, 1973.

Mergui, R. and S. Cohen. "L'Histoire des relations secretes Afrique-Israel," *Africa* (Dakar), no. 156, December 1983.

Mertz, Robert A. and Pamela M. *Arab Aid to Sub-Saharan Africa*. Munich: Kaiser, 1983.

Miller, Jake C. "African-Israeli Relations: Impact on Continental Unity." *Middle East Journal*, vol. 29 no. 2, 1981, pp. 393-408.

Moleah, Alfred T. "The Special Relationship," *Africa Report*, vol. 25 no. 6, November-December 1980.

Moore, John Norton (ed.). *The Arab-Israeli Conflict*. Princeton: Princeton University Press, 1977.

Moore, Michael and G. A. Tyson. "Perceptions and Misperceptions: The Middle East and South Africa." *The Journal of Social Psychology* vol. 130 no. 3, June 1990, pp. 299-308.

Nadelmann, Ethan A. "Israel and Black Africa: A Rapprochement?" *Journal of Modern African Studies*, vol. 19 no. 2, 1981.

Netanyahu, Binyamin. *A Place among the Nations: Israel and the World*. New York: Bantam Books, 1993.

Nyang, Sulayman S. "African Opinions and Attitudes to the Palestine Question." *The Search*, vol. 1 no. 3-4, 1980, pp. 218-241.

Nzongola-Ntalaja. "Africa and the Question of Palestine." *The Search*. vol. 5 no. 1, 1982, pp. 169-199.

Ododa, harry. "Afro-Arab Relations since the 1973 Middle East War." *TransAfrica Forum* Summer 1987, pp. 61-71.

Oded, Arye. "Africa and Israel: African Attitudes toward Resumption of Diplomatic of Relations," Jerusalem: Hebrew University Leonard Davis Institute for International Relations, 1986.

––––––. *Africa and the Middle East Conflict*. Boulder, Co.: L. Rienner, 1987.

––––––. "Africa between the Arabs and Israel." *Hamizrach Hachadash* vol. 25, 1975, pp. 184-209.

––––––. "Africa, Israel and the Arabs: On the Restoration of Israel-African Diplomatic Relations," Jerusalem *Journal of International Relations*, vol. 6 no. 3, 1982-83, pp. 48-70.

––––––. *Africa, the PLO, and Israel*. Jerusalem: Hebrew University Leonard Davis Institute for International Relations, 1990.

_____. "Arab Aid to Africa, 1973-1983." *International Problems*, vol. 24 no. 1-4, 1985, pp. 24-40.

_____. "Islam in Afro-Arab Relations." *Middle East Review* vol. 18 no. 3, Spring 1986, pp. 15-23.

_____. "Slaves and Oil: The Arab Image in Black Africa," *Wiener Library Bulletin*, vol. 27, 1974, pp. 34-47.

Ogunbadejo, Oye. "Black Africa and Israel: Towards a Rapprochement," in C. Legum (ed.)., *Africa Contemporary Record* 1982-83, New York: Africana Publishing Co., 1983, pp. 120-132.

_____. "Qaddafi and Africa's International Relations." *Journal of Modern African Studies*, vol. 24 no. 1, 1986, pp. 33-68.

Ojo, Olusola. *Africa and Israel: Relations in Perspective*. Boulder: Westview Press, 1988.

_____. "Africa's Food Crisis and Afro-Arab Relations," *Ife Social Science Journal*. vol. 5 no. 1-2, 1982, pp. 137-153.

_____. "The African States and the Arab World." PhD dissertation, University of London, 1977.

_____. "Afro-Arab Relations in the 1980's and Beyond," *Jerusalem Journal of International Relations*, vol. 8 no. 4, 1985, pp. 105-118.

_____. "The Arab-Israeli Conflict and Afro-Arab Relations," in Timothy M. Shaw and Olusola Ojo (eds.). *Africa and the International Political System*. Washington: University Press of America, 1982, pp. 139-167.

_____. "Israel-South African Connections and Afro-Israeli Relations," *International Studies*, vol. 21 no. 1, 1982.

_____. "Nigeria and Israel." *Jerusalem Journal of International Relations*. vol. 8 no. 1, 1986, pp. 76-101.

_____. "The Role of the Arab World in the Decolonization Process of Black Africa." *International Problems* vol. 20 no. 2-4, 1981, pp. 73-84.

———. "South African-Arab Relations," *Ofahamu*, vol. 2 no. 3, 1982, pp. 121-132.

Orjiako, Umunna. "Black Africa and Israel: Is it Time for Rapprochement?" *Nigerian Forum*, no. 2, 4 and 5, April-May 1982, pp. 532-539.

———. "The Fragility of Afro-Arab Solidarity." *Nigerian Forum*, no. 2 and 3, March 1982, pp. 500-505.

Osia, Kunirum. "Arab Aid to Black African states and their Relations with Israel," *Journal of African Studies*. vol. 10 no. 3, 1983, pp. 109-116.

———. "Choice in African International Relations: Perspectives on Arab and Israeli Infleunces in Africa, 1967 to 1979." PhD dissertation, The George Washington University, 1981.

———. *Israel, South Africa and Black Africa: A Study of the Primacy of the Politics of Expediency*. Wasington: University Press of America, 1981.

Otayek, R. "Les relations arabo-africaines a l'epreuve de la paix entre Israel et l'Egypte," *Annee Africaine* 1981, Paris: Pedone, 1982.

Ouardighi, Abderrahim. "L'Afrique face a Israel." Rabat: H. A. Bayali, 1974.

Patai, Rafael. *Israel between East and West*. Westport, Ct.: Greenwood Press, 1953.

Payne, Richard. *The Nonsuperpowers and South Africa: A Study of the Primacy of the Politics of Expediency*. Bloomington: Indiana University Press, 1990.

Peleg, Ilan. *Begin's Foreign Policy*. Westport, Ct: Greenwood Press, 1987.

Peres, Shimon. *David's Sling*. New York: Random House, 1970.

Peters, J. *Israel and Africa: the Problematic Friendship*. London: British Academic Press, 1992.

———— . "The Return of Israel to Africa: Israeli-African Relations in the 1980's." in S. Wright and J. N. Brownfoot (eds.), *Africa in World Politics*. Basingstoke: Macmillan, 1987, pp. 181-193.

Rabinovitch, Itamar and Jehuda Reinharz (eds.). *Israel and the Middle East*. New York: Oxford University Press, 1984.

Rafael, Gideon. *Destination Peace: Three Decades of Israeli Foreign Policy*. London: Weidenfeld and Nicholson, 1981.

Roberts, Samuel J. *Survival or Hegemony?* Baltimore: The Johns Hopkins University Press, 1973.

Rodin, Tibor S. "Political Aspects of Israeli Foreign Aid in Africa." PhD dissertation, University of Nebraska, 1969.

Rosenfeld, Steve. "Will Israel and Africa Patch it Up?" *Present Tense*, vol. 5 no.2, 1978, pp. 14-15.

Safran, Nadav. *Israel: The Embattled Ally*. Cambridge: Harvard University Press, 1978.

Sankari, Farouk A. "The Costs and Gains of Israeli influence in Africa," *African Quarterly*, vol. 14 no. 1-2, 1974, pp. 5-19.

Schaar, Stuart H. "Patterns of Israeli Aid and Trade in East Africa," *American Universities Field Staff Reports* (East Africa Series), vol. 7 no. 2, 1968, 2. pts.

Schwab, Peter. "Israel's Weakened Position on the Horn of Africa." *New Outlook*, no. 20, April 1978 pp. 21-27.

Segre, Dan V. "Colonization and Decolonization: The Case of Zionism and African Elites,"*Comparative Studies in Society and History*. vol. 22, no. 1, January 1980.

———— . *The High Road and the Low: A Study of Legitimacy, Authority and Technical Aid*. London: Allen Lane, 1974.

Seliktar, Ofira. *New Zionism and the Foreign Policy System of Israel*. Carbondale, Il.: Southern Illinois University Press, 1986.

Sharawi, H. "Israeli Policy in Africa," in K. Haseeb (ed.), *The Arabs in Africa.* London: Croom Helm, 1985, pp. 285-343.

Shehim, K. "Israel-Ethiopia Relations: Change and Continuity," *North East African Studies*, vol. 10 no. 1, 1988, pp. 25-37.

Shimoni, Yaacov. "Israel, the Arabs and Africa." *Africa Report*, August 1976, pp. 51-55.

Shlaim, Avi and Avner Yaniv. "Domestic Politics and Foreign Policy in Israel." *International Affairs.* Spring 1980, pp. 242-262.

Sigel, Efrem. "Israel and Africa," *Africa Report*, vol. 15 no. 2, 1970.

Simmons, Andre. *Arab Foreign Aid.* Rutherford, N. J.: Fairleigh Dickinson University Press, 1981.

Sisyphus. "Israel's Aid to the Third World: Lessons of the Past and Prospects for the Future." *Middle East Review*, vol. 10 no. 3, 1978, pp. 30-36.

Skinner, Elliott P. "African States and Israel: Uneasy Relations in a World of Crisis."*Journal of African Studies* vol. 2 no. 1, Spring 1975, pp. 1-23.

Sklar, Richard L. "Africa and the Middle East: What Blacks and Jews Owe to Each Other," in Joseph R. Washington Jr. (ed.), *Jews in Black Perspective: A Dialogue.* Cranburg, N.J.: Associated University Presses, 1984.

Slonim, Shlomo. "New Scramble for Africa." *Midstream*, vol. 23 no. 8, 1977, pp. 30-35.

Soffer, Ovadia. *Le diamant noire: comment on devient ambassadeur d'Israel.* Paris: R. Laffont, 1987.

Steinberg, Gerald. "The Mythology of Israeli-South African Nucleur Cooperation." *Middle East Review* vol. 19 no. 3 Spring 1987, pp. 31-38.

Stevens, Richard P. Zionism, *South Africa, and Apartheid: The Paradoxical Triangle.* Beirut: PLO Research Center, 1969.

———. and Abdelwahab M. Elmessiri. *Israel and South Africa: The Progression of a Relationship.* New Brunswick, N.J.: North American, 1977.

"Sudan: Amin, the israelis and Explanations." *Africa Confidential,* 24 December 1972, pp. 3-4.

Sylvester, Anthony. *Arabs and Africans: Cooperation for Development.* London: The Bodley Head, 1981.

Tamarkin, Mordechai. "Israel and Africa: Past, Present and Prospect." *Africa Insight,* vol. 15 no. 2, 1985, pp. 84-88.

Tekoah, Yosef. *In the Face of the Nations: Israel's Struggle for Peace.* New York: Simon and Schuster, 1976.

Teplinskii, L. B. *Tel Aviv Fails in Africa.* Moscow: Novosti Press Agency Publishing House, 1975.

Tomeh, George J. *Israel and South Africa:* The Unholy Alliance. New York: New World Press, 1973.

Tomlinson, John. "Israel's Cooperation with Black Africa," *Focus* (London), March 1984.

Wade, Michael. "Bypassing Africa – and history." *New Outlook,* vol. 19 no. 7, 1976, pp. 23-26.

Wai, Dunstan M. "African-Arab Relations: Interdependence or Misplaced Optimism?"*Journal of Modern African Studies,* vol. 21 no. 2, June 1983.

———. "Afro-Arab Relations: Misplaced Optimism." in UNESCO. *Historical and Socio-Cultural Relations Between Black Africa and the Arab World from 1935 to the Present.* Paris: UNESCO, 1984.

Warburg, G. R. "The Sudan and Israel: An Episode in Bilateral Relations," *Middle East Studies,* vol. 28 no. 2, 1992, pp. 385-396.

Weinberg, David M. *Dialogue pour le developpement" le programme israelien d'aide a l'etranger.* Westmount, Quebec: Comité Canada-Israel, 1987.

Weitzel, Hartmut and Renate Notzel. *Africa and the Arab States.* Hamburg: Institute of African Studies, 1979.1

Weitzmann, Chaim. *Trial and Error.* New York: Harper and Row, 1949.

World Jewish Congress. *African and Asian Media Survey Attitudes on the Middle East Conflict,* 1974.

Yacobi, Gad. Breakthrough: *Israel in a Changing World.* New York: Cornwall, 1996.

Yousuf, Hilmi S. *African-Arab Relations.* Brattleboro, Vt.: Amana Books, 1986.

"Zaire Facing the Future." *Israel Economist.* May 1983.

Zohra, Filali F. *Nature et fondements des relations israelo-africaines: memoires.* Algiers: University of Algiers, Institute of Political Studies, 1972.

A NOTE ON THE AUTHOR

Samuel Decalo is a naturalized Israeli citizen, who majored in Political Science at the University of Ottawa, Canada, before joining the University of Pennsylvania where he obtained his MA and PhD degrees. Specializing in both African and Middle East Studies, he wrote his dissertation on Israel's then-blossoming relations with Black Africa.

After obtaining his PhD Professor Decalo commenced his academic career, being affiliated with several universities, both in the US and abroad. In the United States he taught, among others, at the University of Rhode Island, the Graduate Faculty of the New School for Social Research, Emory University and the University of Florida. He has also been affiliated, for varying periods of time, with the University of the West Indies (Trinidad), the University of Botswana, and the University of Natal, in South Africa. He headed departments of Political Science, and of African Studies, for a total of twelve years.

Professor Decalo is the author of fifteen books, many of which are basic reference works currently in revised third editions, and eighty professional articles. A globally recognized expert on Francophone Africa and civil-military relations, he has visited most African states several times. His best-known book is the path-breaking *Coups and Army Rule in Africa* (Yale University Press, 1976; revised/expanded edition, 1990) that became a staple textbook in hundreds of universities. Another work, *Psychoses of Power: African Personal Dictatorships* (Westview Press, 1989) was acclaimed as an "Outstanding Book of 1989," and won him a coveted prize for academic excellence. Professor Decalo is currently completing two books, *Not by Democracy Alone*, and *Is Africa Different?* The latter compares Southeast Asia's developmental paradigms with Africa's developmental capabilities.

Though Professor Decalo continues to write prolifically on African affairs, he regularly lectures on Middle East politics, and has kept abreast of events in Afro-Israeli relations as attested by the thirteen articles in this volume than span the period of two and one half decades.